How Social Security
Picks Your Pocket

How Social Security Picks Your Pocket

A Story of Waste, Fraud, and Inequities

Joseph Fried

Algora Publishing
New York

Library of Congress Cataloging-in-Publication Data

Fried, Joseph.
  How social security picks your pocket! : a story of waste, fraud, and
inequities / Joseph Fried.
     p. cm.
   ISBN 0-87586-248-9 (soft) — ISBN 0-87586-248-9 (hard cover)
   1. Social security—United States. 2. Social security beneficiaries—United
States. 3. Waste in government spending—United
States. 4. Welfare fraud—United States. I. Title.

  HD7125.F75 2003
  368.4'3'00973—dc22
                                   2003017213

Printed in the United States

for Mom, Nina and David

Table of Contents

For many years, I've counseled individuals and small businesses regarding employee compensation and retirement plans. Often, the subject of Social Security would arise and I'd be asked, "Is Social Security a good investment?" To answer the question, I'd plug a few numbers into my calculator, and show the results to my client:

> Look at this. If a 22-year-old invested all of his payroll taxes in private investments earning just 3.5% above inflation, he could have over $850,000 by the time he retired — in today's dollars. That would buy an annuity of $76,000 per year for the rest of his life. Which do *you* think is better: $76,000 per year or Social Security? [1]

It's a simplistic example, of course, but it gets the mental juices flowing. Why does Social Security pay such a meager amount? Is the program properly designed and managed? Are some people getting less than their share? Are there better alternatives? *How Social Security Picks Your Pocket* answers these and many other important questions.

To write this book, I put on my eye shades, sharpened my pencils, and poured through endless financial schedules, statements, agency reports, and research studies, with all of the skepticism of an eagle-eyed accountant reviewing his restaurant check. The goal? To get the real story behind the numbers. Twenty years of CPA audit experience made it easy. Then, I set out to

---

1. For a single male earning $65,000 per year, and retiring at full retirement age (age 67).

write a book that would take nothing for granted, and take no prisoners. If you're looking for opinions, you'll find a boatload in this book; and they are backed up with facts and followed up with recommendations. If you're looking for perspective, you'll find that too, because program-wide cost estimates have been added, wherever possible.

Some may presume this to be a conservative book because, perhaps, they believe *any* criticism of Social Security may be a "right-wing" attempt to eliminate it, or cut benefits to the poor. I hope these people, in particular, will read this book with open eyes and open minds. If we are truly concerned about common, working people, we must also be concerned about the blundering way Social Security handles their money and distributes their benefits. Social Security is a program of lofty and noble goals, but it is also a system of enormous waste and inefficiency.

In reality, this book is neither conservative nor liberal, nor is it married to any particular philosophy regarding Social Security. You may not agree with every opinion rendered, but this book will lead to new insights about a subject of great importance.

Finally, a word about the book's layout. Some people want to see how amounts are calculated, while others are bored by such details. To keep the book readable, certain information has been exiled to Appendix A. References to this additional information are included in the text.

Appendix B, on the other hand, is for the people who get hot under the collar as they read about the billions of dollars — their money — wasted each year by Social Security. As a stress-reliever, these people may want to call, fax, e-mail, or write to the influential people and organizations listed in Appendix B. Civic activism can be good therapy, and can be a catalyst for the important reforms needed to help Social Security deliver on the promises it has made, but cannot keep.

Risky behavior

Mary and Jill, each only twenty-two years old, started working in 1973 on the same day, for the same pay, but for different employers. Mary worked in the private sector while Jill worked for the State of Ohio. During their careers they always earned equal amounts, starting at $8,500 each in 1973, and ending with salaries of about $45,000 each in 2002.

Economically, these women seemed the same, but they were quite different. Mary had been engaged in risky behavior: she was mixed up with something known as Social Security. Jill, on the other hand, was exempt from Social Security because she was a state employee. She belonged to the Ohio Public Employees Retirement System (Ohio PERS).

After 30 years of work, the women decided to retire, but Mary received some distressing news. It would be another 14 years before she could start collecting her "full" Social Security benefit — of just $1,299 per month. Jill, on the other hand, would start collecting $2,208 per month immediately, at age 52, and would continue to collect that amount (plus annual inflation increases) for the rest of her life.

Admittedly, the enormous difference in the value of their benefits was partly due to a higher required annual contribution to the Ohio plan. But, even after making all adjustments required to make the comparison fair, Jill's expected benefits were worth *more than twice* as much as Mary's. Mary lost about

$155,000 in present-day dollars — a small fortune for someone who never earned over $45,000. (See Figure 1.)

Figure 1

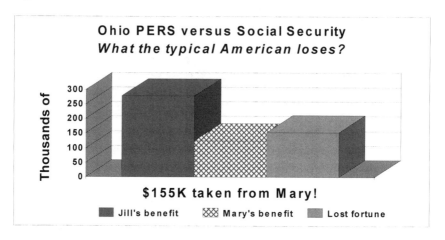

Mary went back to work for 14 long years while Jill engaged in her own risky behavior with Ted, her personal tennis instructor. And here is where the story gets sad. When they were age 66, Mary and Jill died right after attending their own joint birthday party (salmonella in the salmon). Poor Mary had not even collected her first Social Security check, and had nothing to leave to her daughter, who was in college. Jill, on the other hand, had collected retirement checks for 14 fun-filled years and, upon her death, Ohio PERS continued to pay retirement benefits, worth about $85,000 (after tax), to Ted, her designated beneficiary.

In Figure 2, below, the first column shows the benefits paid by Ohio PERS to Ted; the smudge mark in the center depicts the benefits paid by Social Security to Mary's daughter; and the third column shows the difference — a lost legacy.[2]

Millions of Americans lose out

These names and circumstances are made up, but the benefit amounts are approximately the actual ones that would be received by people with those

2. For calculation details, see Appendix A- 1.

salaries and in those retirement systems. In fact, there are millions of Americans like Mary and Jill. They have similar incomes while working, but very different incomes in retirement.

Figure 2

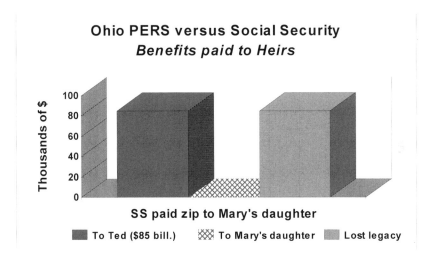

Generally, the ones with the great benefits are government workers, and are exempt from Social Security. The rest of us are forced into Social Security, and have meager benefits. This begs the question: Why can't Social Security provide workers with decent retirement income?

Issue-by-issue, this book will explore the reasons and give you a guided tour of a system of staggering waste and blatant inequities. You'll learn how average retirees are robbed of benefits — benefits that are redirected to wealthier, non-paying beneficiaries. You'll learn about the millions of people who pay lip-service to Social Security — but pay nothing else. They don't participate in the system described as their "worst nightmare."

We will visit the teachers who became janitors for just one day, to qualify for $100,000 in Social Security benefits — each. And, we'll review the amazing 115% tax inflicted on working seniors. Yes, people can actually pay more in tax than they earn.

Your tour will include the growing disability programs. Are you a hypochondriac? Good! You just may qualify for disability benefits. (Check out Section 12.07 of the Social Security "Blue Book.") Did you know that *one third* of all workers getting disability benefits claim to have a mental impairment? Are you up on the latest designer diseases? And, did you realize that only *one in every 500* disabled workers recovers and returns to work — despite our miracle cures, technology, and "reasonable accommodations"?

You'll need your "hard hat" when we visit Supplemental Security Income (SSI), which is a welfare program run by Social Security. It's been classified by the GAO as "high risk" due to its habit of paying benefits first, and asking questions later (or never). SSI has its very own disability program, and should be in the Guinness book for once paying benefits to 181 members of one family — simultaneously. In this program, more than 60% of disabled beneficiaries are paid for claimed mental impairments.

The tour includes some unsavory neighborhoods, rife with crime and corruption. We'll discuss the different schemes and scams used to rip off the system, and the new and threatening trends on the horizon. The Social Security Administration claims that it can't estimate the amount of fraud in its programs. This book challenges that claim.

What Social Security tour would be complete without a discussion of insolvency, the trust fund, and Personal Retirement Accounts (PRAs)? Is the program really broke? Would PRAs help, or hurt? You'll get the lowdown on these matters, plus insights into a great alternative plan that has been serving retirees *longer* than Social Security, right here in America. Comparing the benefits of this alternative plan to those of Social Security is an enlightening, if sobering, experience.

The final stop on the tour is my dream plan for Social Security. It's a little different than any other proposal. Is it "Shangri-La" or Sham-ri-La? That's for you to decide.

(ARE WE ABOUT TO STRIKE AN ICEBERG?)

Ms. Fuller

Social Security used to distribute photographs of its first retiree, Ida May Fuller, a Vermont legal secretary who paid $25 in Social Security taxes, and received benefits totaling $22,889. On her investment, Ida had earnings of about 1100% — each year. The agency doesn't distribute her pictures anymore — might cause hard feelings. You see, today's average rate of return is less than 2%, and heading south. In fact, millions of retirees will have *negative* investment earnings. That's like *paying* a bank to hold your money. How did such a good program get so bad? In truth, Social Security was *never* financially sound. The early days were a sham — a massive Ponzi scheme. In case you don't know what a Ponzi scheme is, let me digress.

Carlo "Charles" Ponzi

Carlo "Charles" Ponzi was born in Italy in 1882, and immigrated to the United States when he was 21. In the year 1919, Ponzi had a brainstorm. He established a business that would make money, supposedly, by exploiting the postal stamp valuation differences of various countries. The business plan didn't make sense and it never worked, but that was not really the point. What mattered was that people *thought* it was a profitable business plan. Indeed,

7

thousands of investors believed Ponzi's claim that he could double their money in just 90 days. Ponzi raked in the dough — up to $1 million per week. That's big money today and was incredible in 1920. The new investors were the only source of income for this "business," and while it was expanding rapidly, the cash flow enabled Ponzi to pay off the earlier investors. They, like the early Social Security beneficiaries, were delighted. Indeed, they did double their money. But, no pyramid scheme can go on forever. Ponzi's plan started to unravel in mid-1920, when newspapers, auditors, and banks started asking questions that made investors nervous — and scarce. Without a growing supply of investors, the pyramid scheme was doomed. Ponzi gave up his business and eventually went to prison.

We need more babies

You might say that Ida May Fuller was one of the first "investors" in the Social Security Ponzi scheme; and like the first investors in the original Ponzi scheme, she had to be very, very happy. For just $25, she received benefits that seemed too good to be true. They were. Such unrealistic benefit payments were only possible due to the contributions of several subsequent Social Security "investors." When Ida May filed her claim, there were more than 40 people working for each person receiving benefits. Later, when those 40 workers filed for benefits, there were fewer investors to support them. Today, there are only 3 or 4 workers for each beneficiary, and soon that figure will drop below 2. We just aren't breeding fast enough to keep the Social Security Ponzi scheme going.

Are old folks the problem?

Please don't misunderstand. Ida May and her generation got a great deal, but they are not the sole cause of our present-day problems. The current worker-to-beneficiary ratio (3.5 to 1) is not as favorable as past ratios, but it is favorable in comparison to future ratios and in comparison to what I call the "natural" ratio. If you think about it, the natural ratio of workers to beneficiaries, in a population with little growth, is approximately the number of years a person works divided by the number of years a person is retired. Let's say that a typical person works 40 years and is retired for about 17 years. That implies a natural worker-to-beneficiary ratio of about 2.35 to 1 (i.e., 40 divided by 17). Of course, it is not that simple. Not every worker lives long enough to reach retirement age, and there are numerous Social Security beneficiaries who never worked at all (more on this, later). When these factors are considered, along with increasing longevity rates, changing work patterns, and immigration, the natural ratio probably drops to less than 2 to 1. The point? We, the current workers, have no right to complain. We don't have the spectacular 40 to 1 ratio that existed in 1935, or the 16 to 1 ratio that existed in 1950, but we are not paying more than our fair share. We are probably paying *less*.

Worse than the Titanic

We are cheating our children by shoving a huge debt forward to them. Based on current trends, Social Security trustees estimate that benefit outflows will start to exceed payroll tax receipts by the year 2018. At that time, the Treasury's general fund, which has been borrowing from Social Security for many years, will have to start repaying its debt to Social Security. That will probably trigger a sharp increase in general income taxes. And, starting around 2042, when Social Security has finished collecting the debt (owed by the Treasury's general fund), it will become insolvent unless there is a massive cut in benefits and/or a sharp rise in payroll taxes. Between 2018 and 2077, we and our descendants will have to come up with $3 to $4 trillion in payroll taxes and $20 trillion or more in general income taxes, just to maintain our current level of benefits. That's a total of about $24 trillion in today's dollars. And even after all that money is spent, we will still be stuck with our unique, "pay-as-you-go" system.[3]

How do you like that? We have crummy benefits and high taxes right now, and it only gets worse for our kids. Put another way, we are heading toward a financial iceberg, but *not* on the Titanic. That was a luxury liner. We are heading toward an iceberg on a battered, old barge.

---

3. For an explanation of the various methods used to measure the Social Security shortfall, see Appendix A-2.

Demographically doomed?

There is a problem, however, with the gloomy analysis offered above. It is predicated on the assumption that we are doomed, demographically, because we are in the tail-end of a Ponzi scheme. And, it presumes that nothing can save us except tax increases or large benefit cuts. That is not necessarily the case. Although Social Security is a perfect example of a Ponzi scheme, that is not the fundamental problem of Social Security. The Ponzi scheme is what *covered up* the real problems.

Do we still drive cars made in 1935?

Social Security was designed in a different era, when people had fewer sources of income, different family structures, and different retirement aspirations. Since that time, the program has not been appropriately updated, due to neglect and politics. And, in truth, it was never efficiently managed — it never had to be, due to the high ratio of workers to beneficiaries. Yes, there are many people who revere Social Security and believe that it epitomizes good government. But the foundation of their belief is an illusion. Now that money is getting tight, the glaring shortcomings are becoming evident.

Nine Specific Design And Management Problems

Below, you'll find a listing of Social Security's major problems and the associated costs. In subsequent chapters, the problems are discussed in greater detail, along with proposed solutions.

NOTE: *The estimates below represent averages of the waste, in today's dollars, for each of the next 75 years.*

1. *Extra benefits for high-income workers with stay-at-home spouses* (estimated yearly waste: $71 billion)

The world has changed a great deal since 1935 — the year that Social Security was created. In 1935, more people got married, stayed married, and had lots of children. In that era, there were no modern freezers or washing machines, TV dinners, or vacuum cleaners, so one of the married partners (usually the wife) stayed home to clean, cook, and nurture those many kids. Because it was difficult for married people to save for retirement (and because of political pressures), Social Security was amended in 1939 to give lucrative "spousal" and "survivor" benefits to the worker with a non-working spouse. Do these benefits still make sense?

Today, many married couples have few or no children, and they have access to modern conveniences that make it possible for each partner to maintain a career. The woman (or man) who stays at home throughout adult life usually does so by choice. And, even if the spouse chooses to stay in the home, we can't assume that the couple is "needy." To the contrary, one-earner couples often earn *more*, not less, than two-earner couples.

Ironically, it is often the single mom or dad, completely ignored by Social Security, who needs the most help. Today, a single woman may raise several children while maintaining her career. Yet, our 1930s-minded Social Security system regards her as privileged, so there are no special benefits for her. (And, benefits she earned may even be transferred to others.)

If we just consider the transfer of extra benefits to people with wages *higher than 70% of other workers*, spousal and survivor benefits will cost the system, on average, an estimated $71 billion for each of the next 75 years.

2. Misguided welfare built into benefit formulas (estimated yearly waste: $29 billion)

There is another method by which retirement benefits are siphoned from the middle class, and redistributed to wealthier retirees who didn't pay for those benefits. It is the bulk-transfer of benefits by means of a unique and crude 3-rate benefit formula. The intention is to transfer benefits to the "poor." The problem, however, is that Social Security measures poverty solely on the basis of a retiree's historical wages. Totally ignored is income — current and past — from interest, dividends, rents, capital gains, alimony, inheritances, limited partnerships, etc. In addition, Social Security completely ignores the wealth of other people in a worker's family. For example, a woman who earns a small salary as a part-time museum worker would be considered "poor" by Social Security, and she would get *extra* benefits — benefits she never paid for — despite her marriage to a rich plastic surgeon, a governor, or Bill Gates.

Can our cash-starved Social Security system afford to keep giving wealthy people *extra* benefits? Is it fair to take thousands of dollars from a middle-class retiree, with no other source of income, and give that money — *her* money — to a married couple making millions? It happens all the time, and it will cost the system an estimated $29 billion for each of the next 75 years.

3. Good welfare — wrong source of funding (estimated yearly waste: $84 billion)

In many cases, Social Security does succeed in getting the extra benefits to those who truly need the support. This assistance, often referred to as "social insurance," should be continued or increased. But, whatever we call it, extra assistance is a form of welfare, and *it is wrong to finance any welfare exclusively on the backs of workers.* Helping people in need, just like national defense, is not exclusively the responsibility of wage earners. Wealthy people with other types of income are also responsible for our needy, and elderly, citizens. However, the rich pay virtually all of their taxes in the form of general income taxes — not payroll taxes. So, when we finance this hidden welfare with payroll taxes, the wealthy get "off the hook" and the Social Security system loses about $84 billion each year.

4. Stealing benefits from those who die young

Unlike most retirement plans, Social Security has very few options for withdrawing benefits. You take the benefits either at full retirement age (scheduled to become age 67) or a few years earlier or later. There is no lump-sum option, no ability to leave benefits to an heir of your choosing, and no ability to get retirement benefits prior to age 62. If you die right after benefits commence, a lifetime of payroll taxes may be forfeited, with nothing left to your heirs.

The lack of flexibility amounts to discrimination against millions of workers, especially the obese and those with other life-threatening chronic health conditions. The discrimination is also manifested along ethnic and gender lines. For example, black males are statistically likely to die at age 67 — the very same year they qualify for full benefits.

Why not give individuals the option of taking monthly benefits, at actuarially-reduced amounts, while they are in their 50's? Why not give people the right to bequeath their unclaimed benefits in the event that they die at a young age? The answer to these questions is the same. Social Security actuaries count on the fact that millions of people will die without collecting benefits. The system needs their money. The lack of flexible options deprives these workers of all or part of their benefits, but it *saves* the system money — at the expense of some of our most unfortunate citizens.

5. Five million workers AWOL because of union politicking (estimated yearly waste: $13 billion)

For historical and *political* reasons about 5 million state and local government workers are exempt from participation in the Social Security program. The unions representing these people have fought tooth and nail to keep them out of Social Security but, ironically, these unions are big promoters of Social Security — *for everyone else*. So far, the state and local government workers have managed to keep their separate retirement plans, largely due to the help they receive from the politicians they generously support.

It is fundamentally unfair for our government to sanction separate and unequal retirement systems in America — a lousy one that is mandatory for most of us, and a lucrative one for the lucky 3 or 4% who are politically connected. The hypocrisy of the unions is offensive. But there is also a financial cost to Social Security. Allowing these workers to go AWOL will cost the system an estimated average of $13 billion in each of the next 75 years.

6. Taxation of benefits — a sneaky double tax for millions (estimated waste: $28 billion per year)

One of the least understood and least equitable aspects of Social Security has to do with the way benefits are taxed. For most retirement plans, including those of state and local workers, taxation is straightforward. Workers pay no tax at all on the retirement contributions withheld from their paychecks; they pay tax only when they retire and start collecting benefits. That is fair, and if Social Security were to use that method, it would result in an *increase* in funds available to the program. But, rather than a straightforward and fair method, Social Security uses a goofy and inequitable method of taxing benefits. The result? Many pay *less* than their share, while others pay a *double* tax on their benefits. How did our elected representatives get away with a double tax? In a word, "confusion." The tax is so complex most seniors, even those on Ginkgo Biloba, have no idea they are paying it.

For some retirees, it gets even worse due to imposition of a stiff work penalty. It is hard to believe, but Social Security beneficiaries can pay an effective marginal tax rate of *more than 100%!* That means *working costs them money.* If we switched to a simple system of taxing benefits (in lieu of taxing contributions), the system would save around $28 billion per year. In addition, millions of taxpayers would be saved from double taxation and costly tax preparation fees.

7. Disability rates are a scandal — Only 1 in 500 disabled beneficiaries returns to work (estimated waste: $17 billion per year)

The worker disability program, which now accounts for about 14% of all benefits paid by Social Security, is a joke. Billions of dollars are squandered by an agency that *knowingly* grants awards to hypochondriacs. The mismanagement of the program is not fully apparent until claim and award trends are studied in detail. It then becomes evident that awards for verifiable impairments (like broken arms, infections, etc.) are becoming more rare, while awards for non-verifiable impairments (like certain forms of mental illness) are skyrocketing. The two conflicting trends somewhat offset each other, thus obscuring much of the massive waste and abuse.

Another huge problem is the failure of the Social Security Administration (SSA) to get disabled people rehabilitated. Despite the Americans with Disabilities Act, "reasonable accommodations," and all sorts of high-tech devices and medicines, only about *one in 500* disabled workers leaves the disability rolls to return to work. Better management of the worker disability program could easily save $17 billion each year.

In addition to the worker disability program, the SSA provides disability benefits within a program called Supplemental Security Income (SSI), which was created in the early 1970s to help low-income Americans. Although SSI is not financed with Social Security trust funds, better management of the SSI disability program could result in additional savings (to the Treasury's general fund) of $6 billion per year.

8. Undetected fraud and erroneous payments (estimated yearly waste: $16 billion)

Fraud affects all aspects of Social Security, but particularly two areas: the worker disability program and the SSI welfare program (discussed above). Faking ailments and concealing income probably constitute the two most serious problems faced by Social Security. Control over the SSI welfare program has been so lax that, in 1997, the GAO proclaimed it to be a "high-risk" program (a designation it carried into 2003). In fact, one analyst refers to this costly program as the "black hole" of our welfare programs.[4] Other fraud schemes

---

4. Christopher M. Wright, "SSI: The Black Hole of the Welfare State," Policy Analysis no. 224 [online] (Washington, D.C.: Cato Institute, 27 April 1995 — [cited 22 August 2002]); available from *http://www.cato.org/pubs/pas/pa-224.html*.

affecting Social Security include collecting SSI while in prison, on the lam, or out of the country; stealing or fabricating identities (to get benefits), and collecting retirement benefits for those who don't exist.

Although the SSA provides estimates of erroneous payments attributable to inaccuracies (e.g., issuing a check to the wrong retiree), it claims that it can't estimate the amount of fraud in its programs. However, Social Security fraud can be estimated by using the same methods employed by private plans and the public systems of other countries. In a later chapter, we show that fraudulent and erroneous payments could result in lost Social Security trust funds totaling $16 billion per year, on average, for 75 years. In addition, fraud in the SSI welfare program could result in an additional yearly loss (from the Treasury's general fund) of $10 billion.

9. Poor investment earnings (estimated waste: $26 billion per year)

Finally, let's not forget the topic that has been so widely discussed in recent years. Funds in Social Security have been invested too conservatively, and this has resulted in a vast loss of potential earnings. In the future, far more earnings will be lost unless prudent changes are made. There is widespread agreement that, over long periods of time, funds invested in the stock market earn higher returns than funds invested exclusively in debt instruments. Although it is possible to have the government purchase equity investments directly, most economists fear the economic impact of direct government ownership on such a massive scale. Therefore, it is more likely that a system of Personal Retirement Accounts (PRAs) would be used as the vehicle for investing Social Security funds in the stock market. A modest system of PRAs could increase system assets by an average of about $26 billion per year.

The Wheel of Waste

Eight of the above-listed problems involve major costs to the Social Security fund or the Treasury's general fund. (Item 4, pertaining to flexible options, actually saves money by depriving certain retirees, and their heirs, of benefits.) The following pie chart summarizes the Social Security funds that are wasted as a result of these eight problems. It should be noted that, in aggregate, this waste dwarfs the sum of annual savings needed to prevent insolvency during the next 75 years (about $118 billion per year).

Figure 3

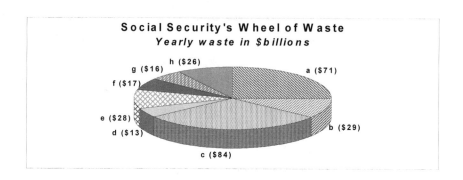

Key to Wheel of Waste (waste in today's dollars, for each of next 75 years)

Refer ence	Description	Wasted SS funds (billions)	Wasted gen'l treasury funds (billions)
a	Spousal benefits to high-rollers	$71	$0
b	Misguided welfare	$29	$0
c *	Good welfare, but wrong funding	$84	($84)
d	AWOL state & local workers	$13	$0
e	Inconsistent taxation of benefits	$28	$0
f **	Disability abuse	$17	$6
g **	Fraud and erroneous payments	$16	$10
h	Lack of good investment earnings	$26	$0
	Total	$284	($68)

*Correcting this problem would save Social Security funds, but cost the Treasury's general fund a commensurate amount.
**Part of the disability and fraud savings pertains to the Supplemental Security Income program, which is financed from the Treasury's general fund. The fraud figures are shown net of estimated collections.

The Wheel of Waste shows that a staggering sum is thrown away each year. The net amount, in today's dollars, is $216 billion per year ($284 less $68). To put this in perspective, the following chart compares it to the amount required to eliminate the Social Security insolvency problem for at least 75 years.

Figure 4

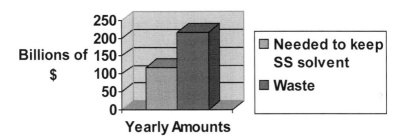

As you can see in Figure 4, above, the annual amount required to eliminate the insolvency problem ($118 billion) is far less than the annual waste associated with Social Security ($216 billion).

ONE UNDERLYING PROBLEM

If there were a hub on our Wheel of Waste, it would be labeled "Congress." Are the specific problems we just outlined Republican issues? Democrat issues? In reality, they are neither. They are simply commonsense problems that cry out for commonsense solutions; but that doesn't mean our politicians will come together to solve them in a bi-partisan way. When it comes to Social Security, *everything is political.* The majority of Democrats see Social Security as *their* property — not to be touched or altered by anyone. Republicans are scared to death that they will be accused of trying to hurt senior citizens. During the stock market bubble of the 1990s, the GOP mustered up enough courage to talk about private investments, but that is as far as they would go.

Earlier, we noted that the income assistance provided by Social Security is often called "social insurance." To understand the political nature of Social Security, consider why its benefit shifting is described as "social insurance" instead of welfare (the "W" word). The architects of Social Security decided that people wouldn't support the program if their money was given away for welfare. Solution? Change the language. Include the welfare but call it "social insurance," and build it into complex, inscrutable benefit formulas and provisions. This deceit has come with a hefty price tag: we can't "means test" before giving out the extra benefits because it might reveal the welfare secret. Instead, Social Security *guesses* who the poor people are, and throws money in their direction. If one of every two dollars gets to a truly needy person, Social Security pats itself on the back.

Are the Yankees for sale?

For the moment, let's be optimistic and assume that our political leaders will come together to truly reform the Social Security program. If that happens, how likely is it that we will keep those reforms, free of politically-inspired amendments? About as likely as the Yankees moving to Cleveland. It's not going to happen.

The overarching problem of Social Security is its lack of independence from Congress. Sure, Congress established a "trust fund" with its own special-issue bonds and its own "trustees." Having this trust fund is a useful way to track how much money has been raised via payroll taxes versus income taxes. But the Social Security trust is not a *true* trust, because the trustees were given no significant power, and the beneficiaries were given no rights whatsoever. Virtually all power remains with Congress.

The mythical trust

This point is clearly made in an article by John Attarian, entitled, "The myth of the Social Security Trust Fund." He notes:

> All trusts must have a "settlor," who sets up the trust and puts property into it; a "trustee," who manages the trust and has legal title to the property in it; a "beneficiary," who holds equitable title to the property and for whom it is managed; property; and terms of trust stating its purpose and duties, the powers of the trustee(s), and the beneficiary's rights.

After noting the lack of a true settlor, the trustees' lack of legal title to trust property, and the lack of beneficiary rights, Mr. Attarian concludes that the Social Security system contains nothing that even remotely resembles a legal trust.[5]

A structural problem: Congress controls the show

The lack of a true trust or similar independent entity means that Social Security is no more than an entitlement program. This is, in fact, acknowledged by the Social Security Administration:

> Like all federal entitlement programs, Congress can change the rules regarding eligibility — and it has done so many times over the years. The rules can be made more generous, or they can be made more restrictive. Benefits which are granted at one time can be withdrawn....[6]

Indeed, Congress micromanages Social Security with the same attention to detail that Martha Stewart gives to a cocktail party — nothing is left to chance and everything is planned in excruciating detail. Have you ever looked at Social Security law? The subsection on benefit payments comprises almost 22,000 words, and it is loaded with special benefit provisions.

What was the alternative?

Congress could have created a true trust, to be run by autonomous trustees who would answer only to principles set forth in some form of irrevocable trust document. The document would set forth broad principles of equity, fiduciary responsibility, and overall funding caps, but details such as the definition of "disability," retirement distribution options, and other administrative matters would be left to the appointed and/or elected trustees. And, once funds were transferred to the trust they would no longer be in reach of Congress. Period.

Unfortunately, Congress could not give up control of a program that distributes so much money to the one segment of our population that enjoys

---

5. John Attarian, "The Myth of the Social Security Trust Fund," *The Freeman* [online] (Irvington-on-Hudson, New York: Foundation for Economic Education, Inc., March 2000 — [cited 24 November 2002]), vol. 50, no.3; available from www.libertyhaven.com.

6. Social Security Administration, quoted in "Strengthening Social Security and Creating Personal Wealth for All Americans" [online] (President's Commission to Strengthen Social Security 21 December 2001 — [cited 28 November 2002]), 30; available from http://www.csss.gov/reports/Final_report.pdf.

voting. As a result, politics permeates every major and minor program decision, and this creates enormous political risk for future retirees and future taxpayers.

Social Security — a vital and noble program

Many people presume that critics of Social Security want to eliminate it. Perhaps some do, but not I. To the contrary, I'd like to see it become a great retirement program — a stand-alone system that people can count on for genuine retirement security. That is why the waste and inequities — and politics — have to go.

To appreciate the need for reform, just consider these matters from the perspective of a few ordinary Americans. Figure 5, below, shows the increase in benefits that could be realized by five individuals (or married couples where husband and wife each work) if we'd simply use one flat benefit rate, and direct benefits to retired workers and the disabled (instead of nonpaying beneficiaries).[7]

As you can see, each individual or couple would realize a significant increase in benefits. Someone with average earnings, as depicted in the middle column, would have a benefit increase of over 20%, and someone earning about $45,000 (column to right side) would have a 40% increase. Those increases are before we even consider the savings that could be achieved through disability reform, fraud reduction, tax reform, and better investment earnings. They're just a beginning.

Mr. Senator, you're under arrest!

We've all heard that Social Security is the "third rail" of politics. Touch it and die! I'd like to offer a new interpretation of that metaphor: any politician who employs the demagoguery of Social Security should be imprisoned. (Death would be too quick.) That is my fantasy. I'd like to see something similar to the new Corporate Corruption Task Force round up the politicians who are inflicting this system upon us and are covering up its many problems. At best, they are negligent. At worst, they are jeopardizing our futures to get a few votes.

---

7. No doubt, many would regard these changes as "radical." However, it should be noted that, for the most part, the retirement plans of state and local workers have always used one flat benefit rate (applied to the worker's salary and service credits), and have directed benefits towards retired workers and the disabled. (This is discussed in greater detail in Chapter IV.) For the calculation of the universal replacement rate, see Appendix A-3.

Figure 5

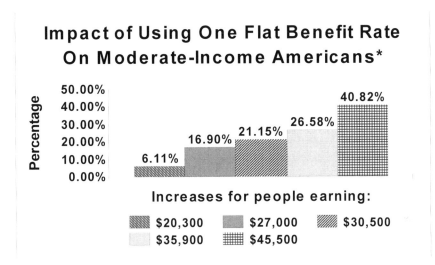

*based on 1999 benefits and rates

CHAPTER III: THE SOCIAL SECURITY SHUFFLE

(HOW BENEFITS ARE MOVED FROM ONE BENEFICIARY TO ANOTHER)

A monumental fraud

Imagine that you are buying milk. You ask, "How much?" and the clerk replies, "It depends. Normally it's $2 per bottle but for some customers we charge $12 or even as much as $20. It's based on what we *guess* your income to be, and it depends on your marital status and health." Outrageous? That's the way Social Security works, but few people realize it because of the way it is structured. You see, the Social Security payroll tax percentage — 12.4% — is the same for all employees. The uniformity of that rate, and 65 years of Social Security disinformation, lead people to assume that benefits are reasonably proportional to taxed earnings. But, as Paul Harvey would say, they need to know "the rest of the story." People need to know that, many years later when they are about to retire, a wealth transfer of enormous proportions takes place. This undisclosed transfer of wealth in the Social Security program constitutes one of the biggest frauds in America. If more people knew about it, it would not be tolerated.

An "average" worker doesn't get an "average" benefit

In Chapter II, we noted that the monthly benefits of many retirees with typical wage histories would increase substantially if we adopted the following radical concept: give them benefits in proportion to the payroll taxes they paid, as workers. A retiree with average wages ($30,500 in 1999) could get a 20% raise; a worker with wages of $45,500 (in 1999) could get a benefit increase of more than 40%. Those increases are before improving Social Security's investment earnings, or reducing its fraud and abuse. Is it too much for a worker with average wages to expect average benefits? Apparently it is, because Social Security needs her money to redistribute to others. That is the main reason Social Security is, for millions of Americans, a mere supplement to retirement income rather than the stand-alone retirement plan that it could be.

Figure 6

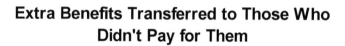

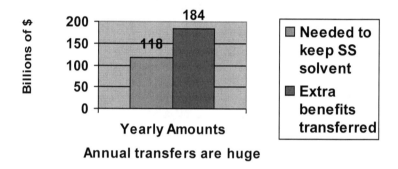

Who pays for the transfers?

Figure 6, above, compares the annual sum of transferred *extra* benefits (i.e., benefits not paid for by the recipient), to the estimated annual amount needed to keep the entire Social Security system (retirement and disability) solvent for the next 75 years. The value of these benefit transfers is enormous; it dwarfs the amount required to "save" Social Security. Perhaps that is why one economist describes Social Security as the "largest income-transfer program in the United States."[8]

Who pays for the extra benefits? To one degree or another, everyone else in the system. Yet, these transfers have been made every month for decades, with very little public scrutiny. Are they compatible with public policy objectives?

---

8. Jeffrey B. Liebman, "Redistribution in the Current U.S. Social Security System," in *The Distributional Aspects of Social Security and Social Security Reform,* ed. Martin Feldstein and Jeffrey B. Liebman (Chicago and London: University of Chicago Press , 2002), 11.

More important, are these transfers fair to those who are footing the bill for them — that is, the other retirees? You, for instance?[9]

In this chapter, we'll discuss the mechanisms used to shuffle benefits between retirees, who's getting the extra benefits, and how much. We'll also discuss why these transfers make no sense whatever. They are so misguided that they amount to a complete waste of Social Security resources. First, however, a little background.

Half truths, right from the start

The Social Security program has never been candid about benefit transfers. To gain widespread support, Social Security was essentially *portrayed* as a collection of individual annuity accounts, entirely based upon the separate earnings of participants. There was no talk of transferring benefits between retirees; rather, people were told that they would get their "money's worth," a concept described as "individual equity." The 1934 President's Committee on Economic Security stated:

> The plan outlined above contemplates that workers who enter the system ... will receive annuities which have been paid for *entirely by their own contributions* and the matching contributions of their employers [emphasis added].[10]

The Advisory Council of 1938 put it this way. Participants "should receive in all cases insurance protection at least equal in value to *their individual direct contributions invested at interest*" (emphasis added).[11] And, in a Social Security Bulletin issued in 1939, it was stated:

> [M]ost annuitants, whether or not they have dependents who qualify for benefits, get much more protection than they could have purchased for the value of their contributions from a private insurance company.[12]

---

9. For the calculation of the annual amount of savings required to keep Social Security solvent, see Appendix A-4.

10. "Report of the Committee on Economic Security" [online] (Social Security Administration, 1934— [cited 31 July 2002]), section entitled *Contributory Annuities-Explanation*; available from *www.ssa.gov/history/reports/ces5.html*.

11. "1938 Advisory Council Report" [online] (Social Security Administration, 1938 — [cited 31 July 2002]), recommendation A, III; available from *www.ssa.gov/history/reports/38advise.html*.

Hell to pay

Unfortunately, the information emphasized to the public was only half true. A more truthful disclosure would have gone something like this:

> Your benefit will be based on a blend of factors, including your marital status and *our* estimation of the amount of income you really need. We happen to believe that the benefits associated with higher *wage* earnings should be only a small fraction of the benefits related to lower *wage* earnings. On the other hand, we completely ignore any other types of income you may have, such as dividends and interest.
>
> Also, we believe that married couples should be given substantial extra benefits, provided one of the partners stays at home. On the other hand, if you and your spouse both work, or if you are single, we'll have to cut your benefits. Don't complain, however. Everyone — for the first few years — will get a good return on his investment, due to this special Ponzi methodology we are incorporating.
>
> Of course, one day there is going to be *Hell* to pay. But, relax. You'll probably be dead by then.

Rationalizations

The inability of Social Security to deliver on the promise of "individual equity" was recognized by its architects during the early years of the program, but they issued rationalizations instead of straightforward disclosures. In *Retooling Social Security for the 21st Century*, economists Steuerle and Bakija note:

> At times they [the 1934 and 1938 Councils] argued in individual equity terms only with respect to the employ*ee* contribution, leaving the employ*er* contribution available for redistributive purposes (an argument economists don't buy since the employer contribution is paid by employees through lower cash wages). At other times, the two Councils recognized the conflict by proposing to support the system in the future with contributions or interest payments from government revenues (emphasis added).[13]

---

12. Lyle L. Schmitter and Betti C. Goldwasser, "The Revised Benefit Schedule Under Federal Old-age Insurance," Social Security Bulletin, vol. 2, no. 9 [online] (Social Security Administration, September 1939 — [cited 31 July 2002]), section entitled *Benefit Patterns*; available from *www.ssa.gov/history/reports/1939no2.html*.

13. Eugene Steuerle and Jon M. Bakija, *Retooling Social Security for the 21st Century* (Washington, D.C.: Urban Institute Press, 1994), 20.

Ultimately, however, Congress and the President decided to let Mr. Ponzi take care of the matter. In that way, they could eat their cake and have it too. There would be a redistribution of benefits to the poor *and* there would be "individual equity," without raising general income taxes. All is possible when you have those 40 workers for every beneficiary.

What has happened in the last 65 years?

Since 1935, the mechanisms used by Social Security to transfer wealth have become simplistic and counterproductive — made obsolete by the enormous changes in individual finance and family structure. The Ponzi scheme is on its death bed, and funding is drying up. Almost no one gets his "individual direct contributions invested at interest." In fact, many get no interest at all, and lose much of what they contributed. So much for "individual equity!" Yes, there has been a world of changes — but Social Security is still operating in 1935. It remains frozen by political paralysis.

The Social Security Wealth Transfer Machine

When it comes time to divvy up the benefits, there are some winners and many losers in the Social Security system, as illustrated in Figure 7, below.

At the top of the drawing, you see the groups that surrender all or part of their benefits to the Social Security Wealth Transfer Machine. Those groups are single people, the so-called "high earners," people who don't live for long after age 67, people who work more than 35 years, and couples where husband and wife each have significant earnings. At the bottom of the drawing are a couple of groups that get extra benefits — in massive quantities. Those are married people with stay-at-home spouses, and so-called "poor" people. These transfers are accomplished by means of four mechanisms, built into the Social Security rules and regulations.

FOUR TRANSFER MECHANISMS

1. A 3-rate benefit formula that constitutes a crude *de facto* welfare device,
2. An obsolete shifting of benefits solely on the basis of marital work sharing,
3. A forced delay of the retirement date, until many of us are in the grave, and
4. A failure to give workers credit for service beyond 35 years

Figure 7

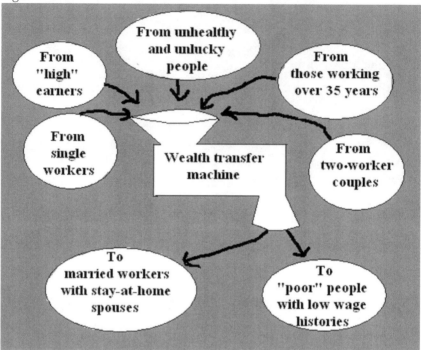

The first two transfer mechanisms involve massive distributions of extra benefits, and are very costly to the Social Security system. On the other hand, the last two items are very costly to many individuals within the system, but do not hurt the finances of the system as a whole. Each of the four mechanisms warrants explanation.

1. Transfers made via a 3-rate benefit formula

To calculate your retirement benefit, Social Security starts by averaging your "lifetime" earnings, adjusted for wage inflation, and limited to 35 years. If you worked more than 35 years, the highest 35 years are used. If you worked less than 35 years, zero-income years are added, to bring your total to 35. Once the average is obtained, benefits are calculated using three very different rates. For the first $7,272 per year of earnings, the benefit is 90%.[14] In other words, a retiree with wages averaging $7,000 per year during his life would get $6,300 per year (i.e., 90% times $7,000), starting at full retirement age. But, the rate is only 32%

---

14. $7,272 is the amount for 2003. It will be adjusted each year for inflation.

for lifetime average earnings between $7,272 and $43,836; and it is a measly 15% for earnings above that range. Mind you, these are benefit rates — not rates of return. A 15% benefit rate is a joke, and is so low that the return on investment is *negative to the extreme.*

Mr. Madonna

Creation of the 3-rate benefit formula was a conscious effort to shift wealth to the needy, but it was premised on two ludicrous assumptions:

- A person can be needy, even if married to a wealthy spouse.
- A history of low *wages* (notwithstanding large amounts of other income) is indicative of need in retirement.

These assumptions are briefly discussed below.

(a) *Income from spouse*

Apparently, Social Security believes that need should be measured at the individual, versus family, level. As a result, the program gives extra benefits to individuals with low wages, even if those "poor" retirees have high-earning spouses. Does this make sense? If a man earns $5,000 per year, but is married to Madonna, he might need our sympathy, but does he need our financial assistance? Is it fair to give him *extra* benefits (that he never paid for) at the expense of others on Social Security?

(b) *Retirement income*

It used to be safe to assume that a person with a history of low wages would need extra help during his retirement. Today, however, an individual's finances are more complex. Wages are still the primary source of income for most Americans, but many now have other types of income — lots of it, from investments, rents, inheritances, partnerships, etc. And, many have these sources of income, plus wage earnings, during their retirements. Should we automatically shift benefits around solely on the basis of historical *wage* levels? We can no longer assume that people who had low wages are poor. In fact, the opposite could be true: some of these people had low wages because *they never needed to work.*

2. Transfers based on marital work sharing (i.e., spousal and survivor benefits)

The second transfer mechanism involves special benefits for certain married people. A married worker with a stay-at-home spouse gets a benefit increase of up to 50% over other workers — regardless of need. It's called a "spousal benefit," and it works like this. At age 62, the worker's spouse can apply for a benefit based on her own work record or, if greater, a benefit equal to one half that of her husband's benefit. She qualifies for that benefit whether or not she ever worked, and whether or not the couple is wealthy. This benefit is rare, or nonexistent, in private retirement plans.

The "survivor's benefit" is another valuable perk provided by Social Security to the married worker who has a stay-at-home spouse. Virtually all retirement plans, public and private, allow workers to have monthly payments made over joint lives — their own and their spouses' lives. But, when a worker makes such an election, an "actuarial reduction" of the benefit is required, to reflect the longer payout period of two lives versus one life. Social Security does not make an actuarial adjustment, and this amounts to a very substantial extra benefit.

Should some get more, for staying at home?

Spousal and survivor benefits were added in 1939 as another short-cut way to get assistance to the "needy." As noted earlier, marriage generally meant lots of children, necessitating that most women stayed at home. That made it difficult to save for retirement. When it created the spousal and survivor benefits, Congress knew that these extra benefits for one-worker couples would sharply reduce benefits for two-worker couples and single workers. Nevertheless, our legislators felt that traditional families had to have help, and fast. Today, it's not the same. Economist Eugene Steuerle, of the Urban Institute, puts it this way:

> Spousal benefits might appear to be a fair way to compensate parents for raising children, but a closer glance quickly dispels this illusion. Since spousal benefits are greater for those married to high earners, higher-income households in general get more for raising their children than lower-income households — producing the dubious result that child-raising in high-income households is somehow more valued by society.
>
> Furthermore, spousal benefits are not even related to the raising of children. Consider an extreme case in which a single mother works while raising children and a wife does not work and has no children. The woman without children might receive a generous spousal and survivors benefit as a

result of marriage, while the single head of household clearly receives nothing additional for raising children.[15]

Another economist, Jeffrey Liebman of Harvard University, has analyzed data which suggest that, on average, the wealthiest 20% of workers receive about 90% more from spousal and survivor benefits (in present-value dollars) than do the poorest 20%. This led him to state:

> Thus, one could argue that the Social Security system implicitly values the time out of the labor force of women married to high earning men more than that of women married to low earners.[16]

Punishing women who work

Another problem with spousal benefits is illustrated in Figure 8, below. It's the unexpected and arbitrary nature of its economic impact. The benefit levels of two couples are depicted, each with total annual earnings of $8,000 (assuming 30 years of work ended in 2000). In the first case, however, one spouse earns all of the income. In the second case, the income is earned evenly, by husband and wife.

Figure 8

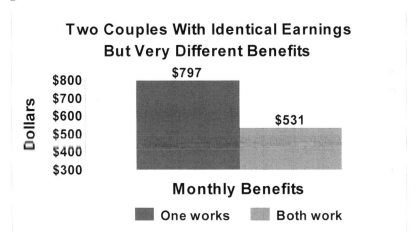

15. Eugene Steuerle, Christopher Spiro, and Adam Carasso, "Does Social Security Treat Spouses Fairly?" *Straight Talk on Social Security and Retirement Policy*, no. 12 [online] (Washington, D.C.: Urban Institute, November 1999 — [cited 27 May 2002]); available from *www.urban.org/retirement/st/Straight12.html*.

16. Jeffrey B. Liebman, "Redistribution in the Current U.S. Social Security System," 32.

As you can see, the couple with one earner has a monthly benefit of $797, which is 50% higher than the benefit amount of the 2-earner couple, *even though total earnings are identical.* Stated in highly technical terms, the 2-worker couple gets the short end of the stick.

3. Transfers made via delay of benefits

Money-back guarantee

As previously noted, the founders of Social Security sold the program on the platform of "individual equity." The appeal of Social Security was irresistible since people were virtually guaranteed more money than they could earn with a private insurance annuity. To show how far this concept went, there was even a *money back guarantee,* so to speak. If you reached age 65, but were not yet eligible for benefits (because you didn't have the then-required 5 years of earnings), you got back 3.5% of your cumulative wages. That may not sound like a lot, but, at the time, the payroll tax rate was *just 2%* of wages (1% for employees and 1% for employers). Therefore, the government was offering a refund greater than the total of payroll taxes paid. And, if you died after reaching age 65, your family received a death benefit of 3.5% of your cumulative wages, reduced by the amount of benefits already received. Unfortunately, the refund for ineligible retirees was eliminated in 1939 (to help pay for those lucrative spousal benefits), and the death benefit was cut to a measly $255 by 1954. "Individual equity" was cast into a ditch.

Flowers for your casket

Today, Social Security has very little flexibility to it. You can't elect to take your payments in a lump sum, as with other programs, and there is only a limited opportunity for early retirement (the age 62, reduced payout option). If you never become eligible for benefits because you didn't work the now-required 10 years, tough luck! The payroll taxes you paid stay in the system. And when you die? Well, the standard $255 your family gets will buy some lovely flowers for your casket.

The lack of benefit options is a disgrace, and it tends to discriminate against people from families or groups with high mortality rates — poor people, overweight people, smokers, blacks, men, people from families with histories of heart disease, etc. Those people, and their families, are cheated out of their benefits — and it's not due to oversight. Remember, the law was *amended* to reduce the payout options. Why? Because the Social Security system relies on the fact that many people will not be around to collect their money. It needs to keep feeding its Wealth Transfer Machine.

If a person wants to retire at age 55, he or she should be able to start collecting benefits (albeit at an actuarially reduced rate). And, if someone dies shortly after starting to collect benefits, the family should get a meaningful death benefit, relative to the sum of taxes paid into the system. These are simply matters of fairness — of "individual equity"; and sooner or later, changes must be made. Meanwhile, however, keep working, keep exercising, and lay off those Big Macs!

4. Transfers made by ignoring wages after 35 years

The fourth benefit transfer mechanism is the 35-year wage limit that is built into the benefit formula. Most people in America start their careers by age 22 or 23, and many start as teenagers. The woman who begins working at, say, age 20, has 47 years to wait until she qualifies for full Social Security benefits. Yet, if she works during all those 47 years, *only 35 will count*. The payroll taxes paid on the other 12 years goes down the drain — and it's not insignificant. If she earned $40,000 per year during the uncounted years, she just gave up $70,000 (i.e., $4,960 of payroll taxes for 12 years, plus 3% interest). Social Security strikes again! The lady's pocket was picked, and she never even knew it. Her money also went into the Wealth Transfer Machine.

If you think this 35-year limit doesn't affect many retirees, consider this. A survey taken in 1999 for the AARP showed that 8 in 10 baby boomers planned to work in retirement.[17] Given the current status of their dot com investments, the 8 in 10 number may now be more like 9 in 10. Each of those aging "boomer" workers will be paying 12.4% in payroll taxes; yet, for many or most of them, the extra taxes paid will not increase their benefits by one dime. We need to start giving retirees full credit for all payroll taxes paid, relative to *all* years worked.

---

17. "Baby Boomers Envision Their Retirement: An AARP Segmentation Analysis" [online] (Roper Starch Worldwide Inc. and AARP, February 1999 — [cited 22 October 2002]), 6; available from *http://research.aarp.org/econ/boomer_seg.pdf.*

How much is transferred?

As noted, the 3-rate benefit formula and the spousal/survivor benefits are the principal mechanisms used to transfer massive resources out of the Wealth Transfer Machine. Of the $184 billion that will be transferred each year, about $77 billion will be transferred via the 3-rate benefit formula, and $107 billion will be transferred via spousal/survivor benefits, as illustrated in Figure 9, which follows.

Figure 9

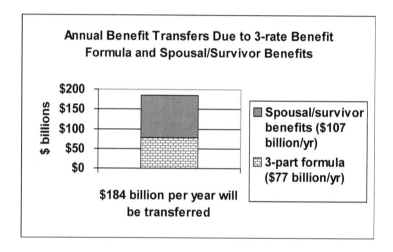

What portion of the transfers constitutes waste?

Figure 10, below, breaks out the $184 billion in a different way — by the amount wasted. How much is wasted, you ask? *All of it.*

The first (left) column of the chart indicates that an estimated $71 billion per year, in the form of spousal and survivor benefits, will be transferred to people with career wages above 70% of the career wage earnings of all other retirees. I'd call that a waste, wouldn't you? We're transferring extra benefits to high-earners who didn't pay for those benefits. Why on earth are we doing this?

The second (middle) column shows that $29 billion will be transferred to people who have, in retirement, substantial incomes from spouses and/or non-Social Security sources such as salaries, pensions, interest, dividends, rents, etc. In fact, these people have more income *before* receiving Social Security than most people (70%) have *after* receiving Social Security. They're not needy people, and they didn't pay for these extra benefits. Again, why are we doing this?

Thankfully, the $84 billion, shown in the last column, is not directed toward people who are wealthier than 70% of the population. These extra benefits (or, at least, most of them) should be paid. However, they should not be paid with Social Security funds because those funds come primarily from payroll taxes. Welfare assistance, no matter how meritorious, is not exclusively the responsibility of middle-class wage earners — the ones who pay almost all of the payroll taxes. Wealthier citizens, who are primarily subject to the income tax (versus the payroll tax), also have responsibility with regard to the welfare of our needy senior citizens. For this reason, we need to get the welfare out of Social Security or, at least, separately fund it with income tax receipts. This would save the Social Security trust fund about $84 billion per year.

Figure 10[18]

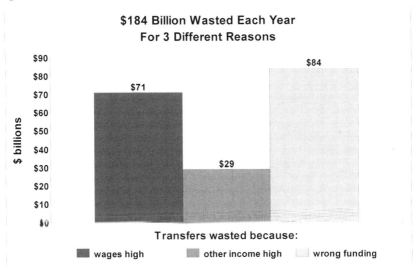

HOW WERE THESE ESTIMATES MADE?

Two economists, Alan Gustman and Thomas Steinmeier, studied the amount and nature of benefit transfers in Social Security by analyzing thousands of earnings records from the Social Security Administration, supplemented by

18. The calculation of these amounts is shown in on page 39.

information obtained from the Health and Retirement Study.[19] They began by grouping respondents by the level of wages they earned as individual workers.[20] By comparing benefits received to payroll taxes paid, they determined that, as a result of the 3-rate benefit formula, there were net transfers from high earners (the upper 30% of wage earners) to low earners. This amount, equal to 10.6% of total retirement benefits, is shown at position 1a in Table 1, below. If we apply that 10.6% net transfer rate to an estimate of the average value of retirement benefits that will be paid in each of the next 75 years (an amount which excludes spousal and survivor benefits), we can project that, on average, about $77 billion will be transferred from the upper 30% of earners to the lower 70% of earners (each year) due to the 3-rate benefit formula. This amount is shown at position 1b in Table 1.

Table 1

Line		a	b
		Net transfers to lower 70% of wage-earners	
		As % of total benefits paid	In billions of dollars
1	On individual basis, without spousal/survivor benefits	10.6	$77
2	Impact of adding spousal/survival benefits	-3.2	-15
3	Subtotal, on individual basis, including spousal/survivor benefits	7.4*	62
4	Impact of grouping on family basis	-1.8	-15
5	Total -- before considering non-wage income	5.6	47
6	Impact of other sources of income in retirement (e.g., earnings, dividends, interest, rents)	-1.7	-14
7	Adjusted distributions	3.9	$33

In the Gustman-Steinmeier research, this amount was 6.8%. Here, the percentage of benefits going to low earners was calculated to be somewhat higher, since the proportion of retirees collecting spousal/survivor benefits will decline in the future.

An unexpected finding

Surprisingly, however, when the researchers added spousal and survivor benefits to the mix, the percentage of benefits transferred to low earners did not

---

19. Alan L. Gustman and Thomas L. Steinmeier, "How Effective is Redistribution Under the Social Security Benefit Formula?" *Journal of Public Economics* 82, no. 1 (Elsevier Science B.V., October 2001), 1-28.

20. All individuals studied were born in 1931 through 1941. Since women born after 1941 are more likely to work outside of the home, the results of the study may be somewhat less applicable to workers born in subsequent years.

increase. In fact, it significantly *decreased,* from 10.6% to 6.8%. Apparently, more of those spousal and survivor benefits went to high earners than low earners. How much more? The amount can be estimated by applying some math to the Gustman-Steinmeier information, and by factoring in anticipated changes in the future mix of worker benefits and spousal/survivor benefits. Using this approach, it can be estimated that the upper 30% of wage earners will receive $15 billion per year more, in proportion to their payroll taxes, than will the lower 70% of wage earners. This is expressed as a negative net transfer to low earners at position 2b, in Table 1.[21]

The key: assess wealth of families instead of individuals

Let's get back the to the Gustman-Steinmeier study. After adding in the spousal and survivor benefits, the researchers decided to rearrange the population of retirees under study. Each married individual was paired with his spouse, and the couples (instead of individuals) were arrayed by average earnings. The objective was to see if some low-earner individuals actually belonged to high-earner family units. In fact, this turned out to be the case and, when arrayed on a family-income basis, the percentage of total benefits transferred to low earners dropped by another 1.8%. (See Table 1, position 4a.) You see, many of the "poor" people, to whom Social Security gives extra benefits, are married to high earners. The 1.8% decrease translates into a $15 billion reduction in transfers to lower earners. This amount is found at position 4b, in[22] Table 1.

Retirees with other types of income

We're not quite done. Gustman-Steinmeier only considered wage histories — not the various types of income available *during retirement.* There is another $14 billion per year (shown at position 6b in Table 1) that will be transferred to those who are ostensibly poor (based on their wage histories), yet have lots of income in retirement from a variety of sources (e.g., pensions, rents, spousal wages). (These must be the retirees that drive the big gray Buicks that, apparently, can only go 25 miles per hour.) The people who will get this $14 billion per year will

---

21. This calculation is explained in greater detail in Appendix A-5.

22. For another interesting finding in the Gustman-Steinmeier study, see Appendix A-6.

be in the lower 70% in terms of their historical W-2 earnings; however, in retirement, these people will have more income *before* collecting Social Security than 70% of retirees have *after* collecting Social Security. In other words, a retired couple in this category would have income of at least $46,000 per year (in year 2001 dollars) *before* collecting Social Security. We're sending $14 billion a year to people *who didn't pay for the benefits* and who make more, before collecting Social Security than 70% of retirees make after collecting Social Security.

Line 7 of Table 1 is the bottom line, which reflects all of the above adjustments. As you can see, net transfers to low earners are just 3.9%, or $33 billion per year.

A problem of gross proportions

If we were to stop here, we could conclude that transfers are not very significant in the Social Security system, since only $33 billion (3.9%) of benefits will be moved each year from high earners to low earners. But that would be a false conclusion because the *netting* of transfers masks much larger *gross* transfers. This is evident from Table 2, below, which presents the same information as Table 1, plus a few additional columns that show the distribution of transfers, using gross transfer amounts for spousal and survivor benefits.[23]

As you can see, Column *c* shows total transfers, column d shows transfers to the wealthiest 30% based on wage histories, Column *e* shows transfers to the wealthiest 30% based on all sources of retirement income (other than Social Security), and column f shows transfers to the lower 70% based on either criterion.

By using these amounts, we find that the $33 billion per year in *net* transfers to low earners, shown at position 7b, corresponds to $84 billion in *gross* transfers to low-earners, shown at position 7f. An additional $71 billion per year will go to "high earners" as defined by wage histories, and $29 billion per year will go to "high earners" as defined by other sources of retirement income. The total transfers are $184 billion per year, as shown at position 7c. As you can see, gross transfers are very large, and often go to high-earning beneficiaries.

---

23. The calculation of the gross spousal/survivor transfer amounts is explained in detail in Appendix A-5.

Table 2

		a	b	c	d	e	f
		Net transfers to lower 70% of wage-earners		Distribution (using gross amounts for spousal and survivor benefits)			
		As % of total benefits paid	In billions of dollars	Total	To high earners (upper 30% based on career wages)	To high earners (upper 30% based on non-SS retirement earnings)	Gross transfers to lower 70% of wage earners
Line							
1	On individual basis, without spousal/survivor benefits	10.6	77	77	--	--	77
2	Impact of adding spousal/survival benefits	-3.2	-15	107	71*	--	36
3	Individual basis, including spousal/survivor benefits	7.4	62	184	71	--	113
4	Impact of grouping on family basis	-1.8	-15	0	--	15	-15
5	Total -- before considering non-wage income	5.6	47	184	71	15	98
6	Impact of other sources of income in retirement (e.g., earnings, dividends, interest, rents)	-1.7	-14	0	--	14	-14
7	Adjusted distributions	3.9	$33	$184	$71	$29	$84

*This amount comprises $55 billion to be paid in proportion to payroll taxes paid, plus an extra $15 billion which constitutes a transfer from the lower 70% of wage-earners to the upper 30% of wage earners.

The impact of other sources of retirement income

I'd like to return to an amount in Table 1, on page 36 (position 6b): the $14 billion that will be transferred each year to those who are ostensibly poor, but who have substantial incomes in retirement. I deliberately brushed by the calculation of this $14 billion amount, in case you are reading this book while operating heavy equipment. The calculation is a bit long, so it is explained in a separate note in Appendix A. However, let me describe, in general terms, part of the information used to make the estimate. Every two years, the SSA puts together a study of income of older Americans based on data from the Current Population Survey of the U.S. Census.[24] Within this study is a table showing how much *non*-Social Security income is available to retirees, age 65 or older. The table classifies retirees into 5 levels (quintiles) based on their Social Security

---

24. Although Social Security benefit quintiles correlate to career wage histories, the correlation is only approximate.

benefits and, implicitly (albeit roughly), on the level of their average wages earned while working. In addition, it lists the value of non-Social Security income available to retirees in each of those five groups. This table is illuminating.

We learn that nonmarried people in the lowest quintile (i.e., those that Social Security deems to be poorer than 80% of all others) have median incomes a little *higher* than those in the next two higher quintiles — in other words, higher than about 60% of the population age 65 or older.[25] For married couples, the results are even more surprising.[26]

Those deemed to be poorest are the wealthiest!

Married couples in the lowest quintile (i.e., those considered to be poorer than 80% of the population age 65 or older) have non-Social Security median incomes higher than those in all other categories. In other words, the married couples getting all those *extra* benefits from Social Security are the *wealthiest* retirees after we consider income from spousal and retiree earnings, pensions, interest, dividends, capital gains, etc.[27] Nearly half of these people, who are "poorest" by Social Security standards, have incomes of at least $20,000 per year, before they collect any Social Security. And, about one in five of these poorest of the poor have annual incomes of at least $50,000 per year, before collecting Social Security.[28] Earth to Congress! Why are you taking benefits from the people who *paid for them* — people who, in many cases, have *no income except Social Security* — and transferring those benefits to people who *didn't* pay for them, and, as we have shown, have significant sources of other types of income? Should you be confiscating retirement benefits and redistributing them to people who are *not* needy? How many millions of times do you plan to make this mistake?

---

25. "Income of the Population 55 or older, 2000" [online] (Social Security Administration, Office of Policy, February 2002 — [cited 19 April 2003]), tables 3.5 and 4.3; available from *http://www.ssa.gov/policy/docs/statcomps/inc_pop55/2000/*.

26. The calculation of the estimated amount at position 6e in Table 1 is explained at Appendix A-7.

27. Undoubtedly, there are several explanations for this phenomenon. Some retirees are married to working spouses. Some people collecting Social Security are, in fact, still employed. Others have significant income from passive sources such as rental properties and investment portfolios.

28. "Income of the Population 55 or older, 2000."

A reality check

If you have a normal, healthy amount of skepticism, you should be asking how millions of Americans can get higher benefits by eliminating wasteful transfers. Who will pay the bill? The answers can be found in a strange-looking graph prepared by economist Jeffrey Liebman in a paper analyzing redistribution of income within Social Security.[29] *Don't jump over this graph* — it is the key to the whole problem.

Figure 11

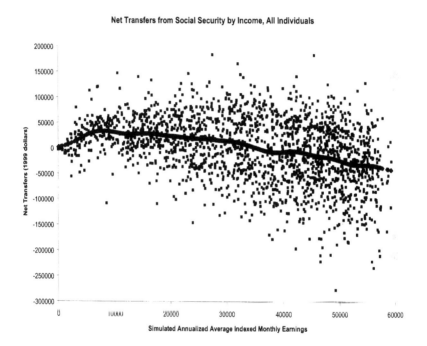

The points have been randomly jittered to preserve confidentiality.

The graph in Figure 11 plots benefits received less payroll taxes paid, by income level, for several individuals.[30] Take a good, long look at this graph. The

---

29. Jeffrey B. Liebman, "Redistribution in the Current U.S. Social Security System," Figure 1.2, p. 24.

bold line running from left to right shows that, on average, net benefits are somewhat higher for low earners than high earners, but that average is merely a theoretical amount. The dots, representing the *individual* net benefits, are what really count. The many dots below the theoretical average line signify retirees, both high earners and low earners, who have probably been ripped off by the system. Many have lost over $150,000 relative to the average Social Security benefit (and *much more* relative to other retirement systems).

The dots *above* the average line, particularly the ones toward the right side of the graph, represent colossal waste in the form of misdirected *extra* benefits (i.e., misdirected welfare). As you can see, many people in the top 20% of the income range receive transfers greater than the average received by people in the lowest 20% of the income range. (In fact, 19% of them do, according to the Liebman study.)[31]

In the graph in Figure 11, each dot above or below the line indicates a potential system failure. Whether you're a liberal, conservative, or kangaroo, when you look at the shotgun scattering of net benefits shown in this graph, you can't help but realize that Social Security (or, more correctly, Congress) has been miserably derelict in its duty to effectively and efficiently distribute benefits. It has simultaneously failed in its efforts to help the needy, and its promise to provide each retiree with "individual equity."

An award

There are so many middle-class Americans who sacrifice greatly to keep our Social Security system afloat; it's about time we gave recognition to one of them. Here is my nominee for outstanding supporter of the Social Security system. He is a representative of millions.

Malcolm Made-up Man was a single, African-American dad who worked two jobs all his life so that he could support his mom and three daughters. Malcolm started working in 1962 for $4,800 per year, and his wages kept up

---

30. More precisely, these net benefits (or net incoming transfers) are equal to the discounted value (at age 65) of lifetime benefits received minus the discounted value (at age 65) of lifetime payroll taxes paid. The net transfer amounts were calculated by using a micro-simulation model based on data from the 1990 and 1991 Surveys of Income and Program Participation, and matching data from Social Security earnings and benefit records.

31. The Liebman graph shown depicts net transfer amounts for individuals. He also presents a graph based on the earnings of married couples. That graph shows a similar, albeit more concentrated scattering, above and below the average.

with inflation until he retired at age 67, in 2002. During the 40 years of his career, Malcolm's pay was reduced by about $300,000 (in present-day dollars) for payment of Social Security taxes. Naturally, Malcolm looked forward to receiving Social Security benefits for many years. Unfortunately, 67 is approximately the age when the average African-American man dies and, in this regard, Malcolm was very average. Malcolm died before collecting a penny of his $300,000 investment, and he left nothing to his family. We thank Malcolm for the $300,000 he gave to keep Social Security propped up. He gave his money without complaint, even though, statistically, it was unlikely he would collect it. We also thank Malcolm's three daughters for not complaining about the $300,000 their father gave to Social Security, instead of to them. Bless them, all.[32]

What we must do

• Pay benefits as a *uniform percentage* of all taxed wage income (with no arbitrary 35-year limit), get rid of spousal benefits, and require an actuarial reduction of benefits where survivor benefits are elected. Using one uniform benefit rate would make Social Security a real pension plan for the suffering middle class, and would help to restore fiscal integrity to the program.

• For those who are needy, whether married, single, with children, or childless, pay additional benefits — but not from Social Security funds. Welfare should be funded with general income tax revenues, although it could be *administered* by the SSA, and combined with the normal retirement benefit. The Supplemental Security Income program, already in place (and discussed later), could be used to distribute this assistance if program controls are greatly strengthened.

• "Means test" with regard to the *extra* benefits given to the "needy," but never with regard to *basic* benefits. Basic benefits (the benefits proportional to the payroll taxes paid) are owed to all retirees, regardless of level of income.

• Give some flexibility to workers so they can get value from their benefits. Stop withholding benefits until people are statistically in the grave. People should be able to get monthly checks while in their 50s (at appropriately reduced rates), provided their reduced benefit is sufficient to keep them above the poverty level. And, where a recipient dies early in the distribution period, his heirs should get a portion of the forgone payments.

---

32. In one regard, Malcolm was lucky. Prior to 1990, Social Security tax rates were lower. If he had paid tax at current rates, his pay would have been reduced by about $350,000 (instead of $300,000). In reality, a person retiring in 2002 could have applied for full benefits at age 65. However, for people born after 1943 the full retirement age is 66, and for people born after 1960 the full retirement age is 67.

• If there is no other reform, we must at least have this one: every American has a right to know how much of his retirement benefits have been shifted to or from others in the program. Retirees should be told (in writing each year) how much their benefits were reduced or increased from the level proportional to the payroll taxes paid. In addition, pre-retirement-age workers should be given a written statement indicating the same information with respect to their projected benefits.

CHAPTER IV: RETIREMENT APARTHEID

("IT'S OUR WORST NIGHTMARE")

Playing it both ways

In recent years, there has been much debate about school vouchers. A plan pushed by President Bush would allow inner city parents to take a small fraction of the tax money spent on their children, and apply it toward the tuition of a school of their choosing. The Supreme Court has ruled the concept to be constitutional but some politicians, prodded by angry teachers, are going to war against vouchers. Their argument? *It would undermine support for public education.*

Knowing this, wouldn't you guess that these same politicians and teachers would rail against anyone taking money out of the Social Security system? After all, that would undermine support for Social Security, right? Well, yes and no. In the case of Social Security, many politicians and teachers are simultaneously fighting a two-front war.

- *Front one*: Nobody should take his/her money out of Social Security to put into personal retirement accounts (not even a small part of it), because that would undermine support for Social Security. "Every percentage point of the Social Security payroll tax that's diverted to private accounts would reduce revenue ... and enlarge Social Security's future shortfall."[33]

---

33. "Everything You Ever Wanted to Know About Social Security's Future But Were Afraid to Ask" [online] (Washington, D.C.: American Federation of State, County and Municipal Employees, AFL-CIO, undated— [cited 8 August 2002]), section entitled, *Why Does AFSCME Oppose Privatization?*; available from *www.afscme.org/wrkplace/ssfuttc.htm.*

45

• *Front two*: There must be an exception for us — teachers and other state and local workers. We should get to take *all* of our money out of Social Security — 100% — because we are "unique" and have "highly specialized needs."[34] Besides, Social Security pays lousy benefits and is heading toward bankruptcy. And, as one retired schoolteacher put it, "It's our worst nightmare."[35]

Well, that sounds reasonable enough, I guess. Public-sector workers are "unique" and "highly specialized." Besides, they're not poor, like the voucher people. Public-sector workers make more than the average inner city slob, and *give more* to their representatives. That should count for something, right?

Retirement apartheid in America

As noted earlier, there are about 5 million state and local workers who have their own pension system in lieu of Social Security.[36] When Social Security was created, in 1935, these public-sector workers were left out of the program due to concerns about the constitutionality of a federal tax on state and local governments. In 1950, the law was amended to allow state and local workers to participate in Social Security, and in 1983, participation became mandatory for all such workers unless their agencies opted out prior to that year. Some state and local agencies did opt out, and that became the loophole which allows for a two-track retirement system in America. For certain Americans there is a great system of retirement programs with real "individual equity" and good investment earnings. For the rest of us there is retirement hell.

---

34. The Segal Company, "The Cost Impact of Mandating Social Security for State and Local Governments" [online] (Washington, D.C.: American Federation of State, County and Municipal Employees, AFL-CIO and Coalition to Preserve Retirement Security, May 1999 — [cited 4 February 2002]), *Executive Summary*; available from *www.afscme.org/action/segaltc.htm*.

35. Bob Shreve, interviewed by the Associated Press, quoted in Richard Miniter, "Forced Payment" [online] *Reasononline*, August/September 1999 — [cited 6 August 2002]; available from *http://reason.com/9908/fe.rm.forced.shtml*.

36. In reality, the "system" for state and local workers comprises several independently managed plans. They all share one important trait, however: benefits which are significantly superior to those provided by Social Security.

Hypocrisy 24/7

Things were going swimmingly for these public-sector employees until, in the late 1990s, some politicians suggested that *newly-hired* state and local workers be required to join Social Security. It was a matter of fairness, they said, and a matter of money, since experts estimated that bringing these people into Social Security would help put off insolvency. Uh-oh! This was a problem. Remember, public-sector workers are represented by unions that overwhelmingly (or is it exclusively?) support a particular political party.[37] And, as we all know, that political party asserts that any criticism of Social Security is the equivalent of slapping an 85-year-old grandma in the face. How would public-sector workers be able to oppose Social Security for themselves, while promoting it for the rest of us?

I can't tell you *how* it is done — just that it *is* being done. Take, for example, the American Federation of State County, and Municipal Employees (AFSCME). This union glorifies Social Security on some pages of its website, while furiously fighting, on other website pages, to keep its members *out* of Social Security. Here are some excerpts:

Social Security is wonderful — when it's for other people
- "Social Security is the nation's great system of income protection...."
- "Social Security links the generations because it's 'pay as you go'...."
- "The Social Security trustees say the system is in good financial shape...."
- "Social Security's near-universality gives Americans a sense of national community...."[38]

But, it's not so wonderful — when it's for AFSCME members
- "AFSCME opposes mandated Social Security for non-covered public workers."[39]
- "Providing the same total benefits will increase total costs [by 35%]."

---

37. Since 1989, the top political donor in the nation has been the American Federation of State, County, and Municipal Employees (AFSCME). It has made political contributions totaling over $30 million, of which 98% went to Democrats and 1% went to Republicans. (The Center for Responsive Politics, as reported by Sabrina Eaton, *The Plain Dealer*, 23 October 2002).

38. "Resolution No: 97, 33rd International Convention, Honolulu, HI" [online] (American Federation of State, County, and Municipal Employees, 24-28 August 1998 — [cited 28 April 2002]); available from *www.afscme.org/about/resolute/1998/r33-097.htm*.

- "Because there is little reserve buildup under this [Social Security] pay-as-you-go funding...annual contribution requirements tend to increase dramatically."
- "[N]ew employees [the ones forced into Social Security] would likely end up in separate retirement plan tiers, or pay higher contribution rates (therefore, getting lower take-home pay) and receive fewer benefits than their fellow workers."[40]

As you can see, there are no accolades here.

Important differences

But AFSCME really shines when it educates us regarding some "Important Differences" between Social Security and plans for public-sector employees. We learn the distinction between Social Security's *"floor of protection"* design (i.e., welfare) and the *"individual equity"* design, used in the plans for public-sector workers. AFSCME says:

> [S]ocial Security's pension benefit formulas are intentionally designed to replace a significantly larger portion of covered pay for *lower wage workers....* By way of comparison, almost all pension programs covering governmental employees (and private sector workers as well) provide pensions under the *"individual equity"* approach; i.e., benefits are directly proportional to earnings and length of covered service ... (emphasis added).[41]

Get it? It's "floor of protection" for us, and "individual equity" for AFSCME. The people in Social Security can take care of the needy while the public-sector employees take care of themselves. Well, at least we got the truth out of them. Social Security is loaded with welfare, and that is one of the reasons *they want no part of it.*

---

39. "AFSCME Opposes Mandated Social Security for Non-covered Public Workers" [online] (Washington, D.C.: American Federation of State, County, and Municipal Employees, first quarter 1999 — [cited 8 August 2002]); available from *www.afscme.org/publications/primetime/pt99103.htm.*

40. The Segal Company, sections I, II, and IV.

41. *Ibid.,* section II.

They're "not paying their share"

AFSCME seems to believe that its members have a unique historical right to avoid any responsibility for "low wage workers." But, others strongly disagree. In a study prepared for and presented by AARP, economist Alicia Munnell notes: "Excluded state and local government employees or taxpayers in their jurisdictions are not paying their share of income redistribution." And, she also adds:

> [They] are not paying their share of financing the unfunded liability associated with the startup of the Social Security program. The parents and grandparents of these state/local workers — like those of covered workers— have received Social Security benefits far in excess of their contributions to the system. This has created a debt that covered employees finance with part of the payroll tax payment. By not participating in the system, state and local government employees and their employers escape this "tax," which is estimated to equal roughly 3 percent of the 12.4 percent payroll tax.[42]

Please don't misunderstand

After reading this, you may be surprised to know that I think AFSCME is right. "Social insurance," "floor of protection," or whatever else you want to call it, does *not* belong in the retirement systems of state and local workers. What AFSCME doesn't grasp, however, is that these forms of welfare don't belong in *our* retirement system, either. So, my beef with AFSCME isn't over the issue, per se, it's with the astounding hypocrisy AFSCME displays.

5 million white settlers

AFSCME is just one of dozens of public-sector unions singing the same tune. They're all working hard to protect 5 million "white settlers" who are nervous about being forced to integrate with 140 million "blacks" from the "homelands." It isn't easy. Just ask F.W. de Klerk. So, from here on I intend to say nothing negative about AFSCME. In fact, I'd like to say something reassuring. We don't really want state and local workers to live in Social Security squalor. We simply want a system like yours. But, we can't get that system as long as

---

42. Alicia Munnell, "The Impact of Mandatory Social Security Coverage of State and Local Workers: A Multi-State Review" [online] (Washington, D.C.: Public Policy Institute, AARP, August 2000 — [cited 8 August 2002]), *Executive Summary*; available from *http://research.aarp.org/econ/2000_11_security_1.html*.

people like you, sitting outside of Social Security, are lining up with opponents of reform.

Social Security transfers are unique

Actually, there is something very important that we can learn from the AFSCME website. It says, "Social Security's pension benefit formulas are intentionally designed to replace a significantly larger portion of covered pay for lower wage workers.... By way of comparison, *almost all pension programs* covering governmental employees (and private sector workers as well) provide pensions under the 'individual equity' approach; i.e., benefits are directly proportional to earnings and length of covered service..." (emphasis added). AFSCME confirms the point we were making in the last chapter: there is no plan, *anywhere* that attempts to redistribute wealth to nearly the degree that Social Security does.

The Social Security benefit-shifting formula is unique, but is that clear to most Americans? Not a chance. I suspect that many (probably most) think that the Social Security actuaries use fairly conventional methods to figure out what people are owed in benefits, as related to what they paid in payroll taxes. But it's not so, and this is the principal reason Social Security benefits are so much less than those of governmental workers.

Figure 12[43]

Social Security Replacement Rates
Benefits as a percentage of wages

Social Security   ■ **Minnesota**   • **New York**

In Chapter III, it was noted that huge amounts of Social Security benefits are shifted from one beneficiary to another via a unique 3-rate benefit formula. On the chart, above, the impact of the 3-rate formula is evident. Benefits, as a percentage of salary, are shown for different salary levels, which increase as we move toward the right. Three plans are compared: Social Security, the Minnesota Teachers Retirement Association, and the New York State Teacher's Retirement System. Can you guess which line depicts Social Security? Here's a hint. The graph of its replacement rates would make a great ski slope the higher the salary, the lower the benefits. Now, look at the lines depicting the replacement rates for public employee plans in those two centers of progressive generosity — New York and Minnesota. The replacement rates don't drop a bit as wages increase because there is no shifting of benefits to low earners. Do you now understand why AFSCME and its members want to stay out of Social Security?

We aren't talking small differences here. The next figure dramatically illustrates the magnitude of the Social Security income shifting.

---

43. Underlying information obtained from online benefit calculators for each of three retirement programs. Internet addresses are *www.ssa.gov* (Social Security), *www.tra.state.mn.us/* (Minnesota), and *www.nystrs.org/*. (New York).

Figure 13

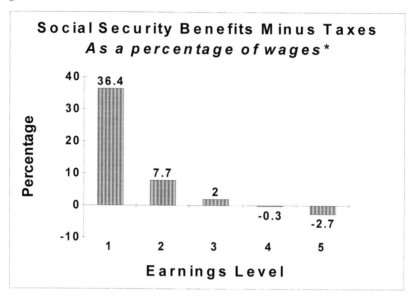

For people born in 1956 through 1960

Figure 13 is based upon data from "Lifetime Distributional Effects of Social Security Retirement Benefits," by Smith, Toder, and Iams.[44] In the chart, Social Security retirees are divided into 5 groups according to career wage levels, with "high earners" shown on the right side of the chart. For each group, the total benefits received minus the total payroll taxes paid, is shown as a percentage of taxable earnings. As you can see, the "low earners" (left side) have net benefits equal to more than 36% of taxable earnings. People in the next group have net benefits of just under 8%. People in the middle income range (wages around $35,000 per year) receive only a 2% net benefit. And people in the upper 40% get nothing. In fact, they have negative net benefits. Put another way, these do not really have Social Security at all. They are simply being used.

44. Graph based on information from Karen Smith and Eric Toder of the Urban Institute and Howard Iams of the Social Security Administration, "Lifetime Distributional Effects of Social Security Retirement Benefits," (Boston College Center for Retirement Research, 17 May 2001 — [cited 4 February 2002]), p.34, table 1b (benefits minus taxes column); available from *www.urban.org/UploadedPDF/410362_retirement-benefits.pdf.*

In the last paragraph, I put quotation marks around "low earners," because we don't really know if these people are, in fact, low earners. As we discussed in the previous chapter, Social Security's welfare delivery system is very crude. Every year it shifts billions of dollars of benefits to people who appear to be poor but are not, because they have wealth from spouses and from a variety of sources in retirement. Can you imagine any other retirement plan that would take a fixed percentage of your paycheck and redistribute a significant portion of it to others *without your knowledge or consent?* They don't do it in the private plans or the plans for public-sector workers. If they did, the trustees would be thrown in jail.

Can we have "individual equity" and help the poor?

We need public-sector workers to join Social Security so that we are all on the same team. We also need to reform Social Security so that it more closely resembles the public-sector plans. In that way, we will all have individual equity — within one public retirement system. But, where does that leave the poor?

It is important to realize that no one is advocating that *needy* people (or people even *slightly* needy) be denied special assistance. Rather, the argument pertains to three issues: who should get the assistance, what program should provide it, and who should pay for it? The answers are clear. First, welfare should be focused on those who really need it. That necessitates "means testing" — not for basic retirement benefits — only for the *extra* benefits that are distributed. When we do it right, the poor can get *more* help — not less. Second, a retirement program is not the proper venue for providing massive amounts of welfare. That should be done in a program designed to carefully monitor the distributions in an efficient and effective manner. And, finally, *all* taxpayers, including the wealthy and the 5 million public-sector workers, should share in the cost. That means we have to finance special assistance programs with general income tax revenues — not payroll taxes. For this reason, any reform of Social Security would probably necessitate adjustments to the federal income tax.

Financial Impact on Social Security

So far, we have explored whether it is equitable for our government to sanction two different retirement systems, one with benefits that are vastly superior to those of the other. However, getting state and local workers into Social Security is a matter of finances as well as fairness. According to a 1999 report by the American Academy of Actuaries, 11% of Social Security's 75-year actuarial imbalance would be eliminated simply by requiring *newly-hired* state and local workers to participate.[45] That would be a savings of about $13 billion per year (11% times $118 billion). Mind you, this reduction would be accomplished without taking away benefits from anyone who is already in a public-sector program.

Why would Social Security improve, financially, by including AWOL state and local workers? We've already discussed two of the reasons: the state and local workers would share in our burden of caring for low-income seniors, and they would help us pay implicit interest on the unfunded liability (the debt that has accumulated since 1935 for people who underpaid payroll tax). A third reason is revealed by the following comments from a speech by Dr. Henry Aaron of the Brookings Institution:

> As a first step, I would extend Social Security to all state and local workers in the U.S. About a third of them are not now paying into the system, and it is a bit of a rip-off. The reason why it is a rip-off is that most of those workers eventually acquire eligibility through part-time work or work before or after their exempt covered employments. Because they have a relatively brief period of employment, they will be seen by Social Security as relatively low wage workers and will receive disproportionately large benefits. So in the name of equity for the rest of us to prevent this situation, all of these workers should be brought into the system on the same terms that apply to the rest of us.[46]

It is inherently difficult to coordinate Social Security with the retirement systems of exempt state and local workers, and Dr. Aaron describes an adverse financial consequence of that difficulty. A $50,000-per-year teacher or policeman picks up an extra $15,000 by moonlighting, and he *looks poor* to the folks at Social Security, who only see the $15,000 (and not the exempt $50,000). As a result, he gets benefits at a rate that is greater than that of others in the program.

---

45. American Academy of Actuaries, "Options for Strengthening Social Security" [online] (presented to Committee on Ways and Means, Subcommittee on Social Security, 18 June 2001 — [cited 3 November 2002]); available from *http://waysandmeans.house.gov/legacy/socsec/107cong/6-18-01/options.htm.*

46. Henry Aaron, in remarks made during presentation entitled, "Avoiding Generational Warfare: Social Security and the Budget" [online] (George Mason University, Fairfax, VA, the Concord Coalition, 20 June 1995 — [cited 5 November 2002]); available from *http://www.concordcoalition.org/entitlements/soc_sec_forum.html.*

This problem and similar problems involving spousal benefits were a great deal more acute prior to passage of the Windfall Elimination Provision (WEP) in 1983 and the Government Pension Offset provision (GPO) in 1977. These laws have provisions which reduce, but do not eliminate, the opportunity for public-sector workers to pick up Social Security benefits at favorable rates. Unfortunately, enforcement of the WEP and GPO reform legislation has been weak. A GAO report issued in May, 2003 notes:

> ...SSA lacks payment controls and is often unable to determine whether applicants should be subject to GPO or WEP because it has not developed any independent source [for verifying who is getting a governmental pension].... [W]e estimated that failure to reduce benefits for federal, state, and local employees caused $160 million to $355 million in overpayments between 1978 and 1995.[47]

To make matters worse, recent reports indicate that thousands of governmental workers have entered into sham employment agreements in an outrageous effort — successful so far — to circumvent the GPO reform provisions altogether. But, that's a story that warrants its own chapter.

Forked-tongue scoundrels

In summary, we have retirement apartheid in this country. A privileged minority enjoys vastly superior retirement benefits, sanctioned by law. In many cases, these elite workers want nothing to do with Social Security unless it is to pick up some lucrative benefits via moonlighting jobs or loopholes. And, to add insult to injury, the unions representing these privileged workers seem to actively resist any change to the Social Security status quo.

In an article entitled, "Forked-tongue Scoundrels," economist Walter Williams suggests some very good questions to pose to opponents of Social Security reform:

> When politicians boast to you about the wonders of Social Security, you should ask them: 'If Social Security is so wonderful, how come people have to be pulled kicking and screaming into it? If it's so wonderful, how come you're petitioning Clinton to spare your municipal employee constituents from being pulled into it?' I bet they will fork you gibberish for answers.[48]

---

47. "Social Security Issues Relating to Noncoverage of Public Employees," GAO-03-710T (U.S. General Accounting Office, 1 May 2003), 5.

What we must do

• The SSA must demand better reporting by government pension plans so that the GPO and WEP reform legislation can be implemented effectively. It may be necessary to impose stiff penalties on governmental plans that fail to accurately report the retiree benefit amounts.

• All new public-sector workers should be brought into Social Security. Once these "white settlers" are forced into Social Security, the momentum toward reform will increase dramatically. In addition, their participation will significantly ease insolvency problems.

• We need to study the public-sector plans, for there is much to learn from them. One such plan is reviewed at the end of this book.

• Demand "individual equity" for all, or "individual equity" for none. Our government should not sanction separate and unequal retirement systems. There must no longer be retirement apartheid in America.

---

48. Walter E. Williams, "Forked-Tongue Scoundrels" [online] *WorldNetDaily*, 4 August 1999 — [cited 6 August 2002]; available from *http://www.worldnetdaily.com/news/article.asp?ARTICLE_ID=20980*.

CHAPTER V: THE WORLD'S HIGHEST PAID JANITORS

(HOW TO MAKE $100,000 PER DAY)

Trading rulers for mops

What do you think is reasonable compensation for a janitor: $20,000, $50,000, or $100,000 per year? Down in Texas, where they like to do everything big, the answer is $100,000 per *day*.

In the first 6 months of 2002, thirty five hundred (3,521) Texas teachers traded rulers for mops on the last day of their careers. As a result of those 8-hour career changes, each will collect, on average, extra retirement benefits worth about $100,000.[49,50] Who will pay for those benefits? Social Security. [51]

As noted in Chapter III, a married retiree can collect a "spousal benefit" equal in amount to one half the value of his/her spouse's normal retirement benefit. For most of us, however, the spousal benefit is payable *only to the extent that it exceeds our own benefit*. For example, if Jim's own benefit is $500 per month, and his wife's benefit is $1,200, Jim will get a spousal benefit of $100 per month (i.e., one-half times wife's benefit of $1,200, *less Jim's own benefit* of $500).

---

49. "Congress Should Consider Revising the Government Pension Offset 'Loophole'," GAO-03-498T (U.S. General Accounting Office, 27 February 2003), 4,6.

50. Per GAO report GAO-03-498T, each teacher is expected to collect an average of $5,200 per year over 19.4 years, for a total of $101,000 per teacher. However, the same GAO report includes a contradictory estimate of just $4,800 per year, which would produce a total of $93,000 per teacher.

51. To be fair, the benefits won't be completely free. The average teacher paid nearly $3 in Social Security taxes in order to qualify for those benefits.

In the case of state and local governmental workers, very different rules used to apply, until 1977. A retiring governmental worker, married to a Social Security retiree, could get the full Social Security spousal benefit *in addition* to his or her own lucrative governmental pension — without offset. In 1977 Congress eliminated this inequity by passing the Government Pension Offset (GPO) — legislation that makes the rules for governmental workers similar to those for Social Security workers. There is one remaining distinction, however, and it is favorable to the state and local workers. Their spousal benefits are only partly reduced, whereas benefits for workers subject to Social Security are fully reduced.[52]

A loophole for "jani-teachers"

As noted, government workers fare relatively well under the GPO reform legislation, in that they retain better spousal benefits than the rest of us. However, this degree of preferential treatment is not sufficient for certain Lone Star teachers. In very recent years, a loophole has been discovered, exploited, and used by many teachers to avoid the GPO reform rules completely. According to the GAO:

> [T]he law provides an exemption from the GPO if an individual's last day of state or local government employment is in a position covered by both Social Security and their state/local pension system. In these cases, the GPO will not apply, and Social Security spousal benefits will not be reduced.[53]

And now you know why the teachers traded rulers for mops. By morphing into "jani-teachers" on the last day of employment, the teachers became subject to Social Security (ostensibly), exempted themselves from the GPO rules, and became eligible for thousands of dollars of benefits.

---

52. Since 1983, the spousal benefits payable to state/local government employees have been offset by only $2 for every $3 dollars received from their own state/local government pension plans. On the other hand, spousal benefits payable Social Security workers are fully reduced (dollar-for-dollar) by their own Social Security benefits.

53. "Congress Should Consider Revising the Government Pension Offset 'Loophole'" 1.

The staggering costs

Since those 3,521 Texas teachers made the one-day career change, in the first 6 months of 2002, 1,274 more have made the switch (or are about to), according to Texas officials. The GAO reports that these identified transactions (plus a handful in Georgia) will end up costing the Social Security system $450 million. And, remember, that is just for the ones we know about. The GAO states:

> [B]ecause no central data exists on use of the GPO exemption by individuals in approximately 2,300 state and local government retirement plans nationwide, we could not definitively confirm that this practice is occurring [or not occurring] in states other than Texas and Georgia....[54]

As for the future, there is reason for alarm. According to the GAO, school officials report increased usage of the loophole. For example, "officials in one school district reported rapid growth — from one worker in 1996 to 1,050 in 2002." And, a "school district that began offering last-day employment this year has received over 1,400 applications from individuals seeking to use the exemption."[55] We have a very costly problem that is getting worse quickly.[56]

Team work

How did thousands of teachers stumble upon this "exemption" during the last few years? You can be sure that it wasn't just happenstance. It took a team effort involving many knowledgeable, hardworking, and not-too-ethical participants. Here are a few of them:

• School districts looking for fees

Some school districts are very aggressive in promoting these one-day career changes. One even advertises a special "Temporary Employment Program" on its website,[57] and the district's superintendent boasts of the results: "It blossomed into something where we have several hundred people who come work for us for one day."[58]

---

54. *Ibid.*, 1-2.

55. "Revision to the Government Pension Offset Exemption Should be Considered," GAO-02-950 (U.S. General Accounting Office, August 2002), 15.

56. It should be noted that none of the cost of this unfolding scandal is reflected in the estimates of Chapter IV, or in the "Wheel of Waste" in Chapter II.

A university incorporates the loophole into standard retirement planning for its staff. It has already booked these special loophole work days through the year 2005.[59]

And, often, there are fees charged by the school districts — big fees. According to the GAO, "These fees are a significant source of revenue — last year one school district collected over $283,000 in fees." In the opinion of Andrew G. Biggs, former staff member of the President's Commission to Strengthen Social Security, these processing charges are, effectively, a "kick-back" of benefits to the school districts that facilitate the last minute career changes.[60]

• Unions (trying to justify those dues?)

According to the GAO, availability of the loophole is "being publicized by teaching associations and groups (websites, newspapers, seminars, etc.) and by word-of-mouth."[61] An example can be found in the *Texas Teacher*, the official publication of the Texas Federation of Teachers (TFT), where teachers are advised to consider transferring to one of the 40 or 50 school districts (out of hundreds in Texas) that can help them use the loophole. Here is an excerpt from that publication, as it appears on the website of the TFT:

> Because of an obscure provision in the law — spell that loophole — you can avoid losing your spousal benefits under Social Security if you retire from an employer that provides both TRS and Social Security coverage. So, you leave your current tight-fisted employer and spend as little as a day.... The Spousal Benefit Offset just goes away.

The TFT also notes that it will provide members with the list of employers who might play the loophole game, if the members call a toll-free number, which is provided.[62]

---

57. Allen Pusey, "Pension Loophole Exploited" [online] *DallasNews.com*, 16 August 2002 — [cited 15 May 2003]; available from *http://www.dallasnews.com/politics/nationalnews/stories/081602dntexGAO.9807b.html*.

58. John C. Henry, Texas teachers use pension loophole to boost benefits" [online] *HoustonChronicle.com*, 15 August 2002 — [cited 30 May 30, 2003]; available from *www.HoustonChronicle.com*.

59. "Revision to the Government Pension Offset Exemption Should be Considered," 16.

60. Andrew G. Biggs, "Close the Government Pension Loophole for Texas Teachers" [online] (Washington, D.C.: Cato Institute, 14 April 2003 — [cited 24 April 2003]); available from *http://www.cato.org/dailys/04-14-03.html*.

61. "Revision to the Government Pension Offset Exemption Should be Considered," 16.

The unions are also pressing legislators to repeal the GPO reform legislation, outright.[63] They claim it is a matter of fairness. According to the *Dallas Morning News*:

> Jeri Stone, executive director of the Texas Classroom Teachers Association, said her organization not only encourages Texas teachers to take advantage of the loophole, but also lobbies against the [unfair] federal provision that was intended to prohibit public employees from collecting both.[64]

Let me see if I understand Ms. Stone's position. The rules which limit spousal benefits for 96.5% of the population (i.e., those of us who are *not* in state/local governmental pension plans) are unfair when applied (even partially) to her association's membership. Apparently, in the view of Ms. Stone, teachers should get to keep their own pensions *plus* spousal benefits, while the rest of us just keep one or the other.

• Politicians in the pocket

In March 2003, important Social Security anti-fraud legislation was defeated (temporarily) by the opposing votes of 166 Democrats and 13 Republicans. The bill, HR 743, included provisions to protect senior citizens and disabled workers from unscrupulous attorneys and other representatives, to halt payment of Social Security benefits to fugitive felons and parole violators, and to expand the availability of civil monetary penalties. Why was it voted down? It also included a provision that would have eliminated the GPO loophole — the technicality exploited by teachers who make these last-day career changes. The defeated bill was resurrected in a subsequent vote, but the pro-teacher politicians were undeterred. Rep. Gene Green (D-TX) sponsored an amendment specifically designed to strip (from HR 743) the language that would have denied benefits to the one-day jani-teachers. Incredibly, Green was able to round

---

62. "Social Security and School Employees," *Texas Teacher*, [online] (Texas Federation of Teachers, May 2002 — [cited 15 May 2003]), available from *http://www.tft.org/docs/txteacher.pdf*.

63. In the Senate, Susan Collins (R-ME) and Diane Feinstein (D-CA) are sponsoring legislation to repeal the GPO reform legislation. In the House, Buck McKeon (D-CA) and Howard Berman (D-CA) are sponsoring an equivalent bill. These assaults on the Social Security system would take us back to the double-dipping days of the 1970's, when public workers could collect their own ample pensions, while collecting spousal benefits intended for those with little or no retirement income of their own.

64. Allen Pusey, "Pension Loophole Exploited."

up 195 votes supporting this outrageous assault on the Social Security system. Although the amendment failed, and the bill is currently pending, the message is clear and unmistakable. Many politicians pay lip service to Social Security, but they are beholden to the powerful government employee unions. When there's a choice between Social Security and the unions, they'll side with the unions every time.

What's next?

The smart money says that the loophole will be terminated this year (after a lot more retiring teachers slip through the closing door). However, it appears that *nobody* is trying to recover the half billion dollars that has already been awarded. In fact, the SSA and the GAO have proclaimed this loophole to be a legal "exemption."[65] But it is time to talk straight. This is no exemption. It is not even a loophole, really. It is a sham: an *illegal* "sham in substance," to be precise.

They ought to be sued

A good overview of the doctrine of sham transactions is found in the opinion of a U.S. District Court involving a petition of the Internal Revenue Service against a taxpayer:

> The sham transaction doctrine originated with the Supreme Court decision of Gregory v. Helvering, 293 US 465 (1935).... Although the taxpayers had followed each step required by the I.R.C. for the reorganization, the Court nonetheless held these losses nondeductible, reasoning that the transaction was a "mere device" for the 'consummation of a preconceived plan' and not a reorganization within the intent of the Code as it then existed.... Because the transaction lacked *economic substance*, as opposed to formal reality, it was not "the thing which the statute intended" (emphasis added).

The District Court went on to distinguish two types of shams.

---

65. To back up its contention that the one-day exemption is lawful, the GAO cites the SSA's Program Operations Manual System, GN 02608.102 (a simple policy statement that makes no legal references). When asked to present its own legal analysis, the GAO declined, citing "attorney-client and attorney work-product privileges." The SSA was asked (by the author) to release any documents in its possession which support the legal opinion expressed in GN 02608.102. None has been provided thus far.

Courts have recognized two basic types of sham transactions: shams in fact and shams in substance. See ACM 157 F.3d at 247 n, 30 (citing Kirchman, 862 F.2d ct 1492). "[S]hams in fact" are transactions that never occurred in reality, that is, transactions that have been created on paper but which never took place...."[S]hams in substance" are transactions that actually occurred but are devoid of *economic substance*....[emphasis added].[66]

The color of money

The essence of each of the above citations is the reference to "economic substance." No matter how perfect and official a transaction might appear, it must have, at the least, a smidgeon of economic substance. Otherwise, it is simply a sham — a sham in substance.[67] And shams are of great concern to every agency of the government — including the SSA. In fact, in one of its own rulings the SSA stated:

> [T]here is a difference between creating a bona fide employment relationship and merely giving to certain purported payments the color of wages for the purpose of qualifying for old-age insurance benefits....
>
> In determining whether a bona fide employment relationship exists, the courts have held that the Social Security Administration has "...both right and the duty to scrutinize with care the actuality of the relationship..." (Quoting Hall v. Ribicoff, CCH, UIR, Fed. Para. 14,374; Thurston v. Hobby, 133).[68]

Did the GAO and the SSA connect the dots?

In their rush to proclaim that the GPO sham is a legal "exemption," the GAO and the SSA appear to have overlooked some facts — facts which prove that there was not a scintilla of economic substance in these one day career changes. Most of the teachers took pay *cuts* to become janitors. (According to the GAO they only made about $6 per hour — $50 per day.) Many actually *lost* money after incurring related expenses. The GAO notes: "Some schools reported that they charge[d] a processing fee, ranging from $100 — $500, to hire these workers." [69] Travel costs were high because many teachers had to transfer to

---

66. Internal Revenue Service v. CM Holdings, Inc., 254 B.R. 578 (D. Del. 2000).

67. I am generously presuming that the teachers actually showed up for the 8 hours and did some cleaning. If not, these one-day stints were "shams *in fact*."

68. Social Security Ruling SSR 76-13a [online] (Social Security Administration, 1976 — [cited 14 May 2003]); available from *http://www.ssa.gov/OP_Home/rulings/oasi/43/SSR76-13-oasi-43.html*.

new school districts to implement the loophole strategy.[70] It was reported that one teacher traveled 800 miles to do his one-day career change.[71] And then there were motel costs. "They drive there [to one of the school districts], spend a night in a motel, go to work one whole day, get their paycheck and then go home. And then they are retired."[72] Let's see. A teacher travels 800 miles, pays for a motel room, pays $100 to $500 in fees, and then earns a total of 50 bucks. Now, there is a job with some real economic substance!

The importance of remuneration

The SSA has already commented on a case involving similar economic issues. In the SSA ruling previously cited, a 71-year-old lady claimed benefits on the basis of work performed for her sister. Although she had been paid, she admitted to having subsequently paid back the wages to her sister. In denying her claim, the SSA noted:

> [A]n even stronger indication that a true employment relationship did not exist was the revelation made by the claimant during the course of her appearance before the Appeals Council that she paid back to her sister whatever her sister paid to her. In actuality, the claimant received no remuneration for the services performed for her sister.[73]

With regard to many of these Texas teacher-janitors, the same thing could be said. "In actuality, these claimants received no remuneration for the services performed," *because they paid it back in the form of fees, lodging, and travel costs!*

---

69. "Congress Should Consider Revising the Government Pension Offset 'Loophole,'"4.

70. Only a small percentage of Texas school districts pay wages subject to Social Security as well as wages subject to governmental pensions, and these are the only districts capable of executing the loophole strategy. As a result, many jani-teachers have to travel a long way to put in their 8 hours of cleaning work.

71. "Revision to the Government Pension Offset Exemption Should be Considered," 16.

72. Charles Dupre, Assoc. Superintendent for business and finance for the Fort Bend School District, quoted in John C. Henry, Texas teachers use pension loophole to boost benefits."

73. Social Security Ruling SSR 76-13a.

Civil or criminal?

At the minimum, the SSA should stop paying benefits awarded on the basis of sham transactions. Let the teachers sue for benefits — we'll see how they justify the "economic substance" of these one-day jobs! Where benefits have already been paid, the SSA should take civil legal action, if necessary, to recover the funds. *The spousal benefits taken as a result of sham transactions must be returned to the Social Security trust fund.*

However, the SSA should also consider making selective criminal referrals, if warranted by the facts. Did the school district that collected fees of $283,000 cross the line? Did the university that scheduled sham work days through the year 2005 go too far? Why are they less culpable than, say, the operators of shady tax shelters, who sell tax breaks on the basis of technically correct, but meaningless, trusts and loan agreements?

Generally, the Social Security criminal statutes (for the worker retirement program) are found in 42 U.S.C. Section 408. However, John K. Webb, Special Assistant United States Attorney, notes: "The existence of specific criminal penalties in the Social Security Act does not preclude prosecution under more general criminal statutes found in Title 18." And Title 18 sometimes provides a more amenable route to prosecution. According to Webb, "[t]his statute does not require fraud as a necessary element, whereas under the Social Security felony fraud statute fraud is a necessary element."[74]

These people were married — or were they?

In Lutwak v. United States, 344 U.S. 604 (1953), conspiracy to defraud the United States was found (under Title 18) where three men went to France, got married (in form only), and returned with brides. The real goal of the marriages was to circumvent immigration law — not to do the other things that married people do. The three men contended that there was no unlawful conspiracy because the marriages were, in fact, perfectly valid. But the Court ruled:

---

74. John K. Webb, "Prosecuting Social Security Fraud: Protecting the Trust Fund for Present and Future Generations," vol. 49, no. 6 of *United States Attorneys' Bulletin* (United States Department of Justice, Executive Office for United States Attorneys, November, 2001), 4.

We do not believe that the validity of the marriages is material. No one is being prosecuted for an offense against the marital relation. We consider the marriage ceremonies only as a *part of the conspiracy* to defraud the United States and to commit offenses against the United States.... [T]he ceremonies were only a step in the fraudulent scheme and actions taken by the parties to the conspiracy (emphasis added).[75]

Could the reasoning used in the Lutwak case be applied to the GPO loophole scam? We need to test it.

The Lutwak v. United States case, redux

Let's replay the Lutwak quotation with just one substitution. We'll replace the references to *marriage* with references to *employment*.

We do not believe that the validity of the *employment* agreements is material. No one is being prosecuted for an offense against the *employment* relation. We consider the *employment agreements* only as a part of the conspiracy to defraud the United States and to commit offenses against the United States.... [T]he *agreements* were only a step in the fraudulent scheme and actions taken by the parties to the conspiracy.

"If the words fit, you must *not* acquit."

Texas teachers strike out, even on a technical basis

It is doubtful that the Texas teachers qualify for this "exemption," even on a superficial and technical basis. Has anyone bothered to read the statute? Section 402(b)(4)(A) states:

The amount of a wife's insurance benefit for each month ... shall be reduced (but not below zero) by an amount equal to two-thirds of the amount of any monthly periodic benefit payable to the wife (or divorced wife) for such month which is based upon her earnings while in the service of the Federal Government or any State (or political subdivision thereof, as defined in section 418(b)(2) of this title) *if, on the last day she was employed by such entity ... such service did not constitute "employment" as defined in section 410 of this title ...* [emphasis added].[76]

---

75. Lutwak et al. v. United States , 344 U.S. 604 (1953).
76. Comparable wording for the husband's benefit is found in subsection (c).

That's cut and dried: the spousal benefit will be reduced if the services rendered on the last day before retirement did not constitute "employment" as defined in section 410 (the section that defines employment for purposes of Social Security). Apparently, the Texas teachers think that their last day services met the section 410 standard. The facts, however, say otherwise.

What "employment" isn't

The easiest way to show that the services of the jani-teachers did *not* constitute section 410 employment is by focusing on one of that section's specific exclusions. According to section 410(a), "such term ['employment'] shall *not* include ... [s]ervice performed in the employ of a State, or any political subdivision thereof ..." unless it is (paraphrasing)

- service for certain public transportation systems,
- service in the employ of the government of Guam or Samoa,
- service in the employ of the District of Columbia,
- service by someone who is not a member of the state or local retirement plan, or
- service included in an agreement under Title II, Section 418.

The Texas teachers had to meet at least one of the five exceptions listed above. Otherwise, they were barred, as state/local employees, from Social Security coverage under Section 410.

Obviously, the first four exceptions did not apply. The teachers didn't drive buses in public transportation, they didn't work for Guam, Samoa or Washington, D.C., and all were members of the teachers' retirement plan. That leaves only exception 5, concerning an agreement under Title II, Section 418.

Section 418 of the Code authorizes the Commissioner of Social Security to enter into agreements with states to extend Social Security coverage to state and local governmental workers.[77] Since the 1950s, hundreds of these agreements have been executed between the federal government and various state and local government employers, such as school districts. Each of these voluntary agreements specifies which state and local workers are, and are not, eligible for coverage under Social Security. The services performed by the Texas teachers during their one-day stints had to be pursuant to one of these agreements under

---

77. These are commonly called "Section 218 Agreements" because they were authorized by section 218 of the Act (which was codified into section 418 of the statutes). To avoid confusion, we simply refer to them as "section 418 agreements."

section 418; otherwise, the teachers failed to meet the technical requirements of the loophole.

The section 418 agreement of the Coleman ISD

Perhaps the ring leader of all Texas school districts peddling the one-day janitor jobs is the Coleman Independent School District (Coleman), located just northeast of San Angelo. It's the district that advertises for temporary help on its website (www.colemanisd.com), and it charges $200 a pop for processing fees. Also, it has the superintendent who bragged of the "several hundred people who come work for us for one day." Since Coleman seems to be state-of-the-art in these matters, a close examination of its section 418 agreement is in order.

The Coleman agreement, executed in 1960, gives Social Security coverage to many employees but specifically excludes certain categories of employment. One of those excluded categories is, "*Employees engaged in rendering services in part-time positions.*"[78]

How is "part-time" defined for purposes of section 418? The SSA's handbook for state Social Security administrators states:

> Generally, a part-time position is one in which the number of hours of work normally required by the position in a week or pay period is less than the normal time requirements for the majority of positions in the employing entity.... A definition may apply on a statewide basis or different definitions may be given for different coverage groups.[79]

According to Susan Mariano, the SSA state and local coverage specialist for the region including Texas, there is no state-wide definition in Texas; the term is defined by the electing school district.[80] With this in mind, I asked a knowledgeable official at Coleman to define the term, and was told the

---

78. Per "Modification No. 347 to Texas State Social Security Agreement" (dated February, 1960), provided by the Social Security Administration, and represented (by an Agency specialist) to be the most recent modification affecting the Coleman ISD. Also, per an Agreement executed in February, 1960 between the President of the Coleman Independent School District and the Director of the Social Security Division of the Texas Department of Public Welfare (provided by the Coleman ISD).

79. "State and Local Coverage Handbook for the Social Security Administration and State Social Security Administrators" (Social Security Administration, August 1995), Section 437.

80. Per telephone conversation between Ms. Mariano and author.

following: A part-time position (for Coleman) could be a job which is one, two, or three days per week. The critical factor is the number of hours worked in the week. Coleman regards a job averaging over 25 hours per week to be full-time; a job averaging less than that is part-time.

The Coleman jani-teachers have a problem

It's pretty clear that most (if not all) of the one-day janitors hired by Coleman were not full-time employees. They were hired by Coleman with the *expectation* that the employment would be completed after just 8 hours — far less than the 25 hours needed to constitute full-time employment. How do we know that these positions were only expected to last 8 hours? We know because we were told this, indirectly, by Coleman's Superintendent. He's the one who said: "[W]e have several hundred people who come work for us *for one day*" (emphasis added). We also know because the "Temporary Employment" ad on Coleman's website directly states that it hires people for "as little as one day." And, finally, we know because all of these new hires were within mere hours of meeting retirement service requirements. Clearly, Coleman had to realize that many or most of these employees would never accumulate the 25 hours required to constitute full-time employment. Therefore, by Coleman's own standard, these were part-time positions — *not* legally entitled to Social Security coverage under Coleman's section 418 agreement and, consequently, not qualified for the GPO loophole.

Were Coleman jani-teachers entitled to any Social Security?

As a matter of academic interest, we could debate whether Coleman's one-day cleaners were qualified for Social Security coverage under *any* provision. In 1990, mandatory Social Security laws were enacted to give coverage to many of the employees excluded by section 418 agreements. However, those mandatory rules do not apply to workers who are qualified participants in a public retirement system. In IRS Publication 963, "Federal-State Reference Guide," it is noted: "If the employee is a member of a public retirement system, the employee is exempt from mandatory social security."[81]

---

81. "Federal-State Reference Guide," Publication 963 (Internal Revenue Service, 2002), I-4.

Perhaps the Coleman employees could qualify for Social Security under some other provision (which eludes me); however, it doesn't really matter because Social Security coverage, per se, doesn't qualify the employees for the GPO loophole. To qualify for the loophole, there must be employment as defined in section 410. Nothing less will suffice. But, cheer up, all you retired Coleman jani-teachers! You can probably apply for a refund of the $3 in payroll taxes improperly withheld from your paychecks.

Coleman's not the only one with a problem

The school districts participating in these scams have not been publicly identified by the GAO.[82] However, on its website (www.atpe.org), the Association of Texas Professional Educators (ATPE) lists five districts "known to have an open-door policy" to those seeking the GPO loophole. One of the five districts is Coleman. The other four are Kilgore ISD, Lindale Consolidated ISD, Sweeney ISD, and West ISD. Copies of the section 418 agreements for these four districts were obtained and reviewed to determine whether they grant Social Security coverage to part-time workers.[83] Two of these four districts (West and Lindale Consolidated) have the same technical problem as does Coleman. That is, they exclude part-time workers. *The spousal benefits awarded to part-time employees in these districts (i.e. districts that exclude part-timers from Social Security coverage) must be returned to the Social Security trust fund.*[84]

---

82. According to the GAO, release of school district names has not been authorized by the Chairman of the Subcommittee on Social Security of the House Ways and Means Committee (per letter to author from GAO, dated June 27, 2003).

83. Based upon the section 418 modification agreements provided by the SSA, and by Ms. Carolyn Fry, the State Social Security Administrator for the state of Texas.

84. In addition to the 5 districts known to have an "open door" policy, ATPE lists 44 other districts that provide Social Security coverage for all or some workers. Some of these districts may also play the loophole game; however, none has been publicly identified, to my knowledge. To test the prevalence of the part-time worker exclusion among these other districts, section 418 agreements for a sample of 10 districts (judgmentally selected) were obtained from the SSA, and reviewed. Six of the ten districts did not provide coverage for part-time employees.

Another technical glitch

Another technical problem (for jani-teachers) can be found in Code section 410 (b), which states:

> If the services performed during one-half or more of any pay period by an employee for the person employing him constitute employment, all the services of such employee for such period shall be deemed to be employment; but if the services performed during more than one-half of any such pay period by an employee for the person employing him do not constitute employment, then none of the services of such employee for such period shall be deemed to be employment.

In other words, an all-or-nothing rule is used. If half of the pay period is devoted to services covered by Social Security (such as janitorial services), all of the services performed in that pay period are deemed to be covered. But, if most of the pay period is devoted to non-covered services (such as teaching), none of the work performed in the pay period qualifies for Social Security coverage.

This rule may not be a problem for the teachers who transferred to a new district before retiring. The 8 hours they worked as custodians were probably the only hours worked in the entire pay period (for that particular employer). But, for workers changing positions *within the same school district*, the section 410(b) rule poses a serious problem. Since most pay periods are 2 weeks or semi-monthly, it seems highly unlikely that a single day of covered service (i.e., covered for purposes of Social Security) would constitute "one half or more of any pay period." In situations where the janitorial duties did not equal 50% of the pay period, there was no employment under section 410, and the GPO loophole requirements were not satisfied. *The spousal benefits taken by employees who taught longer than they cleaned (in the last pay period) must be returned to the Social Security trust fund.*

What is the SSA doing about this?

Normally, SSA evaluates claims for the GPO exemption on the basis of Form SSA-3885, a brief questionnaire completed by the employee. On this form, the retiree is simply asked, in essence, whether he was covered under a state/local pension plan in addition to Social Security on the last day before retirement. If he gives the right answer and signs the form, he qualifies. If he is unable or unwilling to complete the form, the SSA may ask his employer to supplement the employee information by completing a different form (Form SSA-L4163), which includes just 3 questions that pertain to the date and value of the retiree's pension. On neither form will you find any of the following questions, all of which are vital to a meaningful evaluation of a GPO loophole claim:

- Were the services that were performed on the last day of employment (i.e., the janitor duties), eligible for Social Security coverage *under terms of the school district's section 418 agreement?* (If not, the loophole doesn't apply.)
- Was at least half of the final pay period devoted to qualified services? In other words, did the janitor work exceed the teaching work during the final pay period? (If not, the loophole doesn't apply.)
- From the standpoint of the *employee*, was there economic substance in this employment? Specifically, how much did he earn? What were the associated fees? Was there travel and lodging expense? (If there was no economic substance for the *employee*, the loophole doesn't apply.)
- From the standpoint of the *employer*, was there economic substance in this employment? What happened to the regular employee (custodian) on that last day? Were two employees paid for the same (janitorial) duties? How much training was given to the one-day employee? Was the job posted and advertised in accordance with normal district/union policies? (If there was no economic substance for the *employer*, the loophole doesn't apply.)

Judging from the forms used to collect information relative to the GPO "exemption," it appears that most of the important questions *never even get asked* by the SSA. And, apparently, the little bit of information that is collected is not routinely verified. According to the Federal-State Reference Guide (IRS Publication 963):

> A statement from the employer or pension-paying agency showing the employee was in a position on the last day of employment that was covered under social security and also covered by the pension plan is acceptable evidence to show the GPO exemption is met. *SSA generally accepts the employer's statement at face value* when making the determination that the GPO exemption is met (emphasis added).[85]

That's reassuring. The SSA accepts "at face value" whatever the employer tells it — even though there is clear evidence of collusive behavior between employee and employer.[86]

---

85. "Federal-State Reference Guide," Publication 963 (Internal Revenue Service, 2002), 11-6.

Finally, let's stop calling this an "exemption"

> The amount of a wife's insurance benefit for each month ... shall be reduced ... if, on the last day she was employed by such entity ... such service did not constitute "employment" as defined in section 410 of this title ...

That's all it says: The above words, from Section 402, constitute the so-called "exemption" from the spousal benefit reduction rules. These words merely say that spousal benefits will be reduced if the worker is not participating in the Social Security system, as measured on the last day of his/her career. The word "exemption" is not be found in this citation, nor anywhere surrounding it, for in reality this is not an exemption at all. To be an "exemption," it would have to be an affirmative and conscious act of relief or forbearance. There is no implication of such intent here. Rather, there is sloppy wording by legislators who underestimated the cravenness of a few teachers and employers, and their willingness to collude in order to swindle the Social Security system.

A Texas school district stands tall

This chapter has not been kind to Texas teachers and school districts, but it is wrong to paint them all with the same broad brush. No doubt, many would never participate in sham transactions — no matter how much they stood to gain. An example is the Austin Independent School District. As the only district in central Texas that participates in Social Security, it is a potential magnet for teachers desiring to use the GPO loophole. Nevertheless, it does not participate. "We get a lot of calls about that," says Spokeswoman Katherine Anthony, "but our position is that it is fraud, and no, we will not do that."[87] In one concise and

---

86. Have the GAO and SSA implemented new audit procedures in light of the unfolding GPO scandal? The author put this question to the GAO, which responded in a letter dated June 27, 2003. The agency stated: "GAO has not implemented any audit procedures regarding the school districts that we found were offering work to enable individuals to possibly qualify for the GOP (sic) 'loophole.'... We are not aware if SSA has implemented any audit procedures regarding the school districts." The SSA Office of Public Disclosure, in response to a request from the author, would not say if new audit procedures were in place, and did not provide any documents that suggested the existence of new audit procedures.

87. Katherine Anthony, quoted in "Teachers excel in creativity with pensions," unattributed [online] (Austin Community College Classified Employees Association, 17 August, 2002 — [cited 27 May 2003]),]); available from *http://www.austin.cc.tx.us /acccea/ Minutes%208-13-02%20revised.htm;*. Content was verified in direct conversation between author and Ms. Anthony.

clear sentence, Ms. Anthony has addressed the essence of this matter: We must respect both the letter and the spirit of the law. Nothing less is acceptable.

The bottom line

The GPO loophole scam is an outrage. The SSA and GAO must fight vigorously to protect the Social Security trust fund from teachers and employers who collude to defraud the government by means of sham employment agreements. The $450 million awarded to "jani-teachers" must be recovered. In addition, we need to elect legislators who will not subordinate the Social Security system to the whims of the powerful teachers' unions.

In the long run, the best way to eliminate these abusive sham transactions is to have one public retirement system, shared by all. Meanwhile, however, we need to act expeditiously to protect Social Security assets.

- Congress should clarify the law to eliminate the loophole.
- For each retiree who has already used the GPO loophole, payroll transaction details should be audited to see if the last-day services met the technical definition of "employment" under sections 410(a) and 410(b). Those who fail the audit should be asked to return the extra spousal benefits already received.
- For each retiree who passes the technical audit, details of last-day services, compensation, fees, and expenses should be evaluated to determine if there was "economic substance" in the employment (for both teacher and school district). Where there is no economic substance, the teachers should be asked to return the extra spousal benefits already received.
- Retirees who refuse to return the funds should be sued for the benefits, plus interest and penalties. Or, as an alternative, their future benefits could be reduced.
- School districts that received fees for these transactions should be sued, if necessary, to force a return of those fees to the teachers who paid them.
- An assessment of the applicability of criminal statutes should be made.

CHAPTER VI: TWO HIDDEN TAXES IMPOSED ON RETIREES

(MILLIONS OF AMERICANS PAY IT, AND DON'T EVEN KNOW IT)

[O]n April the 15th, the American people will discover the truth about what we did last year on taxes. Only the top 1 — [applause] — yes, listen, the top 1.2 percent of Americans, as I said all along, will pay higher income tax rates. Let me repeat, only the wealthiest 1.2 percent of Americans will face higher income tax rates and no one else will. And that is the truth. [88]

So said President Bill Clinton in his 1994 State of the Union speech, and his word is good enough for me. What I never realized, though, is how *many* people are in the top 1.2%. Perhaps as many as 25% of retirees are in the top 1.2%.[89] If that isn't entirely clear to you, I recommend some remedial study at the Little Rock Institute of Arithmetic Research (L.I.A.R.).

It depends on what the meaning of "tax" is

The 1993 legislation did not raise *taxes* on the middle class; rather, it raised the amount of income subject to taxation. Clinton raised the income threshold — not the tax. It's the vocabulary, stupid! He got millions of Americans to go along with a stiff tax increase — i.e., *income* increase — by making it so sneaky

88. William Clinton, in 1994 State of the Union speech [online] (C-Span.org, 25 January 1994 — [cited 25 July 2003]); available from *http://www.c-span.org/executive/ transcript.asp?cat=current_event&code=bush_admin&year=1994.*

89. Retirees age 65 or more and receiving Social Security.

and complex most of them don't even realize they are paying it. Here is how it works.

Generally speaking, up to 85% of Social Security benefits are taxable if "provisional income" exceeds:

1) $6,925 for married taxpayers filing separate tax returns.

2) $44,000 for married taxpayers filing joint tax returns.

3) $34,000 for single taxpayers.

Provisional income is simply your adjusted gross income, plus any tax-exempt income you might have, plus one-half of Social Security benefits. Prior to 1993, up to half of your Social Security benefits could be taxed. Clinton raised the amount taxed to as high as 85%.

A person with just $7,000 of income could be in the top 1.2%?

Believe it or not, a married person filing a separate return, with provisional income of just over $6,925 (i.e., the sum of his personal exemption and standard deduction for 2002) could be subject to this tax on "the top 1.2 percent of Americans." And, the tax can apply *even where there is no income other than Social Security itself.* In fact, I knew a man whose only income was Social Security (around $18,000). He and his wife always filed separate returns because neither wanted the other to know how much income he/she had. (We all know at least one couple like this.) And each year the man (and, presumably, the woman) paid Clinton's high roller tax.

A "ticking time bomb"

In mid-2000, the House of Representatives voted to roll this tax back from 85% to the 50% rate in effect prior to 1993, but the bill languished in the Senate after a threatened presidential veto. At the time, House Ways and Means Chairman Bill Archer noted:

> [T]his is a ticking time bomb that will explode on millions of seniors over the next generation, because income thresholds are not indexed for inflation. Almost 10 million seniors pay the tax today and more than 20 million retirees will be hit soon. This tax is a clear and present danger to their retirement security.[90]

And, as the old Timex commercial used to say, "it's still ticking!"

In case you think the impact of this tax is minor, think again. This provision nearly doubles the normal tax rates for at least part of your income. The 15% rate effectively becomes 27.75%, the 27% rate becomes 49.95%, and the 30% rate becomes 55.5%. (All rates are those in effect for 2002.) These are marginal rates higher than those paid by multimillionaires. Yet, senior citizens seem to be only vaguely aware of how this calculation works, and how much it costs them. I guess confusion can be a good thing — for politicians. Back in the mid-1990s, many of the same senior citizens who were upset over proposals to increase Medicare premiums by a few bucks per month were oblivious to paying thousands per year in extra taxes on Social Security benefits. Go figure.

Income taxed twice — and not at all

If these high marginal tax rates aren't bad enough, consider the fact that the Clinton increase, from 50% to 85%, is *a double tax* — a tax that was already paid by those senior citizens subject to the Clinton tax. This fact is concealed by averaging these double-taxed victims with the many Social Security retirees who don't pay income tax at all on some of the benefits they receive. But, these two "wrongs" don't average out to make a "right."[91]

Regarding the retirees who *underpay* their tax, the Social Security Advisory Board notes:

> Under present law, Social Security benefits are taxable only if income is above specified thresholds. One alternative [among deficit reduction proposals] would be to phase out the thresholds and tax benefits in a manner similar to that for contributory private pension income.... Phasing out the lower thresholds during 2002-2011, taxing benefits similar to private pensions, and putting all additional revenue raised into the Social Security Trust Funds would eliminate 24 percent of the deficit.[92]

As noted in Appendix A-4, the 75-year open group actuarial imbalance is the equivalent of $118 billion per year, on average, for 75 years. Therefore, a

---

90. "House Approves Rollback of Social Security Benefits Tax: Veto Threatened" [online] *TaxPlanet.com* , 27 July 2000 — [cited 5 November 2002]; available from *wysiwyg://20/http://www.taxplanet.com/legislation/socsecarcher0727/socsecarcher0727.html.*

91. For a simple explanation of the double tax, please refer to Appendix A-8.

92. "Social Security: Why Action Should be Taken Soon," [online] (Social Security Advisory Board, July 2001 — [cited 27 October 2002]), 23; available from *http://www.ssab.gov/actionshouldbetaken.pdf.*

savings of 24% would be the equivalent of $28 billion per year — no small amount. However, would such a change (in tax policy) hurt low-income retirees?

Regarding the impact of a change in tax policy on low-income retirees, the Social Security Advisory Board notes:

> [B]ecause the income tax is structured to protect low income people from being required to pay taxes, beneficiaries with low income would still not pay any income tax on their benefits.[93]

In fact, it has been estimated that 30% of retirees would be exempt from tax, regardless of taxing policy, due to standard deductions and exemptions.[94]

The other sneaky and mean tax

Technically, this one is also not a tax: it just walks and quacks like one. It is the senior citizen earnings penalty. Until recently, if a senior citizen receiving Social Security benefits earned more than a few thousand dollars, his Social Security benefits were sharply reduced unless he was at least age 70. The Senior Citizens' Freedom to Work Act of 2000 eliminated this onerous tax for most seniors but there are many who are still affected. Basically, the earnings penalty (in force today) works like this. If you are getting Social Security benefits, are under full retirement age,[95] and have earned income of more than $11,520 (the amount for 2003), you will have your benefits reduced by $1 for every $2 earned beyond that limit. This is the equivalent of a nasty, 50% federal tax rate, on top of all the other taxes you have to pay. And, sadly, many senior citizens don't even realize that their work income is reducing their benefits.

"Mean" testing

In the Chapter IV, I noted my opposition to means testing with regard to the *basic* benefits owed to retirees. This earnings penalty is a form of means testing, and is a good example of why I oppose it. Actually, we should call it *mean* testing. After all, the person on Social Security who goes to work is, very

---

93. *Ibid.*

94. Ron Gebhardtsbauer, "Social Security Options and Their Effects on Different Demographic Groups" (American Academy of Actuaries, 21 June 1999), 15.

95. "Full retirement age" is between age 65 and age 67, depending on the retiree's year of birth.

possibly, doing so out of necessity — because her Social Security benefits are so pathetic. This assertion is supported by an AARP survey (1999) in which nearly one fourth of baby boomers indicated they would keep working mainly for the income it would provide (and not simply due to vocational interest or enjoyment).[96] We need to ask ourselves this question: If a woman earns wages of, say, $12,000 in addition to $8,000 or $9,000 in Social Security benefits, should we take part of *her* benefits away? No. Means testing should only be used with regard to *extra* benefits (i.e., the welfare part). It should never be applied to a retiree's *basic* benefit.

And now, the amazing 115% tax rate!

This is a quiz. Be alert. Let's pretend you have a good friend in Ohio who is single and age 63, and who has the following amounts of income: wages — $11,000, interest — $500, private pension — $17,500, and Social Security — $16,000.

Your friend needs advice. She wants to help her daughter with college expenses, and has travel plans, but she is a bit short on money. She has a chance to earn $5,000 more by increasing her hours at work. Should she work the extra hours to earn more money?

Before you answer, consider the following breakout of her taxes, statutory and de facto, on the extra $5,000 she wants to earn:

Taxes to pay on $5,000 (2001 tax rates)

Type of tax (statutory and defacto)	Amount	%
Loss of SS benefits due to earnings penalty	$2,500	50.0
Extra federal income tax	2,543	50.9
Ohio income tax	223	4.5
Municipality tax	100	2.0
Social Security tax	310	6.2
Medicare tax	73	1.4
GRAND TOTAL	$5,749	115.0

---

96. "Baby Boomers Envision Their Retirement: An AARP Segmentation Analysis."" [online] (Roper Starch Worldwide Inc. and AARP, February 1999 — [cited 22 October 2002]), 6; available from *http://research.aarp.org/econ/boomer_seg.pdf.*

If your friend works those extra hours, she will pay $5,749 in taxes on the $5,000 she earns. I hope she is not planning on a trip to Maui.

So now, please write your answer below. Should your friend try to earn the extra $5,000, even though she will have to pay $5,749 in taxes on it?

Answer: yes __ no __.

The answer is "yes," of course. You see, despite the apparent tax problem, your friend will have no money problems whatever. Senator what's-his-name, from New England, is proposing a new federal program that will provide counseling to people who are having difficulties in managing their money. Your friend will be just fine.

What we must do

• The Social Security benefits tax is one of the most complicated in the Code — and that is saying something. It is an outrage to burden senior citizens with a tax they can't even understand. In addition, the high marginal tax rates caused by this tax are a disincentive to the elderly who wish to work. And, finally, for millions of Social Security participants, this is a double tax. Let's repeal the 85% tax on benefits.

• For new workers, on the other hand, let's use the same tax method used for other pension plans. That is, the worker pays no income tax on the Social Security payroll taxes withheld from pay. However, when benefits are eventually received, he pays tax on all benefits, just as he does on his other taxable income. This makes a lot more sense for three reasons. Taxes are paid when the money is received (and available to pay the taxes), it is clear and easy to understand, and there is no possibility of double tax. It is true that some people will end up paying more than they do today, but we already have a progressive income tax structure that should eliminate or minimize the tax for those with little total income. In fact, the American Academy of Actuaries estimates that, even if we include the full benefits in the taxable income of retirees, 30% of the recipients will still not pay income tax on those benefits, due to standard deductions and benefits.[97]

• If a senior citizen chooses to work, that's his or her business. The right to retirement benefits should not be affected. The work penalty should be repealed.

---

97. "Social Security Benefits: Changes to the Benefit Formula and Taxation" [online] (American Academy of Actuaries, October 2002 — [cited 15 November 2002]); available from *http://www.actuary.org/socsec/index.htm#2002.*

CHAPTER VII: FROM CRAZY CHECKS TO LAZY CHECKS

(HEALTHY PEOPLE FLOOD THE SOCIAL SECURITY DISABILITY PROGRAMS)

The Supremes create Crazy Checks

Several years ago, a friend of mine, a school teacher, made a startling comment about one of her students. She said that the boy's mother was irate because she, the teacher, wouldn't say he was misbehaving. "She's mad," my friend said, "because her kid won't qualify for benefits unless he has a behavior problem."

I didn't know it at the time, but my friend was telling me about a phenomenon that was spreading through many parts of the country, and gaining notoriety. After a Supreme Court decision in 1990 (Sullivan v. Zebley), the standards used by the Social Security Administration (SSA) for determining disability in children were relaxed. If a child did not have an impairment severe enough to qualify under normal SSA standards, he could still qualify as disabled if his behavior was simply *inappropriate* for his age. Word spread and soon there were reports of parents "coaching their children to put on a demeaning, degrading act: 'to fail simple tests, to wet their clothes, to fight, to show signs of loss of control....'"[98] It was also alleged that poorer parents would "use the special-ed classification as a proof of their child's disability, and consequent eligibility for Supplemental Security Income — $493 a month."[99, 100] Benefit payments for these unruly children were called "Crazy Checks."

---

98. Editorial, "Expect the Worst, Get the Best?" *The Times and Free Press*, 21 June 1999.

99. Kay S. Hymowitz, "Special Ed: Kids Go In But They Don't Come Out" [online] *City Journal*, vol. 6, no. 3, Summer 1966 — [cited 5 November 2002]; available from *http:// www.city-journal.org/html/6_3_special_ed.html*.

A little background

Disability benefits are a huge and costly part of the Social Security system, and are distributed via two distinct programs. Social Security Disability Insurance (SSDI) is the traditional *worker* disability program that distributes benefits from the Social Security taxes withheld from paychecks. Benefits paid are supposed to *roughly* relate to a worker's earnings history. In this book, we refer to SSDI as the "worker" disability program.

As mentioned previously, disability benefits are provided by another program known as Supplemental Security Income (SSI). This program, started in the early 1970s, uses general income tax revenues to pay both disability and old-age benefits to needy recipients. It is a welfare program that exclusively targets recipients who can demonstrate financial need. SSI benefits are not, in any way, related to a worker's earnings history. In fact, you don't even need a work history to collect SSI. In this book, we refer to SSI as the "SSI welfare" program.

Both of the disability programs are administered by the SSA, and the programs have similar standards for defining disability and determining whether a worker has an impairment. Since both programs are financed from your pocketbook, in one way or another, they are each legitimate objects of our attention, and are discussed in this book.

Now, back to Crazy Checks

The SSA reported that, "[b]etween 1990 and 1996, the number of children eligible for [SSI welfare] benefits increased from approximately 350,000 to more than 965,000,"[101] and the Crazy Checks phenomenon clearly accounted for a significant part of that increase. The flagrant abuses in the SSI welfare program were highlighted by the disclosure of abuse in one extended family of about 300 in Georgia.

---

100. Kay S. Hymowitz, "Special Ed: Kids Go In But They Don't Come Out" [online] *City Journal*, vol. 6, no. 3, Summer 1966 — [cited 5 November 2002]; available from *http://www.city-journal.org/html/6_3_special_ed.html.*

The monthly benefit is adjusted for inflation. For 2003 the basic federal benefit is $552 per month. Some states pay additional benefits on top of this.

101. "Welfare Reform and SSI Childhood Disability," a Social Security Factsheet [online] (Social Security Administration, February 1997 — [cited 19 March 2002]), 1.

It takes a village (to top this family)

The SSA had awarded over $1 million in SSI welfare disability benefits to 181 members of an extended Georgia family when Georgia's state disability agency contacted the SSA to express some concerns. It appeared that some individuals were being coached to feign illness — to "malinger." An investigation ensued, during which many of the disabled family members rapidly "recovered." After reviewing the family case files, the SSA Inspector General issued a report. Here are excerpts, pertaining to 2 of the cases reviewed:

> • The psychologist performing the [examination] identified the claimant, an extremely uncooperative child who offered little information about himself, as malingering and capable of significantly better performance than noted in the test results. According to a teacher questionnaire, the child's parents instructed the child to do whatever was necessary to keep the checks coming.
> • [T]here was no evidence of mental retardation, the original disabling condition diagnosed at age 4. [The state agency] noted that every time the claimant tried to talk, the mother would put her hand over his mouth. The teacher's report indicated the child was in regular classes, and there was no evidence of mental retardation.[102]

Publicity about cases such as these created a demand by the public for reform, and in the mid-1990s, Congress responded. The Crazy Checks phenomenon was curtailed with legislation defining a child's disability as an impairment or combination of impairments that cause "marked and severe functional limitation."[103] Behavior disorders and less severe learning disabilities no longer qualified. In addition, Congress prudently passed legislation which denied SSI welfare disability and worker disability benefits "to people whose addictions [alcohol and/or drug] are considered to be a 'contributing factor material to' the determination of their disability status."[104] These law changes took hundreds of thousands of people off of the disability rolls by the late 1990s, and have already saved billions of dollars.

---

102. Office of Inspector General, "Special Joint Vulnerability Review of the Supplemental Security Income Program," (A-04-95-06020) [online] (Social Security Administration, 16 December 1997 — [cited 2 May 2002]), section titled *Malingering*, cases 2 and 4; available from *http://www.ssa.gov/oig/ADOBEPDF/audit_htms/49506020.htm*.

103. "Welfare Reform and SSI Childhood Disability," 2.

104. Public Law 104-121, signed by President Clinton on March 29, 1996.

However, despite the legislative attempts to restore sanity to the process of defining impairments, awards for questionable illnesses are again on the rise. The SSA does not seem able or willing to use common sense in this area. As a result, rising costs threaten the financial health of the entire Social Security system. Worker disability benefits skyrocketed by $6 billion dollars in 2002, an increase of over 10% in just one year.[105] That brought the total of worker and SSI welfare disability benefits to $96 billion per year.

New challenges

As we learned from the Crazy Checks episode, a little looseness in the regulatory definition of "disability" can lead to a flood of applications for benefits. This is particularly true with certain subjective impairments that are hard to define and hard to diagnose.

Mental illness is a broad category comprising several of the most subjective impairments. Despite the reform efforts of the mid-1990s, the number of people awarded benefits for mental disorders started to climb after 1997, as can be seen in the chart below. Statistics show that the number of workers awarded disability benefits for mental disorders increased by more than 37% between 1997 and the year 2001.[106] Presently, one third of all workers receiving disability benefits made their claim on the basis of mental disorders. It is the largest single category of worker disability.[107]

In the SSI welfare disability program, trends are much worse. In the four years between 1997 and 2001, adult disability awards for mental disorders increased by nearly 41%, and disability awards for children with mental disorders increased by almost 60%.[108] (See Figures 14 and 15.) Presently, more than 60% of SSI welfare disability recipients are eligible based on mental disorders.[109] That's 60% of a colossal $30 billion spent on SSI welfare disability beneficiaries — *each year*.[110] And, that $30 billion is more that *ten times* the

---

105. "2003 OASDI Trustees Report" (Social Security Administration, 2003), table IV.A2.

106. Unadjusted gross rates.

107. "2001 Annual Statistical Report on the Social Security Disability Insurance Program" (Social Security Administration, Office of Policy, 17 September 2002), table 29.

108. Unadjusted gross rates.

109. "SSI Annual Statistical Report, 2001" [online] (Social Security Administration, June 2002 — [cited 15 October 2002]), table 21 (total of mental retardation and mental other rows); available from *http://www.ssa.gov/policy/docs/statcomps/ssi_asr/2001/*.

110. $30 billion is the total of federally-administered payments made for blind and disabled SSI beneficiaries from April, 2002 through March, 2003.

amount spent for disability benefits in the program's first full year of operations, in 1974. "Over the next 10 years, the combined federal cost alone for SSI and related Medicaid benefits is estimated at $122,000 *per recipient*."[111] (Remember, there are millions of them.)

Figure 14

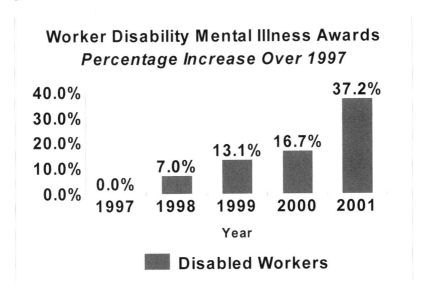

Why does the explosion of mental health disabilities continue, even in the post-Crazy Checks era? Is it fluoride in the water, or something contagious? Were our medical treatments and drugs better twenty years ago than today? And, what explains the fact that mental illness awards in the worker disability program have increased by nearly 10 fold since 1960, while the insured population increased by a factor of less than 3?[112]

---

111. "Supplemental Security Income: Additional Actions Needed to Reduce Program Vulnerability to Fraud and Abuse," HEHS-99-151 (U.S. General Accounting Office, September 1999), 1.

112. By analysis of *Mental Disorders* column in Table 29 of the "2001 Annual Statistical Report on the Social Security Disability Insurance Program" [online] (Social Security Administration, September 2002 — [cited April 2003]); available from *http://www.ssa.gov/policy/docs/statcomps/di_asr/2001/index.html* and *Workers Insured in Event of Disability* column in Table 4c1 [online] (Social Security Administration, 2 February 2002 — [cited 3 April 2003]); available from *http://www.ssa.gov/OACT/STATS/table4c1.html*.

Figure 15

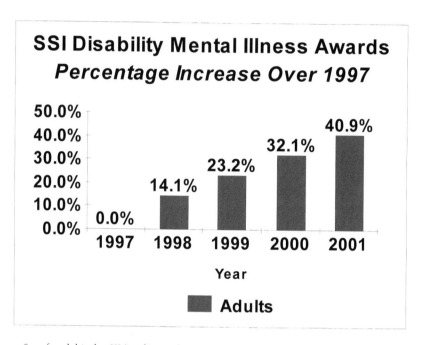

Source for underlying data: SSI Annual Statistical Report, 2001

The legal standards

Part of the problem has to do with the law itself, and how it is administered. At first glance, the legal definition of disability, and the requirements to demonstrate a disability, seem to be very clear — and tough. The law defines a disability as

> ...inability to engage in any substantial gainful activity ... which exists in the national economy ... by reason of any medically determinable physical or mental impairment which can be expected to result in death or which has lasted or can be expected to last for a continuous period of not less than 12 months....[113]

---

113. U.S. Code Title 42, Chapter 7, Subchapter II, Section 423 (d) (1) (A) and (d) (2) (A).

Figure 16

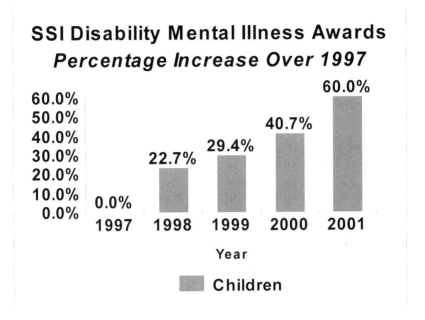

SSI Disability Mental Illness Awards
Percentage Increase Over 1997

Source for underlying data: SSI Annual Statistical Report, 2001

The law also states:

An individual shall not be considered to be under a disability unless he furnishes such medical and other evidence of the existence thereof as the Commissioner of Social Security may require. An individual's statement as to pain or other symptoms *shall not alone* be conclusive evidence of disability as defined in this section, there must be *medical signs and findings* established by medically acceptable clinical or laboratory diagnostic techniques, which show the existence of a medical impairment that results from anatomical, physiological, or psychological abnormalities which could reasonably be expected to *produce* the pain or other symptoms alleged ... [emphasis added].[114]

In other words, there must be
- medical signs and findings of an abnormality which could produce
- alleged pain or other symptoms which are severe enough to result in
- inability to participate in any substantial work anywhere in the national economy.

---

114. U.S. Code Title 42, Chapter 7, Subchapter II, Section 423 (d) (5) (A).

That is the law, and it is straightforward, right? Unfortunately, the administering regulations related to this statute are less clear. They state:

> We must always *attempt* to obtain objective medical evidence and, *when* it is obtained, we will consider it in reaching a conclusion as to whether you are disabled. However, we will not reject your statements ... solely because the available objective medical evidence does not substantiate your statements (emphasis added).[115]

In other words, the SSA will *try* to follow the law but, if it can't — don't worry about it![116]

You too can qualify!

Let's see how the clear standards set forth in Social Security law are actually applied by the SSA. Within the agency's "Blue Book" manual is a "Listing of Impairments" considered "severe enough to prevent a person from doing any gainful activity." Section 12.07 of the Listing of Impairments pertains to Somatoform Disorders, which are defined by the SSA to be "physical symptoms for which there are *no demonstrable organic findings or known physiological mechanisms*" (emphasis added). The SSA states that these Somatoform disorders may qualify a claimant for benefits if there is medical documentation of *any one* of three stated conditions, including:

> ... *unrealistic* interpretation of physical signs or sensations associated with the preoccupation or belief that one has a serious disease or injury [emphasis added].

In other words, you can qualify if the doctor documents that you are a *hypochondriac!*

But — not so fast. You've got to *prove* that you have this make-believe illness. The doctor must also note the presence of "at least two" of the following four conditions:

---

115. U.S. Code of Federal Regulations, Section 404.1529 (c) (2).

116. In minimizing the importance of objective medical evidence, the SSA may be skirting the law because Code Section 423(d)(5)(A) *requires* the presence of medical signs, and those are defined in Regulation 404.1528 as "anatomical, physiological, or psychological abnormalities which can be observed, *apart from your own statements*" (emphasis added).

1) Marked restriction of activities of daily living; or

2) Marked difficulties in maintaining social functioning; or

3) Marked difficulties in maintaining concentration, persistence, or pace; or

4) Repeated episodes of decompensation [depression], each of extended duration.[117]

That means you can qualify as having a severe disability, rendering you unfit for any significant work "which exists in the national economy," if you complain of pains or other physical symptoms that *cannot be supported* with organic findings, and *cannot be explained* by any demonstrable physiological mechanism, provided you are a documented hypochondriac who has trouble dating and trouble concentrating. Gee! Maybe my teenage son can qualify for benefits.

At the doctor's office

One can imagine the charade that must take place between doctor and patient in regard to these Somatoform disorders. The doctor can't really observe anything, except the fact that his patient keeps showing up, complaining of symptoms the doctor can't explain, or even observe. The very fact that the patient keeps making medical appointments for no apparent cause becomes the cause itself. You see, his hypochondria *is* the disorder. As for the other required medical observations concerning the patient's social life, ability to persist in activities, mental concentration, etc., the doctor can do no more than take the patient's word for it, write it down, and *pretend* he made direct medical observations. No wonder disability costs are so high.

Somatoform disorders are just one category of several that are invitations to abuse. In a scathing report on the SSI welfare program's vulnerability to fraud, the GAO states:

> SSI is inherently vulnerable to people who, with the help of others, feign their impairments to obtain benefits.... Our analysis of a sample file of SSI beneficiaries ... shows that the majority [over 60%] of disabled recipients had

---

117. "Disability Evaluation Under Social Security" (aka "Blue Book"), Publication no. 64-039 [online] (Social Security Administration, May, 2002 — [cited 25 November 2002]), part A, section 12.07; available from *http://www.ssa.gov/disability/professionals/bluebook/*.

the types of impairments that SSA and DDS staff considered susceptible to feigning.

The GAO also produced a listing of these easily-faked impairments. That list includes, among others, organic mental disorders, affective disorders (e.g., panic and depression), anxiety disorders, personality disorders, mental retardation, and, yes, somatoform disorders. But not all of the vulnerable impairments are mental in nature. Also listed are blindness, back pains, disorders of the muscles, etc., and various sprains and strains.[118]

Designer diseases

Private insurance companies are already looking with alarm at the rising costs associated with old stand-bys, such as back pain and some forms of carpal tunnel syndrome, as well as newer forms of disability, such as Chronic Fatigue Syndrome, fibromyalgia, and "new 'designer' disabilities, such as mid-life crisis syndrome."[119] (So far, I don't *think* that SSA has paid benefits for mid-life crisis, but when they do, I'll be ready.) Many private insurance companies are re-writing policies in an effort to limit the payment of benefits in certain cases where objective medical evidence is lacking. It is time for the SSA to do the same.

The perfect disability gives rise to Lazy Checks

One of the newer and more controversial impairments is Chronic Fatigue Syndrome (CFS). Is it physical? Is it mental? Who knows! Now, don't get me wrong. I am quite sure that many people with CFS really do feel terribly tired and completely unfit for work — even if their doctors can't find a thing wrong with them. The problem, however, is that an invisible ailment presents an irresistible temptation for some people who want to abuse the system. And for those fakers, the benefits we pay for their Chronic Fatigue Syndrome might be called, "Lazy Checks."

---

118. "Supplemental Security Income: Additional Actions Needed to Reduce Program Vulnerability to Fraud and Abuse," 31.

119. Bill Colopoulos, "Group Long Term Disability: Strategic Concepts for Plan Sponsors" [online] (BenefitsLink.com, Inc., 2001 — [cited 26 November 2002]); available from *http://www.benefitslink.com/articles/ltd.shtml*.

A detailed analysis of CFS teaches us about the Social Security disability programs and how they are administered. The Centers for Disease Control (CDC) states that CFS is indicated in a patient who has:

- Severe chronic fatigue lasting at least 6 months, with no apparent medical conditions accounting for it, and
- any four of the following symptoms: "substantial impairment in short-term memory or concentration, sore throat, tender lymph nodes, muscle pain, multi-joint pain without swelling or redness, headaches of a new type, pattern or severity, unrefreshing sleep, and post-exertional malaise lasting more than 24 hours."[120]

If you notice, it is possible to be diagnosed with CFS under the CDC standard, *without verifiable symptoms or pathologies*. This is because a doctor can't see 6 months of continuous fatigue, headaches, pain "*without* swelling or redness," "unrefreshing sleep," or "post-exertional malaise." Each of these symptoms has to be described to the doctor by the patient. Even the SSA acknowledges this. In a Policy Interpretation Ruling devoted to CFS, the SSA says: "Under the CDC definition, the diagnosis of CFS can be made on an individual's reported symptoms alone once other possible causes for the symptoms have been ruled out." The SSA goes on to say that this CDC standard does not, therefore, meet the legal standards for awarding disability benefits because "there must also be medical signs or laboratory findings.... "[121]

SSA — the tough guys?

The SSA sounds tough, right? Wrong. The SSA correctly requires "medical signs or laboratory findings," but then gives a definition of "signs or findings" which is so loose that the standard becomes a joke.[122] It does this by offering the following category of loopholes that (supposedly) "establish the existence of a medically determinable impairment."

---

120. "Chronic Fatigue Syndrome" [online] (U.S. Department of Health and Human Services, Centers for Disease Control and Prevention, 4 February 2002 — [cited 26 November 2002]); available from *http://www.cdc.gov/ncidod/diseases/cfs/index.htm.*

121. "Titles II and XVI: Evaluating Cases Involving Chronic Fatigue Syndrome (CFS)," SSR 99-2p: Policy Interpretation [online] (Social Security Administration, 30 April 1999 — [cited 3 March 2002]); available from *http://www.ssas.com/ssr99-2.htm.*

122. Actually, the SSA is only half right when it says "there must also be medical signs or findings." In point of fact, the law reads that there must be medical signs and findings. The two terms are not interchangeable. A sign is a directly observable condition, whereas a finding could be deduced indirectly via testing.

Some individuals with CFS *report* ongoing problems with short-term memory, information processing, visual-spatial difficulties, comprehension, concentration, speech, word-finding, calculation, and other symptoms suggesting persistent neurocognitive impairment. When ongoing deficits in these areas have been documented by mental status examination or psychological testing, such findings constitute medical signs or (in the case of psychological testing) laboratory findings that establish the presence of a medically determinable impairment (emphasis added).[123]

Does this mean that, if I *report* that I am having trouble with concentration, or *report* that I am having trouble with my memory, or *report* that I can't figure out a math problem, the doctor will write it down, give me a 15-minute "mental status examination," and, voilà: these are no longer simply my own statements; they have been transformed into "medical findings"? [124]

If you read between the lines, it appears that the Centers for Disease Control (CDC) doesn't think so. When it reported the results of its well-known 4-city survey of the Chronic Fatigue Syndrome, it noted:

No biological markers of CFS have been identified, and no diagnostic tests have been developed; the illness is diagnosed primarily on the basis of symptoms and signs *reported by the patient* and exclusion of other possible causes of prolonged, debilitating fatigue (emphasis added).[125]

In other words, the CDC diagnosis guidelines for CFS don't involve medical signs or laboratory findings *because there are none.*

---

123. Titles II and XVI: Evaluating Cases Involving Chronic Fatigue Syndrome (CFS).

124. If a person is trying to feign problems with concentration, memory, or cognitive skills, it is very easy for him to manipulate a mental status examination so that the results reinforce the claimed impairment. For example, he might be read the names of 3 objects and then asked to recall those 3 objects (to test his memory). To evaluate his concentration, he might be asked to count backwards from 100 by 7. A determined applicant who is feigning CFS symptoms will know exactly how to respond to those questions.

125. "Surveillance for Chronic Fatigue Syndrome — Four U.S. Cities, September 1989 Through August 1993" [online] (U.S. Department of Health and Human Services, Centers for Disease Control and Prevention, 21 February 1997 — [cited 3 March 2002]); available from *http://www.cdc.gov/mmwr/preview/mmwrhtml/00046433.htm.*

A few disclaimers

First, it should be stated that CFS has only recently been recognized as an impairment by the SSA, and so far, very few awards have been made for it. Also, we need to consider that there are, no doubt, many who truly feel tremendous fatigue that makes it extremely difficult to work. And for those people, we truly should feel sympathy. But, I suspect that there are others who simply *think* they have an impairment, and still others who are outright fakers, looking for those "Lazy Checks." No matter which category, however, there are plenty of CFS support groups to back them up (just check the Web), and plenty of attorneys ready to help them prepare their applications (for a standard percentage, of course). In fact, one website even has a "sample" medical report, suggesting the "compelling points" that might be made by doctors in their own reports on CFS.[126] (Attention, Doctors! If you use this model medical report, be sure to replace the sample patient name with that of your own patient.) Here we have the potential for an ongoing and growing financial calamity. If you want to scam the government, CFS just might be the "perfect disability." It has invisible causes and invisible symptoms, for which there are "no biological markers," and "no diagnostic tests."

To this point, we have concentrated on subjective impairments that are difficult for the SSA to deal with. But, even with the relatively clear-cut cases, the SSA fails to prudently control claims.

Flunking Claims Management 101

Normally, SSA disability rulings are top secret, and not revealed to the public. But recently a small number of these have become public indirectly, through lawsuits filed by employees under the Americans with Disabilities Act (ADA). Filing for Social Security disability benefits while suing under ADA provisions seems contradictory because, to assert a claim under the ADA, one must be *fully capable* of doing the desired job, given a "reasonable accommodation." On the other hand, to qualify under the Social Security Worker Disability program one must have a "severe disability" rendering him *unable to work* anywhere in the national economy. Did these litigants want to eat their cake, and have it too? After studying the 43 ADA cases, James M. Taylor,

---

126. "Writing a Convincing Medical Report" [online] (Charlotte, N.C.: CFIDs Association of America, undated— [cited 4 March 2002]); available from *http://www.cfids.org/ archives/2000rr/2000-rr1-article04.asp.*

Managing Editor of Accommodating Disabilities Business Management Guide, reaches some startling conclusions about the SSA. In a detailed analysis of the worker disability program titled, "Facilitating Fraud: How SSDI Gives Benefits to the Able Bodied", Mr. Taylor puts it this way:

> A review of SSDI cases and a look at SSDI statistics show a clear pattern of SSA officials' turning a blind eye to all standards and common sense when passing out benefits.... Despite the clear language and the compelling purpose behind the strict SSDI eligibility standards, SSA has been allowing persons with *minor or nonexistent disabilities* to collect SSDI benefits (emphasis added). [127]

According to Taylor, the 43 jaw-dropping cases are just the "tip of the abuse iceberg," and are indicative of massive program waste:

> The payment of billions of Social Security dollars annually to persons with only minor impairments wastes money meant for retirement and pushes the system more quickly toward bankruptcy.[128]

Here are just a couple of excerpts from Taylor's outline.

The peeved Wendy's worker

There is the case of the Wendy's cook, with a kidney impairment, who quit his job because he was miffed that a new supervisor changed his work schedule:

> When the restaurant's president of human resources learned of the misunderstanding, he contacted the cook, apologized for the misunderstanding, offered the cook his previous work schedule, and offered him back wages for the time that he had refused to report to work. The cook refused to accept the president's apology, offer of reinstatement, and offer of back pay and instead took a job at another restaurant.... Despite the unmistakable proof that the cook was indeed medically qualified to hold numerous restaurant jobs ... SSA continued to grant him SSDI benefits....[129]

---

127. James M. Taylor, "Facilitating Fraud, How SSDI Gives Benefits to the Able Bodied," Policy Analysis no. 377 [online] (Washington, D.C.: Cato Institute, 15 August 2000 — [cited 20 July 2002]), 1,3; available from *http://www.cato.org/pubs/pas/pa377.pdf.*
  128. *Ibid.*, 3.
  129. *Ibid.*, 8-9.

Crocodile Dundee at home — disabled at work

There is the case of the hunting, hiking, camping and scuba-diving railroad conductor who was too ill to work:

> A conductor for the Norfolk Southern Railroad injured his knee and back while working on the job. After successful surgery, the conductor nevertheless applied for a leave of absence and filed for SSDI benefits....
>
> After surgery, the conductor engaged in a wide spectrum of recreational activities. He frequently hiked, fished, camped, hunted, and went scuba diving. Nevertheless, he claimed that he had difficulty putting on his shoes and that, when bathing, he needed help washing his back. His own physician concluded, "I must admit that this man seems to be physically qualified to do almost any type of work...."
>
> Despite the conductor's successful participation in the above-listed rigorous sporting activities, SSA granted him full benefits....[130]

What is most disturbing is the fact that not one of the claimants in Taylor's 43 cases seems even close to meeting the legal requirements for disability; yet, they were awarded benefits.

If the SSA can't handle these cases sensibly, how well will it do in administering the new "designer diseases."

Chaos within the SSA

Have I given you the impression that the SSA is one big fuzzyheaded organization, liberally and quickly awarding benefits? I hope not, because that is not an accurate picture. Actually, the SSA is more like a mosaic of differing philosophies and goals. "There are wide variations in decision making between different regions of the country and different levels of adjudication, raising questions about whether claimants are being treated consistently and fairly" (the Social Security Advisory Board).[131]

Although it is a federal program, and the Social Security program foots the bill, the initial disability decisions are made by agencies within all of the 50

---

130. *Ibid.*, 9.

131. "Charting the Future of Social Security's Disability Programs: The Need for Fundamental Change" [online] (Social Security Advisory Board, January 2001 — [cited 25 October 2002]) *Executive Summary*; available from *http://www.ssab.gov/disability-whitepap.pdf.*

states. And, some states, like New Hampshire, award benefits at twice the rate of other states like Texas.

An even greater disconnect is found between the different levels of adjudication within the SSA. In 2000, about 62% of applications were denied at the initial level. Of those who appealed to the second level (the "reconsideration" level), 84% were denied. At this point, those denied were two-time losers, so you would expect that their chances were slim to none in any further appeals, right? Wrong. Almost 60% of those who appeal to the third level — the Administrative Law Judge (ALJ) hearing level — won![132]

The ALJ hearing level comprises about 1000 would-be Johnny Cochrans, each with 1 or 2 weeks of medical training (far less training, by the way, than that of most state adjudicators at the initial level). These lawyers are defiant in resisting any attempts by SSA officials to apply uniformity and rationality to decision making, or to promote ALJ productivity.

> Many ALJs have viewed SSA's efforts to exert management control over administrative matters as an infringement on their decisional independence. The relationship has deteriorated to the point where the judges recently voted to form a union, with the view that this was necessary to have their views taken into account (the Social Security Advisory Board).[133]

I don't know about you, but I sense a problem within the ALJ hearing room. There, you may find an Administrative Law Judge defiantly resisting SSA guidelines, and a specialist attorney respresenting the claimant. What you won't find, however, is anyone representing you and me. This may explain why someone can be, at once, Crocodile Dundee and disabled.

The truly disabled get lousy service

Our focus, so far, has been on the wasteful awarding of benefits to people who may not be truly disabled. That results in cost increases that affect every worker in the Social Security system. There is another side to this story. The truly disabled, who need help quickly, are also ill-served by the present system. This has been repeatedly noted by the GAO:

---

132. *Ibid.*, 8.
133. *Ibid.*, 18.

Our prior work has shown that SSA's disability determination process has long suffered from a set of serious problems. The process is time-consuming, expensive, fragmented, and complex. Ongoing weakness in making timely and accurate determinations results in beneficiaries often waiting more than 1 year for final disability decisions. Continued inefficiency results in very few beneficiaries leaving the rolls to return to work.[134]

In fact, the GAO has reported that it may take over *three years* for some disabled workers to finally get their benefits.[135] And, often, a lawyer ends up with a percentage. That is a very long time to wait, and a lot of money to pay, for a person who is unable to earn a living.

A fish rots from the head down

We have heaped most of the blame for questionable disability awards on the SSA, and it is well deserved. But the U.S. Supreme Court deserves our attention as well. It seems that about every ten years it has to muck up the disability waters with a dubious ruling. There was the Zebley case in 1990 — the one that led to the "Crazy Checks." And, in 1999, there was the Cleveland v. Policy Management Systems Corporation case. In that case, the Supreme Court indicated, contrariwise to the District Court and Fifth Circuit Court of Appeals, that it is possible for individuals to assert that they are "totally disabled" (and therefore receive worker disability benefits), while simultaneously asserting that they are fully capable of work, if only their employers would make a few "reasonable accommodations." Justice Stephen G. Breyer wrote that it is possible to be disabled for worker disability purposes and not for ADA purposes because "the Social Security Administration (SSA) does not take into account the possibility of 'reasonable accommodation' in determining SSDI eligibility," as is the case under provisions of the Americans with Disabilities Act (ADA). That's puzzling. "Reasonable Accommodation" is *the law of the land*, but the SSA needs not assume that employers are following that law.[136] Given the Court's myopic perspective, perhaps it is time for our legislators to amend this law to *mandate* that the SSA make its rulings under an assumption of "reasonable accommodations."

---

134. "Status of Achieving Key Outcomes and Addressing Major Management Challenges," GAO-01-778 (U.S. General Accounting Office, 11 June 2002), 5.

135. "Efforts to Improve Claims Process Have Fallen Short and Further Action is Needed," GAO-02-826T (U.S. General Accounting Office, June 2001), 24.

Summing it up

The legal standards for determining disability appear to be tough and objective — at first glance. But, apparently, the code and regulations leave far too much wiggle room for the disoriented and confused SSA, and for the technicality-minded Supreme Court. Benefit payments for the worker disability and SSI welfare disability programs totaled about $87 billion in 2001, and they jumped to about $96 billion in 2002. Solutions are needed.

What we must do

- We should only pay benefits for verifiable impairments, based on medical signs or symptoms that are not exclusively derived, directly or indirectly, from the claimant's own statements.
- For workers with strong and obvious disability claims, quick relief should be provided through an expedited process.
- Disability should be defined in the context of the aids, assistance, and other "reasonable accommodations" that employers are required to provide. The law should be amended to reflect this.
- Appeals should be submitted to independent panels comprising representatives of government, workers, employers, medical professionals, vocational experts, and insurance companies. Their decisions should be a matter of public record, provided claimant identities can be concealed. The public has a right and a need to know how disability benefits are awarded.
- If none of the above works to stop the hemorrhaging of money out of the Social Security disability programs (worker disability and SSI welfare disability), let's provide beneficiaries with a private insurance plan option. This option is explored in more detail in Chapter XIV.

---

136. The ADA rules do not apply to smaller employers; however, the SSA is not supposed to award worker disability benefits if the applicant is able to "engage in any substantial gainful activity ... which exists in the national economy." The available employment does not have to be everywhere — just "in significant numbers" in the region where the claimant lives, or in several regions of the country (U.S. Code Title 42, Chapter 7, Subchapter II, Section (d)(1)(A) and (d)(2)(A)).

CHAPTER VIII: DISABILITY — THE OPPORTUNITY FOR A LIFETIME

(ONCE DISABLED, ALWAYS DISABLED)

Only one in five hundred returns to work

In the last chapter, we discussed the growing number of adults and children who are judged to have severe impairments, even where there is little evidence to support those decisions. That is an important reason for the high cost of the disability programs, but it is only half the story. The other major problem is this: Once individuals are awarded benefits, they *almost never return to work*. The GAO puts it this way:

> [T]he agency [SSA] has taken a number of actions to improve its return-to-work practices. But even with these actions, SSA has achieved poor results in this arena, where less than 1 in 500 DI beneficiaries and few SSI beneficiaries leave the rolls to return to work.[137]

Does that make sense to you? Only *1 in 500* disabled people is able to return to work, in our modern world of miracle medicines, technology, and "reasonable accommodations" provided by employers!

To understand why so few people return to work, we have to understand the system. Getting disability benefits is a two-part process. In the last chapter, we focused on the first phase: demonstrating that you have a "severe" impairment (or, at least, one that the SSA considers to be severe). But, it is also

---

137. "Agency Must Position Itself Now to Meet Profound Challenges," GAO-02-289T (U.S. General Accounting Office, 2 May 2002), 12.

necessary to show that your impairment prevents you from working at any substantial job in the national economy. Remember, an impairment, even if severe, does not necessarily prevent someone from earning a living. For example, the carpenter who loses his legs might make an excellent accountant or salesperson. In fact, he might earn *more* after he loses his legs than before.

SGA: The Silly Government Approach

How does the SSA figure out whether someone with an impairment can work? Does it use highly-experienced medical and personnel experts who know which disabilities can be made compatible with various occupations? No, that would be logical. It uses the *SGA*, which stands for Substantial Gainful Activity. Coincidentally, that acronym could also stand for Silly Government Approach.

Here is how the SGA works. If an applicant with a qualifying impairment earns a dollar or more *above* the SGA level (generally, $800 per month in 2003), he has proven that he is able to work, and he loses all of his disability benefits. If he earns a dollar or more *below* the SGA amount, it is presumed that he is unable to work, and he keeps all of those monthly checks, potentially for decades. The GAO summarizes the process as follows:

> Eligibility for Disability Insurance benefits is based on whether a person with a severe physical or mental impairment has earnings that exceed the Substantial Gainful Activity (SGA) level, which represents SSA's *principal standard* for determining whether a disabled individual is able to work (emphasis added).[138]

It's hard to believe, but the "principal standard" used by our government to decide if someone can work is not a medical evaluation, nor is it the opinion of vocational rehabilitation experts. It is whether or not that person earns (and *reports*) a certain level of income. It is an all or nothing test, and it is completely within the control of the person getting the monthly checks. This standard, used in the initial evaluation, is also the standard used to determine whether the person later "recovers." As you probably can guess, very few disabled people are found to be "able to work" using this standard.

---

138. "SGA Levels Appear to Affect the Work Behavior of Relatively Few Beneficiaries, but More Data is Needed," GAO-02-224 (U.S. General Accounting Office, January 2002), 1.

A critical problem with the SGA standard is that it involves the use of one flat earnings level ($800 per month) regardless of the amount of pre-disability income. That earnings level is reasonable — if your pre-disability income happened to be around $800 per month. But, the SGA earnings level is pathetically low for most disabled workers, and may constitute a disincentive for rehabilitation. For example, if a disabled welder previously made $50,000 per year and he manages, via rehabilitation, to work just one day per week, he will probably earn more than the SGA earnings level and lose all disability benefits. Knowing this, his incentive to rehabilitate is diminished, and he might opt to take an early "disability retirement."

Disability pays more than work?

There's another reason why few people return to work. For those who have low wages, the disability benefits may constitute a substantial pay *raise*. This is due to a particular flaw in the Social Security disability program. As noted in Chapter III, the Social Security program involves an enormous amount of benefit shifting, and this is true in the disability program as well as the retirement program. At the low end of the earnings scale, an unmarried disabled person collects a tax-free benefit equal to 90% of his average wages — an amount that probably exceeds the net paycheck he earned while working. And, furthermore, with disability he eventually gets Medicare. In total, the disability benefits and Medicare can greatly exceed what the person was earning, or would earn, were he to return to the work place. Table 3, below, shows how disability benefits compare to wages for a person who would normally earn $7,000 per year.

Table 3

	Joe Worker	Joe Disabled
Gross wages	7,000	0
Less taxes*	(700)	0
Disability benefit	0	6,300
Plus Medicare**	0	3,800
Total	6,300	10,100

*Payroll taxes of 7.65% plus estimated state and local tax of 2.35%
**Cost of Medicare A before age 65 normally would be $319/month times 12 mos. = $3,828.

To make matters worse, Joe Disabled can earn another $800 per month (his SGA amount) without any reduction in benefits. That would bring his total disability income to nearly $20,000. What incentive does he have to recover? No private insurer would write a policy that provides more income for disability than was provided for the same person's work.

Disability benefits for kiddies?

So far, we have only discussed the regular, worker disability program, which is based on a worker's average wages and payroll taxes paid. In the SSI welfare disability program there is even less incentive for beneficiaries to work because many never had significant earnings to begin with. The SSI cash and Medicaid benefits they receive (averaging more than $10,000 per year) may be the highest income they ever had. In addition, a large number of SSI welfare disability beneficiaries are *children*, with no work experience at all and *no earnings potential whatever*. Why these children even qualify for disability insurance, which is traditionally for wage income replacement, is one of the great mysteries of life.

In fact, there once was a political debate about giving disability benefits to kids. When the SSI welfare program was set up in the early 1970s, many legislators opposed the concept of using a wage replacement program for children who, by and large, have no significant earned income. However, the supporters of kiddy disability argued that the families of the disabled kids would need the extra money to provide for the special needs of these children. Their view prevailed and the benefit was written into law; however, no compliance testing was put into that law. *Nobody is checking to see how this money is spent!* We simply assume that the families are spending this money on their disabled children. Although national survey data are not available (apparently), a 1996 survey of Florida families indicated that *only one in ten* (10%) of surveyed families spent all of the SSI benefits on the disability-related needs of their kids.[139]

No treatment, no rehab: just take the money

But, let's get back to the subject of *work*, and the pathetic record the SSA has in getting disabled people to do it. In reports issued in 2000 and 2001, the GAO discussed the problem of getting the disabled back into the workplace and

---

139. "SSI Children: Multiple Factors Affect Families' Costs for Disability-Related Services," HEHS-99-99 (U.S. General Accounting Office, June 1999), 5.

contrasted the SSA's efforts in this area to those of the private sector and of other countries. It was noted that, in contrast to alternative plans, the SSA has a "determination process that concentrates on applicants' incapacities, an 'all-or-nothing' benefits structure, and return-to-work services offered only after a lengthy determination process."[140] And, incredibly, the SSA does not regard treatment as a prerequisite for benefits:

> [I]f an applicant is not receiving treatment, SSA still assesses the applicant's eligibility for benefits and — if the applicant qualifies — awards benefits, *even if the applicant would not qualify for benefits if treated*. And, unless medical treatment is prescribed [by the applicant's own physician], it is not a prerequisite for continued receipt of benefits ... (emphasis added).[141]

Further, "SSA's disability programs *do not require rehabilitation* for beneficiaries, regardless of their capacity to work." And, "the Social Security Act *does not require that an individual work to his or her maximum capacity*" (emphasis added).[142]

Table 4, below, outlines these and other differences between the Social Security disability programs, and alternative plans. Take a few minutes to review it, for it clearly indicates why Social Security has failed so miserably in its efforts to get the disabled back to work.

In the last row of the table, you'll find an aspect of disability we have not yet mentioned: staff qualifications. As you can see, the disability programs of private insurers and other countries have access to highly-experienced staffs that can "assess claimants' eligibility for benefits and provide needed return-to-work services...." In contrast, the SSA teams (organized at the state level) are trained to assess the applicant's eligibility for cash benefits, rather than enhance his ability to return to work. This problem is compounded by the fact that some state disability examiners do not even have higher education degrees. Social Security simply does not have the personnel necessary to "carry out the role of returning disabled workers to productive employment."[143]

---

140. "Other Programs May Provide Lessons for Improving Return-to-Work Efforts," T-HEHS-00-151 (U.S. General Accounting Office, 13 July 2000), 3.

141. *Ibid.*, 20.

142. "Other Programs May Provide Lessons for Improving Return-to-Work Efforts" (revised version), GAO-01-153 (U.S. General Accounting Office, January 2001), 29.

143. *Ibid.*, 22.

Table 4

Why Social Security fails to get the disabled back to work[144]

	Private insurers and other countries	**Social Security**
Definition of disability	Definition shifts over time, from less to more restrictive, "recognizing the possibility of improvement in the capacity to work through provision of supports and services, such as retraining." Usually, after 2 years it is harder for the beneficiary to qualify for benefits. This "provides the insurer with leverage to encourage the claimant to participate in a rehabilitation and return to work program."	"All-or-nothing" definition, creates a problem. "Because the result of the decision is either full award or denial of cash benefits, applicants have a strong incentive to emphasize their limitations... and a disincentive to demonstrate any capacity to work."
Rehab and treatment	Intervention occurs soon after disability onset to identify return-to-work needs. This helps to "set up the expectation that the claimant will return to work." Indeed, he is required to get non-surgical treatment and vocational training, as appropriate, to help him work to his maximum capacity.	Intervention doesn't even begin until after benefits are awarded, and that, as we have noted, can take 1 year or more. Even then, "receiving appropriate medical treatment is not a prerequisite for award or continuing receipt of DI benefits." And, vocational rehabilitation is optional. Social Security has no requirement that a claimant work to "his maximum capacity."
Amount of benefits	"[B]enefits generally replace 60% of predisability earnings." This percentage may be further reduced if the claimant turns down a job, or is judged, by independent experts, to be working below maximum capacity.	Benefits (plus Medicare) may exceed predisability income, substantially. This is a disincentive to work. "[B]eneficiaries with low earnings may find it more financially advantageous to periodically stop working, or work part-time and continue to receive disability payments, than to earn more than SSA's limit..."
Earnings limits	During the first 12 to 24 months, claimants are allowed to supplement their disability benefits with earned income, and "thereby receive total income of up to 100 percent of predisability earnings." After 12 to 24 months, the benefit amount is decreased, so that the total benefit is less than 100%. The idea is to encourage the disabled to get back to work soon after the onset of disability.	A disabled worker can earn up to $800 per month without impacting his benefit. One dollar more, however, and all benefits are lost. This same dollar limit applies to those who previously earned $7,000, and those who earned $70,000. It is not adjusted for previous levels of income.
Staff qualifications	Each insurer "has access to multidisciplinary staff with a wide variety of skills and experience who can assess claimants' eligibility for benefits and provide needed return-to-work services..."	"In contrast, SSA's DDS teams of medical and psychological consultants and disability examiners are hired and trained to assess eligibility of applicants to receive cash benefits rather than to enhance claimants' capacity to work. In some cases, the disability examiners have only high school diplomas. As a result, the staff of SSA and the DDSs do not have the expertise to carry out the role of returning disabled workers to productive employment."

We're not making progress!

As noted, SSA disability programs do not require rehabilitation for beneficiaries, even where that rehabilitation would increase their capacity to work. It hasn't always been that way. Until very recently, we required that disabled individuals "be promptly referred to the state agency or agencies ... for necessary vocational rehabilitation services." In addition, the law "authorized deductions from payments [to beneficiaries] up to amount of benefits on

144. All quoted references in the table are from "Other Programs May Provide Lessons for Improving Return-to-Work Efforts," T-HEHS-00-151, pgs. 3, 7, 10, 16, 20, and 22.

account of refusal without good cause to accept rehabilitation services."[145] Surprisingly, those basic and reasonable requirements — standard provisions in the plans of other countries and private insurers — were *dropped* in 1999, when a new SSA initiative was enacted into law (see, below). It's as if we are driving in reverse.

The Ticket to Shirk

The "Ticket to Shirk" (I mean, "Ticket to Work") program eliminated the mandatory vocational rehabilitation requirements in both disability programs (worker and SSI welfare), and replaced them with a unique, voluntary program. The disabled person gets a ticket (a real, printed one) that he can give, *if he wishes*, to one of several listed businesses that will provide him with vocational training (no job, mind you, just vocational training). The disabled person is promised that, if he redeems his ticket, the SSA will *stop its periodic reviews* of his eligibility. That is, the SSA will stop trying to figure out if he *really* qualifies for the benefits it gives him. This is unsettling. No one who is truly disabled fears the periodic reviews, so the program does little to induce job re-training. On the other hand, a person who is only marginally disabled (or, not disabled at all), will be very attracted to this plan, since his disability claim will no longer be challenged if he just plays along with the Ticket program. And, remember, he *never* has to actually get a job.

Personally, I wouldn't bet the farm on the Ticket to Work program and, apparently, the GAO wouldn't either. It states:

> Even in light of the new Ticket to Work Act, SSA will continue to face difficulties in returning some of its beneficiaries to work, in part due to statutory and policy weaknesses in the design of the [worker disability] program.[146]

The $1 for $2 offset proposal

In the same good legislation that created the Ticket to Work program, Congress authorized the SSA to undertake studies to predict the net effect of a

---

145. U.S. Code Title 42, Chapter 7, Subchapter II, Section 422, prior to amendment in 1999 by Public Law 106-170, Sec. 101 (b).

146. "Major Management Challenges and Program Risks — Social Security Administration," GAO-01-261 (U.S. General Accounting Office, January 2001), 23.

proposed new program called the "$1 for $2 Offset." Basically, the proposal allows a disabled beneficiary to earn the normal SGA level (the amount he can earn and still be considered "disabled"), *and* it allows him to earn amounts beyond that, with a reduction in benefits of only $1 for every $2 earned. The results of large scale demonstration projects are not in, but one researcher, John Rust, of the University of Maryland, provides some early and disturbing insights based on "very preliminary" computer modeling. In a paper released in late 2001, he notes that the financial inducements of the proposed policy would likely cause a "doubling of the DI roles" due to the fact that people would join the ranks of the disabled at younger ages, and would stay "disabled" for a longer period of time.[147] Think of it. If we give a financial incentive, we can create more disabled people, who will stay disabled longer.

In summary

The SSA has done a poor job of motivating the disabled to go back to work. It assesses ability to work by comparing reported earnings to an arbitrary one-size-fits-all earnings limit. There is so much shifting of disability benefits to low-end workers that many receive more by being disabled than they would by working. And, having kids get disability benefits defies logic. Incredibly, the SSA does not always require treatment that would eliminate a worker's disability, it doesn't expect a claimant to work to his maximum ability, and it has no requirement for vocational rehabilitation training that might help the disabled beneficiary return to work. In fact, the SSA is slow to even offer rehabilitation guidance, and its staff lacks the training and experience to effectively give that guidance. The new Ticket to Work program is a feeble attempt to get the disabled into vocational training because it offers no effective inducements. In fact, the Ticket program may become a haven for those seeking to avoid SSA challenges to their disability claims.

What we must do

• Disability benefits must never become more attractive, financially, than wages. Currently, however, Social Security pays some disabled workers

---

147. John Rust, "Modeling Behavioral Responses to Changes in Social Security: A Life-Cycle Framework" (University of Maryland and National Bureau of Economic Research, 3 November 2001, 18.

benefits that greatly exceed their pre-disability work incomes. The solution is to put a percentage cap on disability benefits, as related to past wages. The cap used by most private insurers is 60%.[148]

• Let's drop the SGA earnings standard. A claimant's ability to work should be assessed on the basis of medical and vocational analyses, and on his earnings as they relate to his pre-disability income. We cannot use the same dollar limitation for all workers.

• As noted in Table 4, alternate insurers (i.e., private companies and the systems of other countries) allow claimants to supplement disability pay with earned income, and to receive up to 100% of pre-disability earnings for the first 12 to 24 months. Thereafter, the benefit amount is gradually decreased so that the combination of benefits and earnings is less than 100%. The Social Security program should adopt this approach, to provide an inducement for beneficiaries to return to work.

• Alternate insurers start with a liberal definition of disability and gradually make the definition more restrictive over the two years following the onset of disability. This gives them leverage to induce claimants to rehabilitate and to return to work. In contrast, Social Security uses an "all-or-nothing" definition, which gives applicants a strong incentive to emphasize their limitations, lest they lose everything. Social Security needs to adopt a flexible definition of disability that recognizes the potential of the disabled to gradually improve their skills, and adapt to the workplace.

• We should no longer issue standard monthly checks to the parents of pre-work-age disabled children (current practice in the SSI welfare program). If these families need extra money for disability-related needs, it makes more sense to reimburse them for the actual expenses incurred and documented.

• We need to give vocational rehabilitation guidance earlier, even before benefits are awarded. And, claimants should be *required* to get non-surgical treatment and/or vocational rehabilitation, where appropriate.

• More qualified personnel should be hired by the SSA and state disability offices. College degrees should be required for disability examiners, and these people should be capable of assisting the disabled in returning to productive employment. Recruiting an appropriate number of qualified workers is going to become exceedingly important and difficult given that, by 2009, more than half of SSA's 63,000 employees will be eligible for retirement.[149]

---

148. "Other Programs May Provide Lessons for Improving Return-to-Work Efforts," T-HEHS-00-151, p. 17, footnote 20.

• Disability evaluation and review service contracts should be awarded to private companies as part of a pilot project. The results of the project should be studied to see where cost savings and improved services may be achieved.

---

149. "Major Management Challenges and Program Risks — Social Security Administration," 10.

Chapter IX: The Case of the Solicitous Spouse

(Are People Really Getting Sicker?)

The dream of every man and woman

A "solicitous spouse" takes on new meaning in relation to the Social Security disability program. There are studies which show that a patient tends to report higher levels of pain and lower activity levels if he, or she, has a solicitous spouse. You know — the spouse who makes you that hot cup of tea, adjusts your Lazy Boy just right, and gets your Davy Crocket slippers to keep your toes warm. The findings of one study "underscore the importance of spouse solicitous behavior ... as a "stimulus for chronic pain behaviors." (Translation: people feel more pain when in the presence of a sympathetic person.) Another study notes that "patients observed by a solicitous spouse spent less time walking on a treadmill than patients observed by a nonsolicitous spouse."[150] (Translation: people wear out more quickly when being observed by a sympathetic person.) The implications are that people feel more pain and have less energy when in the presence of those troublemaking, solicitous spouses. (I'm counting on my wife not reading this.) The research doesn't prove a cause and effect relationship, but suggests a strong correlation between reported pain and social reward.

---

150. Donald S. Ciccone, Nancy Just, and Erin B. Bandilla, "A Comparison of Economic and Social Reward in Patients With Chronic Nonmalignant Back Pain" [online] *Psychosomatic Medicine*, vol. 61 (American Psychosomatic Society, 1999 — cited 14 April 2002]), Introduction; available from *http://www.psychosomaticmedicine.org/cgi/content/full/61/4/552.*

Illness and economic incentives

Another study took this a step further, and produced information of more direct relevance to the Social Security disability program. In research performed by Ciccone, Just, and Bandilla, a relationship was found between patient disability rates and both social and *economic* rewards (such as, for example, Social Security disability benefits). The researchers reported that, when all other factors were held constant:

> [P]atients in the high economic reward group missed more days from work, had more domestic disability, and were more depressed than patients in the low economic reward group.

Similar findings were noted when the reward was social, rather than economic, but there was one key difference. Patients with high *social* rewards had higher levels of *nonspecific* pain. (Honey, I feel awful all over.) In addition, they had more *nonspecific* medical complaints. (Sweetie, I'm just too sick to get the newspaper.) On the other hand, patients with high *economic* rewards had pain more *specifically* related to the disability claim. (Doctor, my carpal tunnel hurts too much for me to go back to my typing job.)[151] The researchers concluded:

> Patients with chronic nonmalignant pain are widely suspected of exaggerating or misrepresenting their symptoms in pursuit of economic and social rewards. Although there is no proof that rewards are causally linked to illness behavior, the evidence seems to suggest that patients who receive financial compensation are more likely to be disabled and to remain disabled than patients who are not compensated.[152]

More evidence of an economic impact on disability rates

In an article entitled "Laid-off Workers Swelling the Cost of Disability Pay," the *New York Times* recently reported:

> Millions of low-skilled workers have turned to federal disability pay as a refuge from layoffs in recent years, doubling the benefits cost and, with little notice, making it by far the government's biggest income-support program.

---

151. *Ibid.*, Abstract.
152. *Ibid.*, Introduction.

The article quotes an MIT economist who states:

> Show me a high school dropout, particularly a male, who is over the age of 40 and is not working and there is a 40 to 45% chance that he is on Social Security disability insurance.[153]

Our retirement contributions are used as unemployment benefits. Is this how it is supposed to be?

SSA disability trends don't reflect real health trends

As suggested by the research and reports, a person's feelings about pain and disability may be significantly affected by economic and social incentives, in addition to his medical condition. In fact, the Social Security disability programs are affected by these and several other factors, including politics, court rulings, the general state of the economy, public attitudes and honesty, attorney promotions, and the attitude and efficiency of the SSA. Evidence of some of these factors can be gleaned from a graph of disability awards issued between 1970 and 2001 (see Figure 17).

You might expect a graph of disability rates to display a gradually-descending line, reflecting lower disability rates due to medical advances and improved workplace accommodations. That is not what we see.

These worker disability award rates (gross rates — unadjusted) show evidence of the 1974-75 recession and the introduction of the SSI program (which swamped the SSA and caused it to cut down on the review of claims of all of its programs). These are the factors that cause the graph to go up between 1970 and 1975. The graph then plunges, largely due to 1977 and 1980 law changes, which put restrictions on benefits and mandated the review of more claims. Keep looking and you will see signs of the disability restrictions imposed by the Reagan administration in the early 1980s, and then softened by Congress in 1984. The recession in the early 1990s is evident, as is the mid-1990 control of Congress by the Republicans (and the resultant toughening of standards). The crucial point is this: the rate of disability awards in this enormously costly program is *only loosely related to medical factors*. Disability rates are highly subjective and

---

153. David H. Autor, quoted in Louis Uchitelle, "Laid-off Workers Swelling the Cost of Disability Pay" [online] *The New York Times*, 2 September 2002 — [cited 4 September 2002], available from *http://www.nytimes.com/ref/open/profiles/02INSU-OPEN.html.*

responsive to external, nonmedical factors. That must be kept in mind when setting policy.[154]

Figure 17

Source for underlying data: SSA Office of Actuary, Table 6c7

Is this a graph of disability rates or the Himalayan Mountains?

The Figure 18 graph of SSI welfare disability awards (gross rates) shows even more volatility. Unlike the worker disability program, the SSI welfare disability program is *supposed to* reflect economic as well as disability changes. Many of the factors reflected in the first graph are reflected here, but even more so. Especially noteworthy are the Reagan valley in 1982, the Crazy Checks rise in the early 1990s, and the sharp plunge following the GOP takeover of Congress in the mid-1990s. The rise starting in 1997-8 is what I call the "Lazy Checks" period,

---

154. "2001 OASDI Trustees Report" (Social Security Administration, 2001), 106; and Actuarial Study 114 (Social Security Administration, June 1999).

where the rise in subjective mental illnesses is starting to overtake declines in other areas. The jury is out on where the worker disability and SSI welfare disability programs will go from here. It is in our hands.

Figure 18

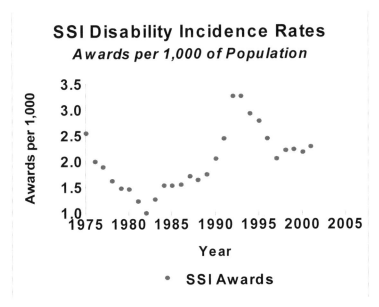

These are gross rates, unadjusted. Source for underlying data: SSI Annual Statistical Report 2001, and U.S. Census Bureau.

What are the real disability rates?

It's almost a formula. Every health-related advocacy group, including the disability groups, wants us to believe that its featured illness is:

- widespread
- growing, and
- impacting a diverse group of people — especially women and children.

You'll never hear one of these groups say, "give donations to us because XYZ syndrome affects very few people, is getting smaller each year, and only harms white males."

The many disability groups out there must be in a real funk these days. For years, they cited pseudo-scientific trend information showing widespread and rising disability, especially among women and children. It turns out the foundation of this trend information was soft; often, the studies did little more than ask people whether they were currently getting government benefits. If more and more were getting benefits, then disability was supposedly on the rise. These "research" results were then recycled back as justification for expansion of government or other programs. But, as you know from the earlier chapters of this book, the fact that someone gets on the disability roles, and stays there, does not mean that he/she belongs there.

Living longer does not mean living sicker

Also, many of these dire forecasts were predicated on an erroneous assumption: the notion that as modern medicine enables people to live longer, there will be more disabled people. Put another way, it is the belief that medicine will keep us alive but we won't be as healthy. Does that make sense? The consensus has clearly shifted. In 1995, one research trio stated that its analysis

> ...would appear to belie the notion that lower adult mortality necessarily implies worse health. We argue further that the reversals observed during the 1980s also call into question whether trends in self-reported health during the 1970s reflected actual health declines.[155]

In 1998, an analysis of various surveys reported:

> [A] growing body of evidence points toward declines in disability rates among the elderly. Some studies show smaller declines than others, but in a variety of disability research employing different surveys and analytic methods, no sustained increase in disability rates has been observed. To the contrary, several sources of survey data, which in earlier years appeared to show either increasing disability or no pattern over time, now show statistically significant declines in elderly disability rates.[156]

---

155. Timothy Waidmann, John Bound and Michael Schoenbaum, "The Illusion of Failure: Trends in he Self-Reported Health of the U.S. Elderly" [online] *The Milbank Quarterly*, vol. 73, no. 2, 1995 — [cited 14 April 2002], *Abstract*; available from *http://www.milbank.org/730206.html*.

A 1998 Rand study performed by Freedman and Martin analyzed disability trends by using four "measures of functional limitations ... that more closely approximate true physiological capabilities...." For all age groups studied, dramatic declines in the rates of disability, for each functional measure, were observed between the studied years of 1984 and 1993.[157]

And finally, in a widely-acclaimed study released in 2001, Manton and Gu analyzed data related to the "activities of daily living" of 42,000 elderly individuals (more bad news for the disability alarmists). They reported that disability rates declined by an astounding 25% from 1982 through 1999 (last year of data), and that the rate of decline is increasing.[158]

Just use your head!

Do we even need to see these studies? Don't we know, intuitively, that people today should be better able to function in the every-day tasks they perform at home and at work? We smoke less, wear seat belts more, and have less asbestos, lead, mercury, and DDT in our lives. We have an array of medicines and pain killers we didn't used to have, and there are non-invasive surgical techniques, titanium hips, MRIs, etc. In addition, those who are disabled should find life easier now. We have ramps for most sidewalks, ramps to get us into the workplace, super-wide lavatories, an assortment of "workplace accommodations," and 20 handicapped parking spaces for each disabled person. Disability rates — real ones — *have to be going down.*

In a Public Policy Forum held on Capital hill in April, 2000, economist David Cutler listed 5 factors that account for the apparent improvement in health: the advances in high-tech medical care, improvements in public health activities, improved conditions of the workplace (less dust, fumes, etc.), better

---

156. Timothy A. Waidmann and Kenneth G. Manton, "International Evidence on Disability Trends Among the Elderly" [online] (The Urban Institute as contractor for the U.S. Department of Health and Human Services, 18 June 1998 — [cited 13 April 2002]), *Executive Summary*; available from *http://aspe.hhs.gov/daltcp/reports/trends.htm.*

157. "Trends in Functional Limitations: Are Older Americans Living Longer *and* Better?" [online] (Rand Center for the Study of Aging, 1998 — [cited 13 April 2002]); available from *http://www.rand.org/publications/RB/RB5021/.*

158. Kenneth G. Manton and Xiliang Gu, "Changes in the Prevalence of Chronic Disability in the United States black and nonblack population above age 65 from 1982 to 1999" [online] *Proceedings of the National Academy of Sciences*, vol. 98, issue 11, 22 May 2001 — [cited 13 April 2002], 6354—6359; available from *http://www.pnas.org/cgi/reprint/ 111152298v1.pdf.*

personal behavior (e.g., less smoking, less greasy foods), and gains in socioeconomic status. (Wealthier, better educated people tend to live longer.)[159] It should surprise no one that we are getting healthier.

But that is not what we see in our Social Security disability programs.

Care for a cigarette?

Instead of the dramatic *reduction* in disability rates that we have every right to expect, long-term worker disability award rates are generally going up — even after adjusting for population aging. In the worker disability program, the number of workers *awarded* disability benefits, as a percentage of the insured population, increased by nearly 5% between 1997 and 2001, and by nearly 25% between 1988 and 2001. The percentage of workers *receiving* disability benefits increased by about 4% between 1997 and 2001, and by nearly 40% between 1988 and 2001. According to Social Security statistics, we have almost 40% more disabled people today than we did just 13 years ago. And that is after adjusting for population and aging trends. Maybe we need to start smoking again.[160]

More evidence

To further illustrate the disconnect between real disability rates and Social Security disability rates, let's again consider the Rand study. The Rand researchers considered disabilities related to four specific functions, for people of just one age bracket — age 50-64. For each of four functional areas — seeing, lifting, climbing, and walking — participants in the Survey of Income and Program Participation were asked questions designed to reveal potential disabilities. For example, they were asked whether they had difficulty seeing the words in ordinary newspaper print, or difficulty lifting a 10-pound bag. The responses received in 1984 were contrasted with those received in 1993. For each functional area, significant improvement was noted. The reported incidence rate declined by 9.2% for walking, 9.3% for climbing, 18.7% for lifting, and 29.7% for seeing. The average decline for the four categories was 16.7%.[161]   Were those

---

159. David M. Cutler, "What's Behind Downward Disability Trends in Disability for Older Americans," text of presentation at Public Policy Forum [online] (U.S. Senate Special Committee on Aging, 13 April 2000 — [cited 26 November 2002]); available from *http://www.agingresearch.org/brochures/medicare/researchatrisk.html.*

160. An explanation of methods and sources used to calculate age-adjusted disability rates is shown in Appendix A-9.

116

results mirrored by any sort of drop in Social Security worker disability awards? No. Instead of going down by 16.7% between 1984 and 1993, Social Security award rates, for people in the same age group and in related impairment categories, skyrocketed. For impairments related to the nervous system and sense organs, the increase was 29%. For impairments related to injuries, the increase was 38%. And, for impairments related to the musculoskeletal system and connective tissues, the increase was 87%. There is no way to reconcile the expected *decreases* (per research) with the huge *increases* per the Social Security programs.[162]

Another problem: the disabled are getting younger

Intuitively, one might assume that, as a result of modern medical advances the average age for the onset of disability is increasing. After all, people should be able to delay the debilitating effects of disability longer, through the use of medicines and other treatments. But, Social Security disability figures show the opposite.

As you can see from Figure 19 below, the average age of those receiving disability benefits is declining. I'll bet the SSA is proud to finally have a graph with a downward trend!

Two conflicting trends. Why?

Why do we have these conflicting trends? On the one hand, most researchers agree that real disability rates are falling, and have been for many years. On the other hand, the number of people joining the Social Security disability programs, and *staying in the programs*, is generally going up, faster than our population is growing. And, people seem to be getting disabled at a younger age. What causes this apparent contradiction? Let's see what the statistics tell us.

161. "Trends in Functional Limitations: Are Older Americans Living Longer *and* Better?"

162. "Annual Statistical Report on the Disability Insurance Program, 2000," table 19; and "Annual Statistical Supplement, 2001," table 4.B5 (Social Security Administration).

Figure 19[163]

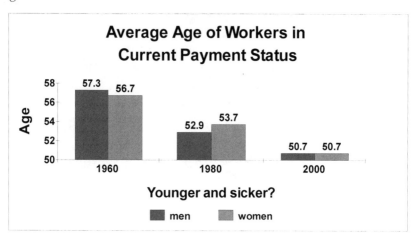

As noted in an earlier chapter, the GAO has developed a list of impairments, shown below, considered "susceptible to being feigned or exaggerated" in the SSI welfare disability program:[164]

- Organic mental disorders
- Schizophrenic disorders
- Affective (mood) disorders
- Anxiety disorders
- Personality disorders
- Somatoform disorders
- Mental retardation
- Epilepsy
- Blindness and low vision
- Chronic pulmonary insufficiency
- Disorders of the back
- Disorders of muscle and ligament, etc.
- Sprains and strains

The last five of these are considered "adult-only," while the rest, the mental-related ailments, are considered to be applicable to children as well as

---

163. "Annual Statistical Report on the SS Disability Insurance Program, 2000," table 16.

164. "Additional Actions Needed to Reduce Program Vulnerability to Fraud and Abuse," HEHS-99-151 (U.S. General Accounting Office, September 1999), Appendix II, table ll.1.

adults. The GAO developed this list of suspect impairments by interviewing "medical consultants and medical relations officers — disability specialists at SSA headquarters, and investigators who specialize in disability fraud." Essentially, it was based upon the educated *hunches* of practitioners in the field. Their hunches were right.

125 percent more mental illness in just 4 years?

Although the SSA stated (in response to a Freedom of Information Request) that it could not produce trend information for final disability determinations on a specific-disease basis, it does publish such data for fairly specific impairment categories. The categories most closely related to the GAO's list of questionable impairments are:

- Mental retardation
- Mental — other
- Nervous system and sense organs
- Respiratory system
- Musculoskeletal system and connective tissues
- Injury and poisoning

By using these categories, in lieu of the specific ailments, we can get a sense of the trends, albeit on a somewhat diluted basis. The results are illuminating.

In the worker disability program, awards related to these categories increased by just under 10% between 1997 and 2001, after adjusting for increases in population and in aging.[165] That's almost 10% more disabled people after just 4 years. But, the real scandal is in the SSI welfare disability program. For the identified categories, there was a 33% increase in awards to adults, and there was a 51% increase in awards to children. The biggest single area of growth related to "Mental-other," which comprises all assorted mental illnesses aside from retardation. For that category, the 4-year adjusted increase in awards was 41% for adults, and a staggering *125% for children.*[166]

---

165. Based on information derived from the "2001 Annual Statistical Report on the Social Security Disability Insurance Program" (previously referenced) and age and insured population information, as described in Appendix A-9.

166. Methods and sources used to calculate SSI age and population-adjusted rates are shown in Appendix A-10.

How it's covered up

Unfortunately (or fortunately, if you are the SSA), these horrific trends are partly offset, and masked, by positive trends for the easily-verified ailments. As noted above, most of the increases in SSI disability awards are related to mental impairments. Awards for most of the other illnesses, the ones that are hard to fake, have been constant or declining. The story is similar in the worker disability program, where virtually all of the major increases are for mental impairments and musculoskeletal problems (back pain). These increases are somewhat offset by declines in infectious diseases and metabolic diseases, etc., so overall trend increases appear moderate. But, disability rates should not be going up *at all*. They should be going *down* — *significantly*.

Don't be confused between people and dollars

We are not talking about an increase in the percentage of *money* spent on disability; such an increase might be understandable because of the rising costs associated with modern medical treatment. Our discussion pertains to an increase in the percentage of *people* who become disabled. This increase makes no sense at all unless there are some weird new diseases affecting backs and brains. Think of the irony. We are spending more than ever on health care, and the new drugs and technology appear to be working. Research tells us that disability rates are declining, yet a growing percentage of the population is seeking government assistance for disabilities.

The fiscal implications

The impact of all of this can be enormous in relation to the long-term fiscal health of the Social Security system. In their 2003 report on the long-term solvency of the Social Security system, the trustees assume a disability incidence rate of 5.6% of insured workers. Here is how they got that figure. They assumed a base rate of 5.2% (based on the age adjusted rate as of January 1, 1996), and increased it by 8% for anticipated changes in the age and gender mix of the working population.[167] Now, if that base rate were 4.0%, instead of 5.2%, the impact on Social Security's long-term fiscal health would be huge — about $17 billion per year for the worker disability program and $6 billion per year for the SSI welfare disability program, on average, for each of the next 75 years. Guess

---

167. "2002 OASDI Trustees Report" (Social Security Administration, 2002), 117.

what. We *had* an average of 4% (even after age adjustments), for 5 consecutive years in the late 1980s — just a few years ago. If we kept our age-adjusted rate at 4% during the 1980s, we should be able to keep it *at least* that low now, and that would save us $23 billion per year. We are spending a bundle on modern medicine and "reasonable workplace accommodations." Let's start demanding *lower* disability rates in return.[168]

What we must do

In the last two chapters we made recommendations related to evaluating medical impairments and getting the disabled worker back into the work place. And, we noted that it might be advisable to privatize all or part of the disability program. To those recommendations let's add this one: On an ongoing basis, we need to reconcile Social Security disability rates to verifiable and objective medical impairment incidence rates. This should be done on an *individual* impairment basis so that questionable disability claim trends are easily spotted and earmarked for investigation. Social Security disability trend graphs should not look like the Himalayans, or any other mountain range. They should, instead, reflect the gradual improvements in medical treatment, and in workplace accommodations.

---

168. An explanation of the disability savings estimate is shown in Appendix A-11.

CHAPTER X: TALES FROM THE CRYPT

(SCAMS OF THE DEAD, DYING, AND LYING)

Mummy Dearest

Bakersfield, California. Sitting on the couch in a lovely dress, Mrs. Wilcher seemed to be watching TV, but was not. She was depressed, her daughter told police — "demonically depressed." She was also dead, and had been for months. In fact, she was a mummy and, apparently, a decent-looking one. It was bizarre, noted the police sergeant, but, "I've seen much uglier than this." Well, if Mrs. Wilcher was still looking good, credit that to Social Security. You see, the daughter had been cashing those monthly checks, and using the money to take care of poor Mum (who, police said, died of natural causes).[169]

Las Vegas, Nevada. Police received a call complaining of foul odors emanating from a storage locker on W. Sahara Ave. Inside, they found a leaky garbage can containing a partially liquefied corpse with a plastic bag wrapped around the head. A short time later, Brookey Lee West was arrested for the murder of her mother, a murder that took place two years earlier. Likely motive? Those monthly Social Security checks. But this time, I would argue, they weren't used to make Mom look beautiful. Brookey was convicted, however she steadfastly maintains her innocence. Her lawyers argued that Mom died a "natural" death, and Brookey simply chose an "unusual" method of disposing of the body.[170]

---

169. "Daughter thought 'mummy' wasn't really dead," Associated Press, 17 January 1997.

Southside, Florida. Louise Brinson's motionless body had been lying on her bed so long that rats built a nest in her thoracic cavity. But, apparently, her "caretaker," Thelma Mahler, didn't notice. Maybe she thought Louise was sleeping; maybe the bedroom lights were dim. My theory, however, is that Thelma was too busy forging endorsements on Brinson's monthly Social Security checks. In the end, Thelma learned an important lesson about Social Security fraud: If you are going to forge someone's name, learn how to spell it. She was sentenced to 6 years in prison, and was ordered to pay restitution of $231,000.[171]

A peculiar problem

These strange cases illustrate a peculiar problem faced by the SSA — knowing when someone dies and, consequently, when to stop sending monthly checks. Is this a significant problem? Well, yes and no. On the one hand, it seems unlikely that many people collect Social Security benefits while hiding the remains of the recently departed. After all, you are not going to have a good Super Bowl party with strange odors seeping into the family room. On the other hand, even when the deceased are properly buried, the SSA may continue to send those monthly checks, due to administrative oversight or deceit. In such cases, it's not unusual for neighbors or relatives to fraudulently cash the checks.

Fraud and other types of payment irregularities are the subject of this chapter. We will consider the various types of problems, give examples, estimate the overall cost, and conclude with recommendations for improvement. First, however, we need to discuss the underlying foundation of the problems.

"20 years of Inattention"

The GAO has stated that the SSA has "an organizational culture that has focused more on quickly processing claims than on controlling program expenditures." And, the GAO has noted that many of the problems facing the

---

170. Glenn Puit, "Slaying Verdict: West Convicted in Death" [online] *Las Vegas Review-Journal*, 20 July 2001 — [cited 24 March 2002]; available from *http://www.lvrj.com/ lvrj_home/2001/Jul-20-Fri-2001/news/16582102.html*.

171. Kathleen Sweeney, "Rat Nest Found" [online] *The Florida Times-Union*, 4 February 1998 — [cited 28 March 2002]; available from *http://www.jacksonville.com/tu-online/ stories/020498/2b2lawAN.html*; and

Allison Thompson, "Fraud Indictment — Caretaker Took Checks as Senior Lay Dead" [online] *The Florida Times-Union*, 3 October 1997 — [cited 28 March 2002]; available from *http://www.jacksonville.com/tu-online/stories/100397/2b1SKELE.html*.

"high-risk" SSI welfare program, which is managed by the SSA, are the result of "more than 20 years of inattention to payment controls...."[172] The Inspector General has made similar assessments, noting that the "... SSA has often placed a greater priority on quickly processing and paying SSI claims with insufficient attention to verifying recipient-reported information.... "[173] With regard to the worker disability program, a recently-prepared independent review found "little evidence that the current quality management system supports a quality-focused culture."[174] If you have any doubt whether these are fair criticisms of the SSA's organizational philosophy and culture, consider the following.

Payments based on "allegations?"

After field office visits, the Social Security Advisory Board, a bi-partisan oversight board created by Congress, noted:

> [T]here is widespread concern about the agency's capacity to properly administer the SSI program.... [E]mployees have told the Board that they sometimes do not pursue certain lines of questioning, such as the details of an individual's living arrangements, because it takes too long to resolve the issues that may be raised.... A number of agency employees have told the Board that many SSI claims are currently being paid based largely on allegations.[175]

The Board concluded, on the basis of these observations, that "the concerns of the GAO and OIG are well founded and that the agency needs to take appropriate action."[176]

172. General Accounting Office letter to Committee on Governmental Affairs, HEHS-00-126R (U.S. General Accounting Office, 30 June 2000), Enclosure II, p. 3.

173. "Congressional Response Report: Integrity of the Supplemental Security Income Program," A-01-02-22095 (Social Security Administration, August 2002), 1.

174. The Lewin Group, Inc., "Evaluation of SSA's Disability Quality Assurance (QA) Processes and Development of QA Options That Will Support the Long-Term Management of the Disability Program," Contract no. 0600-96-27331 (Social Security Administration, 16 March 2001), iv.

175. "Statement on the Supplemental Security Income Program" [online] (Social Security Advisory Board, 30 May 2002 — [cited 15 September 2002]), 2; available from *http://www.ssab.gov/ssi2002.pdf*.

176. *Ibid.*, 3.

"Only a few months of concealed work activity"

To get a sense of the thought process of SSA management, consider some of its recent testimony to Congress. Under a new disability Trial Work Period provision, an individual may work for up to nine months and still get benefits, no matter how much he makes. (Normally, there are limits on earnings.) The SSA's Inspector General, James G. Huse, Jr., recently proposed to deny this 9-month trial period to individuals who were subsequently caught concealing their earnings. In testimony before the Subcommittee on Social Security of the House Ways and Means Committee, he stated:

> [T]his program [the Trial Work Period program] has become a jackpot to those who receive disability benefits fraudulently. When caught and prosecuted, these unscrupulous individuals are permitted to keep thousands of dollars in stolen benefits.[177]

However, it appears that SSA administrators may hold a contrary view. Fritz Streckewald, an Acting Assistant Deputy Commissioner, made the following remarks at the same Subcommittee meeting:

> The IG's proposal could result in lengthy retroactive cessations after many months of legitimate entitlement despite *only a few months of concealed work activity....*
>
> We believe that the current civil monetary penalties and other existing requirements and sanctions in the law, which encourage reporting of wages, are generally sufficient to defer [*sic*] fraud in this area, although we are exploring the possibility of imposing civil monetary penalties in cases of fraud by omission [emphasis added].[178]

It would seem that, to this SSA official, a few months of underground earnings is no big deal, although he allows for "exploring the possibility" of

---

177. James G. Huse, jr., Inspector General, in testimony before the Subcommittee on Social Security [online] (U.S. House of Representatives, Committee on Ways and Means, 10 May 2001 — [cited 9 September 2002]); available from *http://waysand-means.house.gov/legacy.asp?file=legacy/socsec/107cong/5-10-01/107-30final.htm.*

178. Fritz Streckewald, Acting Assistant Deputy Commissioner, Disability and Income Security Programs, in testimony before the Subcommittee on Social Security [online] (U.S. House of Representatives, Committee on Ways and Means, 10 May 2001 — [cited 9 September 2002]); available from *http://waysandmeans.house.gov/legacy.asp?file=legacy/socsec/107cong/5-10-01/107-30final.htm.*

imposing civil, monetary penalties. It makes you wonder if the agency is aware that, under 42 U.S.C. Sec. 408, such concealments may be felonies, punishable by a $10,000 fine and 5 or more years in prison.[179] [180]

By all means, let's NOT help law enforcement!

There are other proposals, made by the agency's own IG, that don't sit well with the SSA. The agency is reluctant to help law enforcement officers identify criminal suspects (by revealing names and SS numbers), unless the suspected crime directly involves an SSA program. The SSA fears that it could result in "serious erosion of individuals' personal privacy rights...." Regarding the denial of Social Security benefits to fugitive felons, the SSA feels that the idea has merit but "we need to proceed carefully.... [T]here would be policy, legal and operation issues that must be addressed."[181] Question: are these Social Security officials driving around in VW vans decorated with flowers and peace signs?

The "universe of fraud"

Perhaps the clearest sign of an "attitude problem" is the SSA's stance on fraud estimates. For years, the agency has refused to provide estimates of the overall cost of fraud in its programs, in defiance of its own inspector general who has stated that it is "imperative that the universe or magnitude of fraud be identified." Recently, the Bush administration also tried to solicit this information — without success. (Although the Administration may not realize that its request was ignored.)[182]

The SSA declares that the "universe of fraud" can never be known; therefore, it focuses on the "outputs of our efforts to achieve improvements in deterring, identifying and resolving fraud."[183] In other words, the SSA tells us

---

179. Despite the apparent reservations of the SSA, Congress has drafted legislation that would withhold the benefits of the Trial Work Period provision from those found to be fraudulently concealing work activities. This legislation, embodied in HR 743, is likely to become law in 2003. This same legislation would deny worker retirement benefits to fugitive felons.

180. Can a failure to report financial information be a crime? See Appendix A-12.

181. Fritz Streckewald.

182. To see how the Bush Administration's request was sidestepped by the SSA, see Appendix A-13.

183. "FY 2002 Annual Performance Plan" [online] (Social Security Administration, 2002 — [cited 30 June 2003]), 116-118; available from *http://www.ssa.gov/performance/2002/2002perfplan.pdf.*

how much it will spend on investigations, how much fraud it hopes to uncover, and how much fraud it did, in fact, uncover. However, it doesn't estimate the amount of fraud that was missed by its bungling. The serious deficiency of this approach can be illustrated with the chart below, reproduced from the SSA's 2003 Annual Performance Plan. This chart shows the anticipated and actual fraud dollars that the SSA recovers.

Figure 20[184]

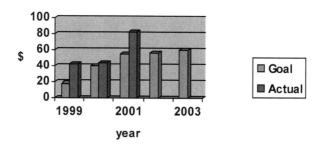

OASDI Dollar Amounts Reported from Investigative Activities (in millions)

As you can see, the SSA anticipates finding more stolen benefits each year, and each year it surpasses all expectations. From this we could conclude that the SSA is doing a great job. On the other hand, we could also conclude that the theft of Social Security funds is skyrocketing. To put it in perspective, consider this same track record within a municipal police department. Each year it would set the goal of discovering more homicides, and each year it would beat that goal by uncovering an even greater number than expected. Sooner or later, there'd be corpses everywhere.

The SSA's refusal to estimate fraud makes no sense. As the IG points out, "insurance, retail, and banking industries have baselines to estimate potential

---

184. "FY 2003 Annual Performance Plan" [online] (Social Security Administration, 2003 — [cited 30 April 2003]), 52; available from *http://www.socialsecurity.gov/performance/ 2003/.*

dollars lost to fraud."[185] For that matter, so do the Social Security systems of some other countries. Estimating fraud is an essential first step for any program that is serious about fighting the problem. It focuses public attention, it helps to identify the specific problem areas, it lets us know if we are making progress in fighting the fraud — and, it can be done.

Estimation efforts in the United Kingdom

In the mid-1990s, the Brits undertook a serious effort to estimate the extent of fraud in their various Social Security programs. Beneficiaries, selected using statistically valid sampling techniques, were extensively interviewed and rigorously audited to determine whether they met the requirements of the programs. These findings were then projected to the population at large. The results of the reviews, conducted between 1995 and 1997, showed negligible fraud in the area of retirement pension. However, in the disability program and the "Income Support" program (equivalent to our SSI welfare program), the fraud found was substantial. (See Table 5, Findings from the U.K.'s Estimates of Fraud.)

Table 5[186, 187] Findings from the U.K.'s Estimates of Fraud

	Disability	**Income Support**
% of cases with confirmed or strong suspicion of fraud	12.2	11.1
% of expenditures lost to fraud	6.7	12.1

185. "Inspector General Statement on the Social Security Administration's Major Management Challenges" [online] (Social Security Administration, December 2001- [cited 30 April 2003]); available from *http://www.ssa.gov/finance/2001/mgmtchallengez1.htm*.

186. Written questions and answers, Hansard (House of Commons) [online] (United Kingdom Parliament, 20 April 1998 — [cited 26 November 2002]), column 543; available from *http://www.parliament.the-stationery-office.co.uk/pa/cm199798/cmhansrd/vo980420/text/80420w35.htm*.

187. Percentage of payments lost to fraud calculated by dividing estimated annual loss due to fraud by total expenditure for the relevant program and year. Sources: written questions and answers, Hansard (referenced above), and Benefits Agency Annual Report and Accounts 1996/97 — [cited November 2002]; available from *www.dwp.gov.uk/publications/dss/1997/ba/benagency_aandr_9697.pdf*, 37.

These were the results just for cases where fraud was confirmed or there was strong suspicion of fraud. When the fraud results were combined with the routine error rate (for the U.K. disability program), the overpayment rate soared to a shocking 27%. This led to a political firestorm, including angry denunciations from the floor of Parliament regarding the outrageous implication that "disabled people are fraudsters...."[188] And, when the Labor Party took over in 1997, much of the program was eviscerated; for example, all reviews of the disability program were dropped. But, undeniably, the estimates led to increased public awareness, positive debate, and numerous and effective anti-fraud efforts, including high-profile advertising campaigns. Now, it is time for the U.S. to shine a spotlight on the fraud and errors in its Social Security program. Instead, we get SSA propaganda.

The SSA could make an Enron auditor blush

Every year the SSA puts out figures that show astounding accuracy in its dissemination of funds. For example, in its Performance and Accountability Report for FY 2001, it reports that the percentage of SSI welfare payments, made without overpayment, was 93.6 in 2000; and the percentage of retirement and worker disability payments, made without overpayments, was 99.9 in that same year.[189] Not bad for government work! But, also, not true. Here is the rest of the story, as stated by the Inspector General in a separate report:

> SSA bases its payment accuracy rate on a detailed analysis of a sample of cases. However ... it still relies on beneficiary *self-reporting* events that can affect eligibility and/or payment amounts. The payment accuracy review does not include the *medical factors* that affect benefit eligibility. Further, the review does not count all types of improper payments as 'inaccurate' for purposes of payment accuracy. For example, *payments made after a beneficiary's death* are not

---

188. Minutes of debate, Hansard (House of Commons) [online] (United Kingdom Parliament, 17 June 1998 — [cited 26 November 2002]), column 291; available from *http://www.parliament.the-stationery-office.co.uk/pa/cm199798/cmhansrd/vo980617/debtext/80617-04.htm*.

189. "FY 2001 Performance and Accountability Report" [online] (Social Security Administration, 2002 — [cited 2 November 2002]), 146 and 150; available from *http://www.ssa.gov/finance/2001/fy01acctrep.pdf*.

counted as 'inaccurate' during the payment accuracy review [emphasis added].[190]

"Payments made after a beneficiary's death are not counted as 'inaccurate'"? By this logic, our cemeteries could be filled with current Social Security recipients, and we would still have 99.9% payment accuracy. To illustrate how absurdly high these accuracy estimates are, the Inspector General (IG) added this little analysis:

> Based on the payment accuracy rate, we expected $140 million in overpayments for the OASI program in FY 2000. However, actual overpayments *identified* were $1.47 *billion* [emphasis added].[191]

In other words, the overpayments the IG stumbled upon, through investigations and serendipity, were ten times greater than the program-wide amount implied by the SSA's super-high accuracy rate.

Decisional accuracy

We just discussed what the SSA calls "payment accuracy." In regard to the worker disability program, reviews are also made of *decision-making* accuracy, on a sample basis, at both the initial level and internal appeals level. These decisional reviews also do not make inquires that would be expected to uncover fraud; however, they involve a complete review of the files, including the medical assessments made. In 1999, 96.5% of initial allowance decisions were found to be accurately made;[192] while only 85% of such decisions were found to be accurate at the appeals level.[193] Based on the number of decisions made at each level, we can roughly estimate an overall decisional accuracy rate of about 93.5%, before consideration of fraud. We'll use this information later, to roughly estimate the dollar value of the overpayments made in Social Security programs. First,

---

190. Office of Inspector General, "Semiannual Report to Congress 10/01/01-03/31/02," SSA pub. no. 85-007 [online] (Social Security Administration, May 2002 — [cited 15 June 2002]),16; available from *http://www.ssa.gov/oig/ADOBEPDF/sar102001032002.pdf.*
191. *Ibid.,* 17.
192. "FY 2001 Performance and Accountability Report," 148, amount for 1999.
193. Office of Inspector General, "Performance Measure Review: Reliability of the Data Used to Measure the Office of Hearings and Appeals Decisional Accuracy," doc. A-12-00-10057 [online] (Social Security Administration, April 2002 — [cited 20 June 2002]), 5; available from *www.ssa.gov/org.*

however, let's review the various types of fraud affecting the Social Security programs.

MAJOR CATEGORIES OF FRAUD

Within the three Social Security programs — retirement, worker disability, and SSI welfare — are the following major categories of fraud:

- Collecting retirement benefits for those who don't exist
- Stealing or fabricating identities
- Collecting SSI while in prison or on the lam
- Collecting SSI while out of the country
- Faking ailments and collaborator fraud
- Faking finances

1. Collecting for those who don't exist

We started this chapter with some unpleasant cases where corpses were hidden to prevent disclosure of the deaths to authorities. More often, however, the bodies are properly buried, but the family and/or friends are a "little slow" to let the SSA know. In most cases, the SSA finds out about the death anyway, from the funeral home, post office, financial institutions, or from DACUS (its Death Alert, Control, and Update System). DACUS is used to identify unregistered deaths from federal and state data bases. Sometimes, however, there is a snafu, and the SSA is not notified. This may occur because the death takes place outside of the U.S., the funeral home doesn't notify, the state records don't reconcile, or the decedent's mail is intercepted. Recent proposals would require states to notify the SSA within 30 days of a death. Presently, it takes 90 to 120 days.

Here are a few examples.

101-year-old dad is in "top secret" experimental facility

An investigation was conducted by the SSA because a man refused to disclose the whereabouts of his 101-year-old dad, a Social Security recipient. While being interviewed, he claimed that his father was in a "top secret" facility specializing in geriatric diseases and only accepting subjects over 100 years of age. He refused to reveal the location of the facility. For some reason, these comments made the Social Security agent suspicious. An investigation ensued, and it was revealed that the father had died 20 years earlier, due to a cause that was never established. The son pled guilty to making false statements, was sentenced to 21 months in prison, and ordered to pay restitution of nearly $100,000.[194]

Why cleaning your house doesn't pay

Because Dr. Jane Matuzel died while outside of the U.S., in Ontario, Canada, the SSA didn't receive notification of the death, and continued to pay benefits for 16 additional years. Those checks were cashed by her daughter, Amaryllis Corbett, who told a federal judge she didn't believe she was doing anything wrong by taking the money. Perhaps that is why Amaryllis didn't think she had to show up in court on the first day of her trial. Federal marshals were dispatched to get her and found her inside her house, "hiding behind a pile of trash." (Apparently, the trash piles in her house were not quite big enough to conceal her.) Amaryllis received a 30-month sentence, and was ordered to pay restitution of $369,000.[195]

2. Stealing or fabricating identities

In March, 2002, the GAO reported that identity fraud was soaring, with a 500% increase in Social Security number misuse in recent years.[196] The Federal Trade Commission estimates that there were nearly 10 million victims of ID theft in 2002 alone, at a cost (to individuals and businesses) of about $53 billion.[197] According to the National White Collar Crime Center, there are primarily two forms of identity theft: "true name" and "account takeover" fraud. In the case of

194. Office of Inspector General, "Case of the Month" [online] (Social Security Administration, March 1999 — [cited 23 March 2002]); available from *http://www.ssa.gov/oig/investigations/caseofmonth/caseofmonth1999.htm#March*.

195. "Woman Gets 30 Months for Social Security Fraud," vol. 3, no. 42 in the series *Fraudinfo Newsletter* [online] (Austin, Texas: Association of Certified Fraud Examiners, 12 December 2001 — [cited 6 November 2002]); available from *http://www.cfenet.com/media/archivedetails.asp?num=3-42*.

196. "Identity Theft: Prevalence and Cost Appear to be Growing," GAO-02-363 (U.S. General Accounting Office, March 2002), 5.

197. "FTC Releases Survey of Identity Theft in U.S. 27.3 Million Victims in Past 5 Years, Billions in Losses for Businesses and Consumers" [online] (Federal Trade Commission, 3 September 2003 – [cited 6 September 2003]); available from http://www.ftc.gov/opa/2003/09/idtheft.htm.

true name fraud, a consumer's personal information is used to establish new accounts in his/her name. Account takeover fraud involves gaining access to someone's existing accounts to make fraudulent charges.[198] Although it usually involves the theft of a Social Security number, most of the crime involves credit card fraud, as opposed to the direct theft of Social Security benefits.

Collecting information is accomplished by several means. Some crooks go "dumpster diving" to get copies of bank checks and statements, or credit card information. Others get the information by eavesdropping when the person is on the telephone or at an ATM. Others get information by "shoulder surfing," which is peering over the victim's shoulder as she or he types personal information.

More sophisticated identity thieves solicit information via e-mail. They spam letters which promise great benefits if the victim will respond with some personal information. Of course, the benefit never comes since the real objective was simply to get the personal information. Another source of information, believe it or not, is the government itself. "Crooks are having a field day with website listings of Social Security numbers gleaned from government records." One of the main government sources is the SSA's Death Master File, an Internet listing of numbers assigned to the now deceased.[199]

If you don't mind being shocked, frightened, and dismayed, just enter the key words "fake" and "ID" into the Google search engine. A barrage of fake ID sites will appear, each touting its authentic-looking wares. For example, one offers "ID cards, degrees, diplomas and certificates" for "any, state, province or country." It has "authentic" "federal ID, police ID, Social Security ID, employment ID," and "birth certificates," among many other cards. It states that you can "fool anyone, anytime, anywhere," and that "no one will know the TRUTH but yourself." "All ID cards are professionally designed by an ex-DMV staff," and, "genuine security holograms and seals" are no problem.[200] In light of the 9/11 attack, these websites are now feeling some major heat and, at least a few appear to be closing down. Hopefully, they will all be gone some day — right after I pick up one more degree.

---

198. "Identity Theft" [online] (NW3C Research Section, undated— [cited 30 November 2002]); available from *http://www.diogenesllc.com/identitytheft.pdf.*

199. Dennis Blank, "Data from federal records used to commit identity theft" [online] *Government Computer News*, 2 October 2000 — [cited 28 March 2002]; available from *http://www.gcn.com/vol19_no29/news/3046-1.html.*

200. For example, see the website of photoidcards.com; available from *http://www.photoidcards.com/.*

In a recent report, the SSA's Inspector General noted that, "one in 12 foreigners receiving new Social Security numbers had done so using fake documents." He added that 100,000 Social Security numbers were improperly issued to noncitizens in 2000, alone. The SSA has attempted to check the records of the Immigration and Naturalization Service before issuing Social Security numbers to noncitizens, but has had little success in getting this information, according to the Inspector General.[201]

An example of identity theft:

The Three Stooges Crook

Michael Penker and his several aliases used as many as six Social Security numbers to falsely establish up to 108 lines of credit. With these, he received over $1 million in cash advances and credit purchases. In Nevada, Penker established a corporation named "D, C & H, Inc.", and had several cashier's checks, drawn on the bogus credit lines, payable to either D, C & H, Inc., or "Dewey, Cheatham & Howe," the fictional Three Stooges' law firm. After he had one Texas bank issue a cashier's check to Dewey, Cheatham & Howe, Michael apparently changed his mind, contacted the bank and asked that it reissue the check, payable to a different name. A suspicious bank employee (apparently a Three Stooges fan) contacted the FBI, triggering an investigation that ended in the downfall of the crook. After Penker pleaded guilty to identity fraud, money laundering and use of fraudulent Social Security numbers, he was ordered to pay restitution of over $1 million, and to serve about 4 years in prison.[202]

3. Collecting SSI while in prison or on the lam

Generally, Social Security law prohibits payment of any benefits — retirement, worker disability, or SSI welfare — to those in prison for 30 days or more. In addition, the Welfare Reform Act of 1996 prohibits payment of SSI welfare benefits to someone who is fleeing to avoid prosecution or custody or confinement for a felony crime, or to someone who is violating a condition of

201. Robert Pear, "Social Security numbers not secure," *New York Times*, (presented in the *Cleveland Plain Dealer*, 20 May 2002), Sec. A.

202. "Defendant Convicted in Three Stooges Reference Scheme Sentenced in Federal Court," press release [online] (U.S. Department of Justice, 11 January 2001 — [cited 23 March 2002]); available from *http://www.usdoj.gov/usao/txn/PressRel02/ penker_sen_pr.html.*

probation or parole. It is hard to believe, but it was legal to pay SSI welfare benefits to fugitives until 1996, and *it is still legal* to pay retirement and worker disability benefits to fugitives.[203]

In a report dated August 28, 2000, the Inspector General of the SSA noted that, despite the prohibition on payments of SSI welfare benefits, thousands of fugitives were still being paid, with a projected cost as high as $283 million. In addition, the estimated ongoing overpayments are expected to remain as high as $135 million *per year*, until better matching of SSA and state records is achieved.[204]

And now, a word on behalf of our fine fugitives and prisoners

When a person is fleeing the law or going to jail, he must have an awful lot to worry about, and probably won't find time, or may even forget, to notify the SSA that his checks should be suspended. Therefore, it might be a good idea for the SSA to handle this problem without expecting help from the fugitive or prisoner. Hmmm? This will necessitate communication between the SSA, penal institutions, and various agencies of law enforcement, including state authorities. An example:

SSI welfare checks lead to accused rapist

At least we got our money's worth from *these* SSI welfare checks, for they led authorities right to the New York City apartment of Anthony Cummings, a fugitive from charges that he raped and molested a 3-year-old girl. "Federal marshals and our guys just knocked on his door and asked if he was Anthony Cummings," said a spokesperson for the Social Security Inspector General. Cummings cleverly replied, "Yeah, that's who I am." It is estimated that Anthony received up to $20,000 in benefits before being apprehended.[205]

---

203. Legislation designed to eliminate the payment of worker retirement and disability benefits to fugitive felons was referred from the House to the Senate in April, 2003, and is expected to become law in 2003.

204. Office of Inspector General, "Identification of Fugitives Receiving Supplemental Security Income Payments," Audit Report A-01-98-61013 (Social Security Administration, August 2000), A-4.

205. David Pace, "Fugitives grab millions in benefits" [online] *Associated Press*, 27 December 2000 — [cited 28 March 2002]; available from *http://www.s-t.com/daily/12-00/12-27-00/a02wn018.htm.*

4. Collecting SSI while out of the country

To qualify for SSI welfare benefits, you do not necessarily have to be a citizen. However, you are supposed to actually live in the United States. (Let's hope the ACLU is not reading this.) After absences of 30 days or more, benefits are cut off; however, many recipients "forget" to notify the SSA that they are gone.

In May, 2001, the Inspector General reported on a 1998 study of SSI welfare recipients who had not used their Medicaid services for at least 15 months. It was discovered that at least 20% of the foreign-born recipients had periods of ineligibility because of U.S. absences. (For the U.S. born recipients, the ineligibility percentage was only 0.2.) Later, a more generalized study of eligibility standards led the SSA to estimate that, for the year 1999, between $234 million and $357 million was overpaid to recipients tested.[206]

SSA staff in border states such as Texas have expressed dismay and frustration with evidence of abuse in this area, and with the lack of enforced penalties. Also, there is frustration over the fact that people who falsify their residency information can get back into payment status *merely by subsequently establishing residency for 30 consecutive days.* In the late 1990s, the Inspector General conducted a pilot project in El Paso, Texas, to test methods for identifying potential residency fraud. Recipients were asked to provide documentation to show proof of residency. During the pilot project, SSA staff saw many indications of residency abuse.

SSA staff comments about residency fraud

- A woman owned her home in El Paso and gave that address to SSA as her residence. However, the recipient rented her house to others. [An] investigator found that the woman had not lived in her house in one and one half years and was residing in Mexico.
- A claimant admitted he comes to pick up his check, stays 3 days [in El Paso] then goes back to [Ciudad Juarez].
- In the end, most of [the suspended cases] are going to be put back into pay status. We will reduce the SSI payments to pay for the overpayment. So the effect is the Government is paying its own self back.

---

206. Office of Inspector General, "Effectiveness of the Social Security Administration's Special Project Reviews of Supplemental Security Income Recipients," Evaluation Report A-09-99-62010 (Social Security Administration, May 2001), p. 6, footnote 5.

• The recipients and the community believe [SSA is] not willing to take harsh steps when [recipients] commit residence fraud. The community should be advised of the penalties associated with SSI residency fraud.[207]

Again, it must be asked: Is the SSA serious about controlling fraud?

5. Faking ailments and collaborator fraud

Lisa Marie Judware died just four days after being rushed, unconscious, to Alice Hyde Medical Center. A year earlier, on her first birthday, doctors had place a pacemaker in her chest in a futile attempt to control her seizures — seizures which she did not even have. You see, the only disease Lisa had was a mother who repeatedly suffocated her, to keep her sick. Only this time, it went a little too far, and Lisa was dead. Hard to believe, but that is exactly what a Malone Co. jury concluded when it convicted Brenda J. Snyder of second-degree murder for smothering little Lisa to death. Brenda was also convicted of the assault and reckless endangering of Lisa's brother, Jonathan, who suffered repeated suffocations, but survived. Prosecutors argued that the woman suffocated and abused the children to make it appear that they had breathing disorders. In that way, they continued to qualify for SSI disability benefits of more than $1300 per month. Brenda is serving a sentence of 55 years-to-life.[208]

Of course, very few people would actually make their children sick, to get benefit checks or for any other reason. But, *feigning* illness, often with the assistance of collaborators such as unethical doctors and lawyers, is not uncommon. A large part of the problem has to do with the public's attitude. Regarding insurance fraud, in general, it has been noted:

> Career criminals, often working with unethical lawyers, doctors and others, commit a large portion of insurance fraud. But policy holders trying to make a quick buck by padding claims or misrepresenting facts commit the rest of it. And many of them see nothing wrong with this practice.[209]

---

207. Office of Inspector General, "Southwest Tactical Operations Plan: Impact on Field Office Operations," Audit Report A-06-97-22009 [online] (Social Security Administration, 8 January 1998 — [cited 28 March 2002]), section titled, *Findings*; available from *http://www.ssa.gov/oig/ADOBEPDF/audit_htms/69722009.htm.*

208. Denise A. Raymo, "Snyder case on TV tonight" [online] *Press Republican Online,* 13 January 2002 — [cited 24 March 2002]; available from *http://www.pressrepublican.com/Archive/2002/01_2002/011320024.htm.*

This attitude is revealed by some polling on the topic of insurance fraud. A 1997 survey showed 36% of all Americans think it's OK to pad an insurance claim to make up for past premiums. In urban areas this rose to 42%.[210] Another study showed that 21.2% of those interviewed had a high tolerance for fraud, blamed insurers for the behavior of their customers, and wanted little or no punishment for those who commit the fraud.[211]

To detect disability fakers, the SSA has successfully used its Cooperative Disability Investigation units (CDIs). Each CDI unit comprises an agent from the Inspector General's office (who acts as team leader) and various state law enforcement and disability personnel. Between 1998 (when the units became operational) and mid-2002, these units conducted investigations resulting in over 2,700 denials.[212] Nevertheless, this is a very limited success. In May, 2002, the GAO concluded that, despite the efforts of the SSA, it has "had difficulty ensuring that decisions about a claimant's eligibility for disability benefits are accurate."[213]

Once a person is awarded benefits, the SSA performs periodic reviews, called Continuing Disability Reviews (CDRs), to see if the person is still entitled to benefits. Despite these efforts, the GAO continues to report that "SSA has achieved poor results in this arena, where fewer than 1 in 500 DI beneficiaries and few SSI beneficiaries leave the disability rolls to work."[214] Undoubtedly, many of these workers are making fraudulent claims.

209. "Insurance fraud: everyone pays the price," in the series *Insurance Backgrounder* [online] (Bloomington, Illinois: State Farm Insurance, July 1997 — [cited 6 November 2002]); available from *http://www.statefarm.com/media/insback.htm*.

210. *Ibid.*

211. *Ibid.*

212. James G. Huse, Jr., Inspector General of the Social Security Administration, "Statement for the Record" before the Subcommittee on Human Resources [online] (U.S. House of Representatives, Committee on Ways and Means, 25 July 2002 — [cited 11 August 2002]); available from *http://www.ssa.gov/oig/executive_operations/ testimony_speeches/07252002testimony.htm*.

213. "Agency Must Position Itself Now to Meet Profound Challenges," GAO-02-289T (U.S. General Accounting Office, 2 May 2002), 7.

214. *Ibid.*, 12.

They weren't retarded, but they sure were stupid!

Social Security examiners noticed some troubling similarities among various applicants for disability benefits. Several of these people, claiming to be retarded, had the *same* problems. "[M]any claimants could not say how many legs a dog had, or what the color of a white horse was.... " Was it a coincidence, or a pattern? An investigation ensued, and 36 fakers were charged with swindling the Feds and New York out of about $1.3 million.[215] At least 34 of the 36 fraudsters were ultimately convicted and ordered to pay restitution.

6. Faking finances

There are *three* basic reasons people conceal assets or income with regard to Social Security programs. As discussed in Chapter VIII (with regard to the worker disability program) the SSA foolishly uses the claimant's earnings level to determine whether he is capable of working. If he earns $801 per month, he is capable of working, *and loses all benefits.* If he earns $799 per month, he is not capable of working, *and keeps all benefits.* If he reports exactly $800? (Sorry. I have to save something for the sequel.) The point is this. The motivation of people to work (and to *report* those earnings) is diminished by this earnings standard because beneficiaries know that one extra dollar of monthly earnings could cost them thousands of dollars in benefits.

Second, with regard to the SSI welfare program, people conceal income and/or assets because it is a means-tested program, and any substantial income or assets (from any source) could result in a denial of benefits.

The third reason people conceal income is to avoid a reduction in *redundant* benefits. Disability benefits are generally reduced to the extent of redundant benefits from other governmental disability programs, such as workers' compensation. If the SSA finds that you have such income, your disability benefits are reduced or eliminated. In an audit conducted by the Inspector General in 1999, it was noted that "SSA's policy is to rely on each beneficiary to voluntarily report" subsequent receipt of workers' compensation, so that the disability benefit can be appropriately reduced. Audit tests showed a failure to

---

215. "Spitzer Announces 36 Charged with Stealing $1.3 Million in Federal-State Disability Payments," press release [online] (Office of N.Y. State Attorney General, 27 April 2001 — [cited 13 February 2002]); available from *http://www.oag.state.ny.us/press/2001/apr/apr27b_01.html.*

report rate of *at least 62%*, resulting in overpayments estimated to be hundreds of millions of dollars.[216]

One way people hide income is by using multiple identities — one to get benefits and another to earn income. There is an example of this, below. Income is also concealed by working in the "underground economy." In addition, relationships with supporting partners may be concealed, so the SSA will not consider the partner's income when awarding benefits. The underground economy and the use of hidden relationships are discussed in greater detail in the next chapter.

There has been some increase in staff devoted to investigating fraud and abuse, but little progress has been made. The GAO reports:

> SSA's work credit and measurement system has historically rewarded staff for processing cases rather than thoroughly verifying applicant eligibility or preventing fraud and abuse. We believe the system needs to be revised to include specific performance measures to hold managers accountable for verifying recipient information and combating program fraud and abuse.[217]

Some examples which illustrate the concealment of income:

Strange love triangle wrecks man's disability scheme

After obtaining a worker disability award in 1976, a man continued to work for 23 years under a phony Social Security number. He, or rather, his phony identity, then applied for retirement benefits. The SSA noticed that both the disabled identity of this man (using the true Social Security number) and the retired identity of this man (using the false number) were married to the same woman. The man pled guilty to his fraud, and received a 3-year suspended sentence. He was also ordered to pay restitution to the SSA for part of its loss of $144,000.[218]

---

216. Office of Inspector General, "Worker's Compensation Unreported by Social Security Beneficiaries," Audit Report A-04-98-64002 (Social Security Administration, December 1999), 6.

217. General Accounting Office letter to Committee on Governmental Affairs, GAO/HEHS-00-126R (U.S. General Accounting Office, 30 June 2000), Enclosure II, 4.

218. Office of Inspector General, "Case of the Month" [online] (Social Security Administration, September 1999 — [cited 23 March 2002]); available from *http://www.ssa.gov/oig/investigations/caseofmonth/caseofmonth1999.htm#September*.

"If those SSA people could see me now!"

So said a "disabled" man while working on the roof of a customer's house. While collecting worker disability benefits, this man ran a home improvement business and fixed up cars for resale. He concealed the earnings from the SSA, because they exceeded the earnings limit and would have "proved" his ability to work. The man eventually shot himself in the foot, so to speak, when he filed a Small Claims Court complaint against a former business associate. In that complaint the disabled man outlined hundreds of hours of his work, for which he was owed $5,000. When confronted with the evidence, the man pleaded guilty to Social Security fraud, was incarcerated, and ordered to make restitution in an amount over $100,000.[219]

The SSA shares the blame

Although we are concentrating on benefits obtained fraudulently, there is another side to this story. Some disabled beneficiaries complain that, even when they inform the SSA of financial and relationship changes, benefits don't get increased or decreased. With regard to the SSI disability program, the Social Security Advisory Board notes:

> At a hearing before the Ways and Means Social Security Subcommittee, one witness commented, "the disability community often views the potential for overpayments as a distinct work disincentive." The experience of people with disabilities is that "numerous reports to SSA and their request to adjust benefits often go unheeded by the administration."[220]

It must be tempting for people to cheat, when the SSA displays such indifference.

How much does it cost us?

As noted, the SSA has steadfastly refused to provide estimates of program-wide fraud; it only provides estimates of erroneous payments attributable to

219. Office of Inspector General, "Case of the Month" [online] (Social Security Administration, January 2001 — [cited 28 March 2002]); available from *http://www.ssa.gov/oig/investigations/caseofmonth/caseofmonth2001.htm#January.*
220. "Statement on the Supplemental Security Income Program" [online] (Social Security Advisory Board, 30 May 2001 — [cited 12 October 2002]), 9; available from *http://www.ssab.gov/ssirept2001.pdf.*

inaccuracies. The table below provides a rough *guesstimate* of all erroneous payments (inaccuracies and fraud), based on SSA-published error rates and the fraud estimates initially produced for comparable parts of British Social Security. As you can see, an estimated $26 billion per year will be lost, in each of the next 75 years, in the disability and SSI welfare programs. (An estimate for the retirement program is not provided, but that loss would, presumably, be significantly less.)

Table 6

Guesstimate of cost of fraud and other erroneous payments for each of the next 75 years

	SSI Welfare	Disability	Total
Payment errors (100%-93.6%*)	6.40%	--	
Decisional errors (100%-93.5%**)	--	6.50%	
Fraud***	12.10%	6.70%	
Subtotal	18.50%	13.20%	
Times estimated average annual expenditure for each of 75 years****	X $63 billion	X $145 billion	
Estimated totals	$11.6 billion	$19.1 billion	$30.7 billion
Less estimated collections*****			
	-1.7 billion	-2.7 billion	-4.4 billion
Estimated fraud and overpayments, net of estimated collections	$9.9 billion	$16.4 billion	$26.3 billion

*SSI overpayment accuracy rate is from the SSA FY 2001 Performance and Accountability Report (for year 2000).

**This is a weighted average of initial and appeals decisional accuracy rates (discussed earlier).

***Estimate is from the British initial estimates previously referenced (assuming our rates to be somewhat similar).

****The $145 billion per year in long-term disability benefits was calculated by annuitizing (for 75 years at 3%) the present value of disability costs (per 2003 Trustees Report Table IV.B6), after reduction for estimated administration costs. The long-term amount of SSI welfare benefits is presumed to increase, from the current level, in the same proportion as worker disability, since almost all SSI welfare benefits are paid for disability.

*****Per the SS Advisory Board's March, 2002 report on collection efforts, $1.9 billion in overpayments was collected in 2001. In that year, about $29 billion was paid in SSI benefits and $60 billion was paid in worker disability benefits, for a total of $89 billion. Since we have estimated that the long-term amount of payments for these two programs will be $208 billion ($63 billion for SSI and $145 billion for worker disability), the $1.9 billion in collections has been increased by the fraction 208/89. This gives us our collections estimate of $4.4 billion per year.

As noted, the above guesstimate is rough, but I make no apologies. Only the SSA, with its considerable resources and access to confidential information, can produce reliable estimates. It is disgraceful that it refuses to do so.

A word about collection rates

On the previous pages we have cited many cases where fraud was detected, and restitution was *ordered*. Of course, ordering restitution is not the same as collecting it. Of the billions in estimated annual fraud and overpayments, only a fraction is discovered through investigations, and only a fraction of that amount is collected. The Social Security Advisory Board states:

> Between 1991 and 2001, the annual amount of overpayments collected by the agency grew from $1.1 billion to $1.9 billion, but the amount of overpayments detected more than doubled, from $1.4 billion to $3.5 billion. During this period the amount of SSA's total outstanding overpayments grew by 133%, from $3 billion in 1991 to $7 billion in 2001.[221]

What we must do

- The first step is to develop and publicize meaningful estimates of fraud and overpayments, in total and in each program. These would alert the public to the fraud problem, and would become yardsticks by which to measure progress in reducing fraud. Comprehensive sampling and auditing, similar to that in the British program, would help us develop the estimates.
- The SSA's Inspector General must continue and expand its efforts to investigate fraud, to audit the programs, and to publicize its findings. Cross-checking of the Social Security data base with the computer files of other federal and state agencies has been one of the most effective tools for identifying problems. The CDI reviews of disability cases have also been effective. These efforts warrant more financial resources.
- The SSA should revise disability regulations which invite abuse and fraud due to the inclusion of conflicting, confusing and subjective standards. The burden of proof has to be shifted back to the claimant. That is, he must demonstrate, via clear medical evidence, that he has an impairment.
- Where financial, familial, and residency information is required, the SSA needs to start auditing and verifying. It is not sufficient to merely accept the word of the claimants. Strict penalties, including jail time, must be imposed for false claims and statements. Penalties should be publicized, to serve as a warning to would-be abusers.
- In the mid-1990s, the SSA started a telephone tip line which has received thousands of calls. This good start needs to be expanded in two ways: by publicizing the tip-line, and by adding a *monetary reward* for information leading to the discovery of fraud or abuse. No abusive claimant or SSA employee should feel safe from the anonymous tipster.

---

221. "SSA's Obligation to Ensure That the Public's Funds are Responsibly Collected and Expended" [online] (Social Security Advisory Board, March 2002 — [cited 2 October 2002]), 20; available from *http://www.ssab.gov/stewardship3.pdf.*

- In the final analysis, public morality is the best defense against fraud. Presently, surveys show that large percentages of the public feel it is okay to cheat insurance companies and government programs. *Ad campaigns*, educating the public to the immorality of such actions, and to the dire consequences, should be started. How about recruiting some big-name Hollywood stars to tell people how Social Security cheaters end up hurting those who really need those benefits?

- To test the SSA's effectiveness in controlling fraud, and in other administrative responsibilities, pilot projects involving the *privatization* of key administrative functions, should be implemented. Results of the privatized pilot projects could then be compared to the general SSA administrative results.

- A national identity card, a topic of interest since 9/11, would greatly reduce identity theft. In addition, better data base sharing between the SSA and INS (Immigration) is needed.

- Surreptitious testers should be established to probe the SSA's internal control systems. These testers would try to get Social Security numbers and benefits, using false documents and statements. Their success or failure rate would serve as an indicator of the size and nature of the problem at hand.

- The SSA needs to recruit top-notch personnel and motivate its employees to provide service to taxpayers as well as beneficiaries. Randomly selected samples of the case work of each SSA employee should be reviewed thoroughly by traveling teams of quality control experts. Positive and punitive incentives should be developed to encourage workers to diligently look for fraud.

CHAPTER XI: SECRET MONEY, SECRET RELATIONSHIPS

(TWO TRENDS THAT ARE WREAKING HAVOC ON OUR BENEFIT PROGRAMS)

Fall of a Princess

In my home town, Cleveland, the director of our public housing authority was a highly-respected woman named Claire. When she arrived in 1990, she was much praised and well-compensated. In 1993, Claire needed someone to run a new housing project, so she decided that the housing authority would pay a New York bank up to $750,000 to obtain the services of one of its employees, named Ira. Later, some disturbing revelations came to light. First, analysts said that the $750,000 was about ten times the going rate for this sort of arrangement. Second, Ira had a previous criminal record. And, third, it was reported that Ira was someone Claire had "known for years and with whom she had an on-again, off-again romantic relationship...."[222] (Eventually, they were married.) The point is this. If Claire and Ira had been formally married when the contract was issued, a possible conflict of interest would have been assumed, and the contract would have been scrutinized. It would have been obvious that, by paying so much for Ira's services, Claire would benefit personally. But they weren't formally married, and most people did not learn of the relationship until after the contract was awarded, and the housing project subsequently failed. It was then that people started to wonder if Ira was paid excessively due to his close friendship with Claire. We will never know, for this scandal was soon overshadowed by more serious legal charges, for which Claire has been convicted in a court of law.

---

222. Editor, "CMHA Director Faces the Strong Prospect of Losing the Good Reputation She Has Worked Hard to Earn," *The Plain Dealer*, 10 February 1998.

Claire now lives in public housing of another sort — the kind with concrete floors and steel bars.

The problem no one talks about

Many sociologists debate the merits of marriage as opposed to informal cohabitation, particularly as this issue pertains to the raising of children. But there is a rarely-discussed side effect to this trend away from the formality of marriage. A lack of formality can conceal relationships that have fiscal, as well as personal, implications. In the case of Claire and Ira, the unknown relationship had implications for the efficient administration of a housing program. Likewise, undisclosed relationships can have implications for the efficient administration of the Social Security programs. This is due to the fact that Social Security regulations are based on the old-fashioned assumption that married people share children, income, and expense; single people do not.

In the previous chapter we discussed several forms of Social Security fraud, including fraud accomplished through the concealment of income. Often, the income is concealed by working in the "underground economy," but income can also be concealed by hiding a personal relationship. These two problems are hardly addressed by our governmental assistance programs yet result, arguably, in more overpayments than any other form of abuse or fraud.

PART ONE — SECRET RELATIONSHIPS

According to the 2000 U.S. Census, the number of unmarried couples sharing a household increased 72% between 1990 and 2000,[223] to a total of about 5.5 million.[224] As we all know, these unmarried couples often share income, expenses, and children as if they were married. Census figures show that about one third of births in the U.S. are to "unmarried" women, but this statistic may be misleading. One extensive research study shows that most unmarried

---

223. "Statistics About Unmarried Partners, Cohabitation, Living Together, and Marriage," [online] (Boston, Massachusetts: Alternatives to Marriage Project, based on U.S. Census 2000 — [cited 6 April 2002]); available from *http://www.unmarried.org/statistics.html.*

224. "Unmarried-Partner Households by Sex of Partners," Table PCT14 [online] (U.S. Census Bureau, 2000 — [cited 26 September 2002]), Census 2000, Summary File 1 (SF-1) 100% file; available from *http://factfinder.census.gov/servlet/BasicFactsServlet.*

mothers are "romantically involved" with their child's father at the time of birth; and almost all are "friends." Deciding whether some of these couples are in de facto marriage arrangements, or de facto parenting arrangements, is not easy. However, given the dramatic rise in informal relationships and the fiscal and social implications, it is important that we try to understand the phenomenon.

Marriage according to the SSA

If a man and woman live together but are not officially married, does the SSA consider them to be married? The SSA handbook, in Section 2122.2 (which pertains to SSI welfare benefits), states that a man and woman (who are not officially married) will be considered married if "they are holding themselves out as husband and wife to the community in which they live..."[225]

For the regular (worker) retirement program, the rules are somewhat stricter. According to Section 1717 of the handbook, you must submit evidence of ceremonial marriage *or* written statements (from husband, wife, and a blood relative of each) asserting that there is a common law marriage. [226]

In either case, marital status is largely based upon representations of the couple, and the determination they make can greatly affect their qualification for Social Security benefits. Consider the following hypothetical illustrations:

The Social Security implications of being "married"

Illustration 1:

Carol is 35 and disabled. She inherited a home worth $500,000, and a Mercedes worth $70,000 (which she uses to go to the doctor), but Carol has no earnings, and has never worked; she owns little other than the house and car. She has lived for the last ten years with Mike, who makes $100,000 per year. She applies for SSI welfare disability benefits, which are only provided to the poorest of people, those with little or no earnings. When asked if she is married, she replies, "No, we don't hold ourselves out as husband and wife." The SSA takes her word for it, and she is classified as unmarried. Since they are not married, Mike's income is not deemed to be her income, and she is awarded benefits. And, by the way, she may also qualify for Medicaid and food stamps.

---

225. SSA Handbook [online] (Social Security Administration, March 2001 — [cited 5 April 2002]), section 2122.2; available from *http://www.ssa.gov/OP_Home/handbook/*.
226. *Ibid.*, section 1717.1.

Illustration 2:

Carol (yes, the same one) is now 65, and still living with Mike, who has just retired and is getting Social Security benefits. A year later, Carol goes to the SSA office and applies for benefits as his common law spouse. To "prove" her marriage, Carol simply submits statements from Mike and two other relatives, and she is awarded benefits equal to 50% of Mike's benefit. (In other words, Mike and Carol together will now get 150% of Mike's amount.) If Mike dies before Carol, her monthly benefit will then be increased to equal the full amount of Mike's benefit for the rest of her life. Carol never contributed a dime to the Social Security system, and was never really poor. Still, she received monthly benefits from age 35, and will continue to do so until she dies.

Hidden marriages

As you can see, there may be a financial motive for a couple's decision to "hold itself out" as married. I suspect that, as the last trace of social stigma attached to unmarried cohabitation melts away, some couples will decide their status mostly in terms of overall financial benefits. On the one hand, they may opt to be "married" (formally or common law) to blend their income tax rates, or to get Social Security spousal benefits. On the other hand, being "single" may maximize the receipt of AFDC, SSI welfare, food stamps, and "earned" income tax credits. And they even may switch back and forth. If you feel this viewpoint is too cynical, consider some research conducted with respect to welfare mothers. In one survey, conducted by interviewing 214 single mothers in four American cities during the mid-1990s, it was reported that:

> Eighty-six percent of mothers were currently receiving *covert* contributions from family or friends, boyfriends, absent fathers, or from other sources ... [emphasis added].[227]

This study tells us two things. First, 86% of the mothers were cheating and probably *breaking the law*. And, second, many of these single mothers were not as *unmarried* as they were claiming, in view of the "contributions" they were

---

227. Kathryn J. Edin, "The Myths of Dependence and Self-sufficiency: Women, welfare, and low-wage work" [online] (University of Wisconsin, Institute for Research on Poverty, Fall/Winter 1995 — [cited 6 April 2002]); available from *http://www.ssc.wisc.edu/irp/pubs/focusold/foc172.htm*.

receiving. If 86% of these people lied to welfare agencies regarding support, shouldn't we be skeptical regarding their claims of single status?

More direct information is available. In a report entitled, "Cohabitation: An Elusive Concept," Teitler and Reichman review extensive survey data concerning unmarried parents, compiled in the ongoing Fragile Families and Child Wellbeing Study. They note:

> Recent results from the ... Study demonstrate that most unwed fathers are involved with the mothers and their children at the time of the birth and that they have intentions to remain involved as parents in the future.[228]

And, even where the fathers were absent from the home, the study found that many still had close relationships with the mothers of their children:

> Though many unmarried couples do not live together, *most do view themselves as collaborative family units* [emphasis added].[229]

In fact, over 82% of the 3,700 "unmarried" couples studied were "romantically involved," and over 90% were, at least, "friends." And, remarkably, these percentages were almost the same in the case of people receiving public assistance.[230]

So, we seem to have a problem. Many people are acting married, but not necessarily declaring it. And when they don't, our social service agencies have to pick up the financial slack.

Hidden parents

So far, we have only considered the hidden relationship of marriage. Yet, there is another relationship that can be concealed by different means. It is the parental relationship. You see, when the SSA evaluates a child's application for benefits (which would have to be SSI disability benefits), that child's income is "deemed" to include that of any parent *in the same household*.[231] If dad, for instance,

---

228. Julien O. Teitler and Nancy E. Reichman, "Cohabitation: An Elusive Concept," Social Indicators Survey Center, working paper no. 01-4 [online] (Columbia University School of Social Work, 29-31 March 2001 — [cited 14 August 2002]), 1; available from *http://www.siscenter.org/cohabitation.pdf.*

229. *Ibid.*, 4.

230. *Ibid.*, figs. 1D and 1E, and table 3.

231. SSA Handbook, section 2169.

does not officially live in the household, his income does not count, except for a portion of the direct support payments actually made to the child's mother. And, often, the mother does not get those payments, or claims not to get them. This SSA "deeming" rule constitutes a financial incentive to the parent (usually the dad) to get out of the home (or, at least, to *claim* to be out of the home), so that his earnings don't prevent the child from getting benefits. As you can see, the crucial matter in this case is *where the parents live*. Whereas, the crucial matter in the case of marriage is how the man and woman *hold themselves out*.

Help Wanted: peeping Tom

Would couples really lie to the SSA about where they sleep? Well, that is hard to determine without hiding in the bushes outside their apartments. However:

> Anecdotal evidence reported by Fragile Families interviewers suggests that there was some under-reporting of cohabitation in order to conceal partners from government agencies ... [in other words, more cheating].[232]

And, any false claims regarding "absentee" dads are of significant concern in light of other research done by Fragile Families. It shows that 76% of the unmarried fathers interviewed had regular earnings in the week before the interview. (And, almost 30% of those dads had additional *underground* earnings.)[233] Those "regular earnings" (and the underground earnings) would probably be enough to preclude the child from qualifying for benefits. In their analysis, Teitler and Reichman note that "the Fragile Families data have dispelled the myth of the absent father...."[234] Maybe I'm a cynic, but I have a feeling that the myth of the absent dad, and the myth of the cohabiting but unmarried dad, will live on for as long as we have governmental programs granting benefits to people who make such claims.

---

232. Julien O. Teitler and Nancy E. Reichman, 10.

233. Christina Norland, "Unwed Fathers, the Underground Economy, and Child Support Policy," research brief no. 3 (Princeton University, Fragile Families and Child Wellbeing Study, January 2001).

234. Julien O. Teitler and Nancy E. Reichman, 1.

Is the SSA on top of this matter?

Is the SSA vigorously checking into the marital and parental status of applicants? The answer can be found in a report from the Social Security Advisory Board cited in the previous chapter, but worth revisiting. After interviewing hundreds of Social Security employees, the Board stated:

> [T]here is widespread concern about the agency's capacity to properly administer the SSI program.... [E]mployees have told the Board that they sometimes do not pursue certain lines of questioning, such as the details of an individual's living arrangements, because it takes too long to resolve the issues that may be raised.... A number of agency employees have told the Board that many SSI claims are currently being paid based on allegations.[235]

Clearly, the SSA cannot deal with the breakdown of formal marriages into cohab arrangements. People in undeclared marriages and parental arrangements will continue to take benefits to which they are not entitled. And, given the trends, this problem is likely to be far worse in coming years than it is today.

PART TWO — SECRET MONEY

How often do you see $100 bills at the grocery store?

Not too often, I imagine. But did you know that over 63% of the value of all U.S. currency in circulation is in the form of $100 bills? It was less than 20% in 1967. Does this tell us anything? Since the underground economy operates almost exclusively in currency (cash), an increase in large denomination currency is generally regarded as a sign of a growing underground economy.[236] Most economists estimate that this unreported activity equals about 10% of our GDP, and some economists estimate that up to 25 million Americans (about one of every six in the workforce) earn a significant part of their earnings from it.[237]

---

235. "Statement on the Supplemental Security Income Program" [online] (Social Security Advisory Board, 30 May 2002 — [cited 15 September 2002]), 2; available from *http://www.ssab.gov/ssi2002.pdf.*

236. "The Underground Economy" [online] (Washington, D.C.: National Center for Policy Analysis, 13 July 1998 — [cited 26 March 2002]); available from *http://www.ncpa.org/ba/ba273.html.*

"Underground economy" defined

Some people reserve the phrase "underground economy" for the criminal activities people engage in, such as prostitution, selling drugs, or stealing. On the other hand, activities that are normally legal, but hidden from government agencies, are considered to be part of the "informal economy." I have a problem with this euphemistic phrase because I think it sounds too nice, too innocuous, and too legal. It is hard for me to see how a person who fraudulently gets $6,000 or more *each year* in SSI benefits is better than the guy stealing a radio. So, in this book, the phrase "underground economy" means any exchange of goods or services for money, if that transfer is unlawfully concealed from a governmental agency by using currency, false identification, or other means.

The underground economy and lost net revenues

The underground economy affects the Social Security program by reducing Social Security net revenue. Net revenue is the excess of payroll taxes collected over benefits paid. When someone fails to report taxable earnings, Social Security loses 12.4% (the combined payroll tax amount) times the amount of unreported income. Of course, Social Security will have an off-setting savings (some day) to the extent that benefits attributable to the unreported income will not be paid. But, the savings to Social Security (i.e., benefits it doesn't have to pay) will rarely be proportional to the lost revenue, due to two factors. First, the benefits paid by Social Security on upper earnings are only one sixth as much as benefits paid on lower earnings. That means an individual who under-reports earnings usually improves his rate of return on payroll taxes paid. Second, about one fourth of payroll taxes collected is used to pay implicit interest on about $10 trillion in unfunded liability. (This amount is our bill for earlier generations who didn't pay enough to justify the value of the benefits they received, and it's our bill for fraud, abuse, and erroneous payments.) When someone under-reports earnings, Social Security loses the 25% that would have been applied to the unfunded liability.

---

237. "The Unmeasured Underground Economy" [online] (Washington, D.C.: National Center for Policy Analysis, 2001 — [cited 6 April 2002]); available from *http://www.ncpa.org/pd/economy/pd122198b.html*.

How much net revenue is lost?

The underground economy is estimated to be about 10% of GDP — in other words, one trillion dollars (10% of 10 trillion dollars). Even if only half of the underground income is subject to payroll taxes, the loss of Social Security gross program revenue is a staggering $60 billion per year, before adding in Medicare and general income tax. If we assume that 25% of that $60 billion would have been used by Social Security to pay implicit interest on the unfunded liability, and the rest was used to pay benefits, the system loses $15 billion in net revenue per year. Thus, anything that can induce people to fully report their wages would greatly benefit the system and help to restore the program's financial integrity. By the way, the $15 billion in estimated losses (due to the underground economy) is not reflected in the "Wheel of Waste" in Chapter II, because it would partially overlap with the estimate of fraud.

The underground and overpayment of disability and SSI welfare

There is another way in which the underground economy affects the Social Security programs. As discussed in Chapter VIII, a disabled beneficiary earning over $800 per month will not qualify for benefits. This income rule discourages some beneficiaries from working (or from working very much), but others want to eat their cake and have it too. They earn the money but conceal it by working for cash or by using a phony ID. In this way, they still appear to qualify for disability benefits. In the case of SSI welfare benefits, even small amounts of earnings (as little as $85 per month) can impact the size of the monthly benefit. Again, there is an incentive to conceal earnings to keep benefits. Because the allowable earnings ceiling for SSI welfare is very low, one suspects that cheating may be common. Indeed, studies show that people receiving welfare, including SSI welfare, frequently have a significant amount of unreported income. One author put it this way:

> [R]ecent studies document that women on welfare do in fact work many hours outside the home, but do not report their earnings or employment to welfare agencies or to conventional cross-sectional sources such as the Current Population Survey.[238]

---

238. Elaine McCrate, "Welfare and women's earnings" [online] (Thousand Oaks, CA: Sage Publications, 1997 — [cited 6 April 2002]); available from *http://construct.haifa.ac.il/~danielp/soc/elaine.htm.*

In one study of 50 women in Chicago, over half were found to have unreported full or part-time work.[239] Another research team, studying 214 welfare recipients, found that 46% "were engaged in covert work." Most of these people "worked off the books or under a false identity...." The balance of the covert workers were involved in "selling sex, drugs, or stolen goods."[240] In addition to the unreported work, the welfare recipients under study had other sources of support. In fact,

> [a]*ll of them* [of the 214 being studied] had additional income from unreported work, under-the-table payments from the fathers of their children, or gifts from boyfriends and relatives (emphasis added).[241]

Finally, in a different study, a research team noted:

> [A]ll of twenty-five interviewed recipients supplemented their benefits through unreported work or the underground economy, *on average doubling their incomes* (emphasis added).[242]

Could this unreported work be the reason the sky did not fall when welfare was reformed in the mid-1990s?

In fact, for many of the interviewed welfare mothers, the total received from welfare, SSI welfare benefits, covert jobs, and support exceeded what was readily available in the job market. And this was a disincentive to getting work. One woman interviewed (in the study of 214 welfare recipients) put it this way:

---

239. LaDonna Pavetti, "How Much More Can They Work? Setting Realistic Expectations for Welfare Mothers," A report to the Annie E. Casey Foundation [online] (Washington, D.C.: Urban Institute, July 1997 — [cited 6 April 2002]); available from *http://www.urban.org/welfare/howmuch.htm*.

240. Kathryn J. Edin, "The Myths of Dependence and Self-sufficiency: Women, welfare, and low-wage work" [online] (University of Wisconsin, Institute for Research on Poverty, Fall/Winter 1995 — [cited 6 April 2002]), 3.; available from *http://www.ssc.wisc.edu/irp/pubs/focusold/foc172.htm*.

241. Christopher Jencks, "Do Poor Women Have a Right to Bear Children?" [online] *The American Prospect*, vol. 6, no.20, 1 December 1995 — [cited 8 April 2002]; available from *http://www.prospect.org/print/V6/20/jencks-c.html*.

242. Elaine McCrate, 3.

> Once you get sucked into the system there is no way to get out because they are paying for your food, your [housing, your medical care], and it is hard to find a job that does all that for you.

All sympathy aside, surely, a free hand-out is always an easy solution, when someone else is paying.

It's not just the poor

When it comes to the underground, there is no one more guilty than that pillar of the American economy, the small business owner. IRS studies have shown that about one half of the unpaid taxes related to undeclared individual income is attributable to sole proprietors. Self-employed individuals who operate formal businesses report only about 68% of their business income, and those operating casually, on a cash basis, only report about 19% of their income.[243] In the future, it's likely to get worse.

The future — a high-tech underground?

"The self-employed will find it easy to evade the current tax system," according to Richard Rahn, author of *The End of Money*. An American contractor, like a writer, lawyer, musician, consultant, etc., will be able to attract U.S. business on a website hosted on a server in a foreign country — one with a low tax rate. Orders will come in via the website, and billing and administrative matters will be handled through it. Rahn says that, to evade government tracking, customers might pay with an anonymous digital currency, issued by a private bank. The scam would be illegal, but hard to detect.[244] Many corporations are already trying to avoid (or evade?) taxes by shifting income offshore (through the use of subsidiaries). And, "[t]he IRS estimates there may be as many as 2 million Americans with money in the Bahamas, the Caymans, Antigua and Barbuda — small nations that are sun-splashed tourist stops with strict bank secrecy laws." A Treasury Department Revenue Agent notes: "U.S. citizens dodge taxes with secret bank accounts, and then pay living expenses with cards that can easily access the money, sometimes through automatic teller

---

243. "Analyzing the Nature of the Income Tax Gap," T-GGD-97-35 (U.S. General Accounting Office, 7 January 1997), 1.

244. Richard Rahn, *The End of Money*, quoted in James Freeman, "IRS, R.I.P.?" [online] *USA Today*, 9 August 1999 — [cited 26 March 2002]; available from *http://www.usatoday.com/news/comment/columnists/freeman/ncjf16.htm*.

machines, sometimes via the Internet."[245] If these trends continue to grow, there could be an enormous loss of tax revenue — both income and payroll.

Can we reduce the underground economy?

There is little question that tax rates are directly related to the size of the underground economy. The higher the tax rates, particularly marginal rates, the bigger the underground economy. This is evident from a look at other countries where the tax rates are higher, and the unreported income is much greater. In the U.S., the underground economy is estimated to be about 10% of our GDP, while in Europe, where the taxes are higher, it ranges from 10 to 30%.[246] Some have proposed lowering tax rates to help promote wage reporting, and others even recommend eliminating the income tax and replacing it with a national sales tax, which would be simpler and more collectible. It is something worthy of serious consideration.

A second factor, which gets far less attention, is the complexity associated with payroll processing. Some businesses go underground to avoid the enormously complex and costly payroll processing requirements. Imagine the small contractor who hires a few guys every year and does construction work in several different localities. Every week or two he has to calculate the payroll tax and make deposits. Every month or two he has to fill out and file returns to report federal, state, and city taxes collected (perhaps in multiple cities). He has workers' compensation and employment insurance to calculate and report, and he may have child support to collect and distribute. There may be Earned Income Tax Credits to calculate and, at year end; there are scads of returns, and W-2 forms to prepare. Is it any wonder that he may simply slip a few bills "under the table?" Let me be clear: violators should be punished. But, our government would collect a lot more payroll tax if it could reduce the paperwork burden.

There is a third way to reduce the underground economy: By making Social Security an *investment*, rather than a *tax*. If a person feels that every extra reported hour of work will eventually increase her retirement benefits, she will be more inclined to work that hour, and to report that income. Personal Retirement

---

245. Bill Sloat, "Online service targeted by IRS," *The Plain Dealer*, 10 November 2002.

246. Bruno S. Frey and Friedrich Schneider, "Informal and Underground Economy," working paper no. 2000-04 [online] (Johannes Kepler University, Department of Economics, 2000 — [cited 27 November 2002]); available from *http://ideas.repec.org/p/jku/econwp/2000_04.html*.

Accounts (discussed in Chapter XII) are one way to turn the Social Security tax into an investment.

Summing it up

Secret money and secret relationships are costly to the Social Security system. Couples who do not formalize their relationships have flexibility in satisfying ambiguous Social Security rules, and the number of such couples is getting larger. The underground economy affects the Social Security program in different ways. It causes a loss of net revenues on the unreported wages, it can be used to conceal income that shows a person is not truly disabled, and it enables applicants to get SSI welfare benefits for which they do not qualify. Studies suggest that a large percentage of beneficiaries in means-tested welfare programs, such as SSI welfare, engage in covert work activities.

What we must do

• Of course, marriage and cohabitation issues are controversial, and there are privacy concerns. Nevertheless, recipients of public assistance have no right to misrepresent their finances by concealing beneficial relationships. At the very minimum, we need to get full and truthful disclosure from people seeking benefits, if we are to protect the greater public welfare. Claimants should be asked pointed questions, and their answers should be verified wherever possible. And they should be advised that they will be held accountable (penalties and jail time) for providing blatantly false information.

• Reducing the size of the underground economy would greatly benefit the financial integrity of Social Security as well as the Treasury's general fund. It would simultaneously lead to increased payroll tax collections, increased income tax collections, and to a decrease in the income-tested benefits paid (such as SSI welfare and disability). Some promote the concept of lower marginal income tax rates, to encourage reporting of wages. It would probably have a positive impact. But there are two other factors that cause individuals to go underground. One is the incredible complexity and costliness of payroll processing requirements. We need to find ways to streamline the reporting process so that employers are more likely to report the earnings of workers. This is particularly true for businesses that hire casual workers. The other way to reduce the underground economy is by making Social Security more like an *investment* than a *tax*. When people believe that they are getting their "money's worth" out of Social Security, they will be more inclined to report their earnings.

A corrupt boarding school

How do I feel about Personal Retirement Accounts (PRAs)? Well, think of it this way. If your daughter were attending a horrible, mismanaged boarding school, where the students receive poor educations, bad food, and live in squalor, would you prefer that she stay at the school 7 days per week, or just 5? That choice is similar to the one offered by most of the PRA proposals. You can keep putting *all* of your payroll taxes into the Social Security "boarding school," or just part of it. *Of course* PRAs would be an improvement!

Political Payola

However, there are two caveats. First, PRAs are not a substitute for comprehensive reform of the Social Security system. They won't clean up the wasteful disability programs, or the "high-risk" SSI welfare program, which is riddled with abuse. PRAs won't compensate for the billions of dollars transferred each year from the middle-class to the upper-class, and from middle-class to 5 million exempt government workers. And, by themselves, they won't eliminate our insolvency concerns.

The second caveat has to do with the price we pay for PRAs. I'm not talking about transition costs or cash flows. I'm talking about the political payola that Social Security defenders will, undoubtedly, demand in exchange for our (partial) freedom. If getting PRAs means making the core system even more inequitable and wasteful (yes, I *think* it is possible.), count me out. And, let me warn you, some of the PRA proposals include political "sweeteners" that are really middle-class "poison pills." We don't need PRA proposals such as these. More on this, later.

PRA basics

During recent years, there has been much discussion of Personal Retirement Accounts as a replacement for or supplement to Social Security. In December, 2001, the President's Commission to Strengthen Social Security (the Commission) put forth three proposals for reforming Social Security — each involving a system of PRAs. The various proposals (from the Commission and others) take many forms but *generally* involve three components: private ownership, prefunding of accounts, and investment diversification.

Under most of the proposals, a worker would have the option of putting a small portion of his payroll taxes into a separate account — a PRA. That money would belong to the worker, but could only be used for retirement. To make sure that the Social Security trust fund is not adversely affected, the worker's normal Social Security benefits would be appropriately reduced. The worker would be allowed to invest his money in at least a few low-cost, diversified portfolios from which funds could be withdrawn, at a certain minimum age, in the form of an annuity or, possibly, a lump-sum. Upon the death of the worker or retiree, the account would pass to his heirs.

Proponents believe that PRAs could boost our retirement benefits, encourage worker productivity and national savings, and help, somewhat, with long-term solvency issues.

Scaring Seniors is Sooo Much Fun

If you've followed the debate, you know that the issue of PRAs is highly-charged and quite confusing. There are numerous Social Security critics and defenders, and each side contradicts what the other side says. There are a couple of reasons for this. First, we are discussing estimates extending out 75 years and involving numerous demographic and economic assumptions. Small changes in the assumptions cause large changes in the results.

In addition, there is a lot of political spin being applied to the numbers. If you need evidence, just consider that memo accidentally released in early 2002 from the office of Rep. Marcy Kaptur of Ohio. After acknowledging that the information being disseminated was "not entirely factually accurate," the unidentified Kaptur staffer said:

> Talk about scaring seniors — this may be a little over the top. But it is sooo fun to bash Republicans.[247]

Of course, there is demagoguery on the other side, as well. Reformers have rarely had the courage to directly criticize the massive and arbitrary wealth transfers, built into the Social Security benefit formulas. They have focused — over focused — on just two issues: the threat of insolvency and the need for the better investment rates that could be earned through investment diversification. These are legitimate issues for reform, but not necessarily more so than other issues.

Wisdom from Shecky Green

Why do I support the PRA concept? It is really quite simple. I'd like to know that part of my payroll taxes goes toward a *real* investment, earning a fair rate of return. And, when I die, I want the unused portion to go to my family; I don't want it to be lost in the smoky hocus pocus of Social Security regulations. I'm tired of the financial beating I get from Social Security, and I want it to stop or, at least, be reduced. It reminds me of comedian Shecky Green's old joke about his nemesis, Frank Sinatra. Shecky claimed he loved Frank because he once saved his life:

> In 1967 in front of the Fontainebleau Hotel ... five guys were beating me up and I hear Frank say, "That's enough."[248]

Well, in regard to Social Security, I'd appreciate hearing those words from the U.S. Congress.

The Shecky Green argument, elegant though it is, may not be compelling for some of you. After all, a lot of people have major reservations about PRAs.

---

247. Stephen Dinan, "Social Security Memo Gives GOP Smoking Gun" [online] *The Washington Times*, 24 May 2002 — [cited 6 September 2002]; available from *http://washtimes.com/*.

248. Robert B. Weide, "But Seriously, Folks," [online] (Whyaduck Productions, Inc., 2001 — [cited 27 September 2002]; available from *http://www.duckprods.com/projects/butseriouslyfolks.html*.

Let's address each of the common criticisms that have been directed toward PRAs, to see if they hold water. Then, we'll examine each of the three PRA proposals put forth by the Commission, including the parts that the Commission does *not* want you to know about.

EIGHT CRITICISMS FROM PRA OPPONENTS

- PRAs are too risky in relation to the investment reward.
- They won't really help national productivity and savings, and may even hurt.
- Administration costs are too high.
- How do we pay for the transition costs?
- The ability to bequeath PRAs is no big deal; Social Security has survivor benefits.
- The insolvency threat is easily solved, so we don't need reform.
- Social Security is "progressive," and helps the needy.
- PRAs would drain resources from the Social Security program.

1. PRAs are too risky in relation to the investment reward.

In most of the proposals, the PRA would be an option, not a requirement. And, even if a worker chose to establish a PRA, he would not be required to invest in stocks — at all. No one need fear being forced into anything risky. To the contrary, most PRA proposals would not even allow participants to invest in individual stocks or aggressive mutual funds. And, at least one proposal goes even further in an effort to wring out all risk. It would limit investments to high-interest bank notes, guaranteed by the government. Under that scenario, there would be virtually zero risk.

But, is a risk-free portfolio a good thing?

No. There is widespread agreement that a risk-free portfolio, devoid of equity investments, is likely to underperform. Economists Genakoplos, Mitchell, and Zeldes put it this way:

> The real economic benefit to privatization comes from the attendant diversification that would be made available to households that cannot participate on their own in diversified capital markets. According to economic theory, every household whose income is uncorrelated with stock returns

should include some stock in its portfolio in order to take advantage of the higher returns stocks provide compared to bonds and other safe assets.

And they conclude:

> We recognize that privatization has several other important benefits, including increased portfolio choice, reduced political risk, possibly reduced labor supply distortions, and an intangible increased sense of ownership and responsibility.[249]

This leads us to criticism number two.

2. PRAs won't help national productivity and savings.

In "Privatizing Social Security: The $10 Trillion Opportunity," economist Martin Feldstein argues:

> Although the transition to a funded system would involve economic as well as political costs, the net present value of the gain would be enormous — as much as $10-20 trillion.[250]

Why? Because a fully privatized and prefunded system would give workers tangible ownership of their retirement assets, and this would be an enormous motivation for increased worker earnings (and, as noted in the previous chapter, for increased reporting of those earnings). According to Feldstein:

> The Social Security rules are so complex and so opaque that many individuals may simply disregard the benefits that they earn from additional work and act as if the entire payroll tax is a net tax no different in kind from the personal income tax.[251]

---

249. John Genakoplos, Olivia S. Mitchell, and Stephen P. Zeldes, "Would a Privatized Social Security System Really Pay a Higher Rate of Return?" NBER working paper no. w6713 [online] (Cambridge, Massachusetts: National Bureau of Economic Research, May 2000 — [cited 24 September 2002]), 152 and 156; available from *www.nber.org.*

250. Martin Feldstein, "Privatizing Social Security: The $10 Trillion Opportunity," *SSP* no. 7 [online] (Washington, D.C.: Cato Institute, 31 January 1997 — [cited 21 May 2002]); available from *http://www.socialsecurity.org/pubs/ssps/ssp7es.html.*

251. *Ibid.*

In other words, people aren't motivated to work harder so that they can "invest" more in Social Security, as presently constituted. They see the payroll tax for what it really is — a tax that bears little relationship to what they will eventually get out of Social Security.

As for national savings, Feldstein notes:

> [T]aken together these studies do imply that the Social Security program causes each generation to reduce its savings substantially and thereby incur a substantial loss of real investment income. Even a conservative estimate that each dollar of Social Security wealth displaces only 50 cents of private wealth accumulation implies that the annual loss of national income would exceed 4 percent of GDP[252]

A privatized system, Feldstein says, would eliminate this impediment to savings by substituting real savings for make-believe Social Security "pay-go" savings. Some economists question Feldstein's conclusions, but most concede that savings would increase somewhat — at least during the funding transition period. On the other hand, it is hard to find an economist with credible evidence that PRAs would cause a decrease in productivity and savings.

3. Administration costs would be too high?

If not handled properly, administration costs *could* eat away at investment returns, and eliminate the benefit of a PRA. However, this problem can be minimized. The key is to keep it simple.

An example of a simple plan is the Thrift Savings Plan, used since 1986 by federal employees. The Thrift Savings Plan allows employees to invest in any combination of three funds — a broad stock index fund, a bond index fund, and a fund paying interest at the rate prevailing on long-term federal debt. The Plan is administered by a governmental board, insulated from political influence by giving members fixed terms in office. To further insulate against political influence, money is actually managed by private-sector firms, selected via competitive contract. The Plan is simple and cheap! Annual overhead charges average just one tenth of one percent (0.1%) of managed assets.

Of course, not all PRA participants will want to limit their investments to trustee-organized indexed funds. For these individuals, how do we control

---

252. *Ibid.*

administration costs, while promoting consumer choice and efficient financial markets?

In its December, 2001 report, the Commission recommends a "two-tier structure" to balance the need for efficient administration with the desire of participants to have several investment options:

> Initially, all collections are invested into "Tier I" of the program. In Tier I, workers choose from a range of funds that are currently offered by the Thrift Savings Plan, plus three additional balanced funds and an inflation-protected bond fund.... When employees have accumulated a threshold account balance (say, initially, $5,000), however, they are allowed to invest that threshold balance plus subsequent contributions in a range of "Tier II" qualified private-sector funds.... The Governing Board chooses the threshold amount that is required for people to move their balances into Tier II so that it would be feasible for such accounts to be charged low transaction costs without the need for price caps....
>
> Funds in both Tiers cannot charge sales "loads" or other marketing fees on entry or exit. Instead, all fees must be included in one annual charge and clearly stated as a percentage of assets.[253]

By using this two-tier structure, administration costs can be controlled, while consumer choice is maintained.

4. What about the transition costs?

If there is an economist who truly thinks that prefunding part of our Social Security debt adds to the total national debt, I'd like to send his diploma to the FBI for testing. We presently have an unfunded Social Security liability — a debt of about $10 trillion or more. If we allow people to trade part of their future benefits (plus interest) for ownership in their own retirement accounts, our total costs don't increase by one dime. We are simply trading one type of debt for another. Milton Friedman, winner of the 1976 Nobel Prize in Economics, makes reference to the "phoniness" of this issue, and states that "there are no 'costs of transition'."[254] And Michael Tanner, Senior Analyst with Cato Institute, states:

253. "Strengthening Social Security and Creating Personal Wealth for All Americans" [online] (President's Commission to Strengthen Social Security, 21 December 2001), 46; available from *http://www.csss.gov/reports/Final_report.pdf.*

254. Milton Friedman, "Social Security Chimeras" [online] *The New York Times*, 11 January 1999 — [cited 27 November 2002]; available from *http://www.ioptout.org/articles/990111.asp.*

We should understand that the design of a new system has nothing to do with the liabilities that (rightly or wrongly) have been accrued in the past. The government's obligation to current (and even future) retirees is unchanged by a decision to privatize the system. What does change is the willingness to acknowledge currently unfunded liabilities.[255]

Well said.

5. Social Security provides good monthly survivor benefits.

But be sure to read the fine print. In a piece put out by the Social Security Office of Retirement Policy, it is proudly noted that there is "a guarantee that *qualified* dependents will receive benefits under Social Security...." (emphasis added).[256] The reader is then referred to "Appendix C" to see what makes a dependent "qualified." Here is what I learned.

- Ralph and Laura are newlyweds. Ralph becomes ill on their honeymoon and dies. Does Laura get monthly survivor benefits? No. Not married 9 months.
- Bob and Mary have been married 10 years. Bob dies in a skiing accident. Does Mary get benefits? No. She isn't age 60, or older.
- Ted and Alice have been married 40 years, and each is over 60. Alice dies. Does Ted get monthly survivor benefits? No. You can't even get survivor benefits unless they exceed your own retirement benefits, and Ted was already getting his own benefits.

If you missed the last one, don't feel bad. The Social Security Administration forgot to mention the "simultaneous benefit" exclusion in its "Appendix C."

Of course, when single people die, their benefits almost always go back into the Social Security "Wealth Transfer Machine."

---

255. Michael Tanner, in testimony before the U.S. Senate, Senate Finance Committee, Subcommittee on Social Security and Family Policy [online] (CATO Institute, 2 August 1995 — [cited 24 August 2002]); available from *http://www.cato.org/testimony/ct-sp82.html.*

256. "The Galveston Plan and Social Security: A comparative Analysis of Two Systems" [online] (Social Security Administration Office of Retirement Policy, 1999); available from *http://www.ssa.gov/policy/docs/ssb/v62n1/.*

We need the right to inheritance — not survivor benefits

Social Security's rules for survivor benefits are so complicated and full of holes that you simply can't count on them. But, even the most comprehensive package of survivor benefits would not be a substitute for inheritable funds.

On this very point, two economists, Jagadeesh Gokhale and Lawrence J. Kotlikoff, reach a startling conclusion after studying the impact of Social Security on wealth accumulation:

> All told, Social Security appears to be raising wealth inequality ... by roughly one-fifth, substantially increasing the share of total wealth held by the richest members of society, and greatly reducing the flow of bequests to the next generation.

How could this be? The Gokhale-Kotlikoff research, which used actual lifetime earnings data within a bequest computer modeling program, shows:

> Social Security exacerbates wealth inequality by leaving the lifetime poor with proportionately less to save, less reason to save, and a larger share of their old-age resources in a non-bequeathable form than the lifetime rich. In so doing, Social Security denies the children of the poor the opportunity to receive inheritances.[257]

The establishment of a system of PRAs would mitigate this problem by enabling millions of low-income and middle class workers to bequeath significant funds to their children. This point is well summarized by author and political commentator David Horowitz:

> Unlike those who depend on Social Security, the rich get to control their retirement funds as personal assets and, therefore, to pass them on to their children.... Let's give the working class the same privilege and power over their retirement funds that the "ruling class" has over its.[258]

---

257. Jagadeesh Gokhale and Lawrence J. Kotlikoff, "The Impact of Social Security and Other Factors on the Distribution of Wealth," in *The Distributional Aspects of Social Security and Social Security Reform*, ed. Martin Feldstein and Jeffrey B. Liebman (Chicago and London: University of Chicago Press , 2002), 106.

258. David Horowitz, "Social Security Reactionaries and Reformers" [online] *Jewish World Review*, 7 August 2001 — [cited 29 June 2003]; available from www.papillonsart-palace.com/socialR.htm.

6. The insolvency problem is no big deal; there is no need for change.

If we were to stop adding new people to Social Security, and simply let the current crop finish their careers and retire, we would have to come up with $10.5 trillion to pay the benefits, according to best estimates. That's not chicken feed; in fact, it is about $75,000 for every worker in the United States. Critics of PRAs are wrong to understate the insolvency problem, or to call for "business as usual." On the other hand, they are correct to say that a higher investment yield on PRAs is not a complete solution to the insolvency problem. Other reforms and adjustments would still be required.

7. Social Security is "progressive," whereas PRAs are not.

The Social Security scheme for doing things is not exactly "progressive"; it is more like *chaotic*. As noted in Chapter III, Social Security transfers billions of dollars, each year, from the middle class to the upper class. This happens due to the crude assumptions Social Security makes regarding who is (and is not) "poor." For the moment, however, let's just assume that Social Security really is progressive.

A truly progressive system

There is another system that is even more progressive. It's called Cuba. There, the gap between rich and poor is much smaller than in America. Must be a great place, Cuba. The point? Eliminating gaps should never be the main focus. Instead, we need to give everyone the tools and opportunity to advance.

Recently, I read a report that said the poor of America prospered significantly during the 1990s. Ominously, however, the report added that the "gap" between rich and poor increased. My reaction? I am truly happy that the poor prospered. As for the "gap," I couldn't care less. If a system has the potential to help everyone, let's not oppose it simply because it may end up helping some more than others.

And, finally, let's remember that closing economic gaps is not the business of a retirement system, anyway. It is the proper business of a means-tested, public welfare program, *financed with general income tax revenues*. Mixing welfare and retirement together is a recipe for waste and disillusionment. In other words, it's a recipe for Social Security.

8. PRAs will drain resources from Social Security.

It depends on how we look at it. Certainly, there would be an erosion of Social Security resources if we let a participant divert money to her PRA *and* keep her full Social Security benefits. However, no serious PRA proposal includes such a recommendation; in all cases, there would be some sort of reduction. The question is, how should benefits be reduced, and by how much?

The fairest way is to reduce benefits by the percentage of adjusted payroll taxes diverted to the PRA.[259] If, for example, a worker diverted 15% of his adjusted payroll taxes to a PRA, his traditional Social Security benefits would be reduced by 15%. This method is fair because people getting the least value from Social Security would pay the least for the privilege of getting a PRA. For instance, a single, black, chain-smoking man with medium or high income can expect to earn almost nothing on the Social Security taxes he pays. Therefore, if he diverts 15% of his adjusted taxes to a PRA, his effective cost will be 15% of "almost nothing."

If the reduction of benefits described, above, is still not sufficient to prevent an erosion of Social Security resources, it might be necessary to use a larger reduction factor. For example, a diversion of 10% of payroll taxes to a PRA might necessitate a 13% reduction in benefits, a diversion of 20% of payroll taxes might necessitate a 26% reduction, etc. The bottom line is this: PRAs can be designed so that Social Security funds available for traditional benefits are unaffected.

Finally, note that there are other methods proposed for reducing benefits. One of these, involving use of a flat interest rate charge, is discussed later in this chapter in regard to a proposal put forth by the President's Commission.

Fight criticisms — all are leaking water

Our preliminary review has concluded, and we have not found a compelling argument that should preclude the use of PRAs. However, careful consideration is warranted with regard to the criticisms concerning investment risk, administration costs, and draining of resources. To minimize investment risk, PRA rules would have to limit investment choices. To minimize administration costs, a simple and centralized system such as that used in the federal Thrift Savings Plan should be an available option for participants. And, to avoid

---

259. The payroll taxes would have to be adjusted by some sort of notional (theoretical) interest rate, so that taxes diverted early in a worker's career would carry more weight than those diverted later in her career.

draining resources from the traditional Social Security system, an appropriate reduction of benefits should be made, to compensate for the funds diverted to the PRA.

An important milestone was reached in December, 2001, when President Bush's Commission released its report on reforming Social Security. The report begins by making strong arguments for the general concept of PRAs. For example, it notes that workers seem to have a natural predilection for ownership and control of their retirement assets:

> [I]n many countries where participation in personal accounts was voluntary, many workers opted for a personal account even when 'on paper' it appeared that they would have received higher benefits through the traditional system.[260]

And, regarding risk, the Commission argues:

> Personal accounts would diversify the risk inherent in the Social Security system by allowing individuals to split risks between political risks ... and financial risks.... Workers demanding absolute security can, through personal accounts, have risk *substantially below that of the current system* simply by choosing to invest in government bonds (emphasis added).[261]

After making a good case for the general concept of PRAs, the Commission outlines three specific PRA proposals. The first one is reasonable, but the other two would simply make a bad system worse. They must be rejected.

Commission Proposal 1

This is a very simple proposal. The core program is not changed in any way. Workers are given the option of redirecting up to 2% of taxable payroll from traditional Social Security to a PRA. The worker who makes the election has his

---

260. "Strengthening Social Security and Creating Personal Wealth for All Americans" [online] (President's Commission to Strengthen Social Security, 21 December 2001), 30; available from *http://www.csss.gov/reports/Final_report.pdf.*
    261. *Ibid.*

traditional Social Security benefits reduced by the amount put into the PRA, compounded at a real interest rate of 3.5%. (That means if inflation is, say, 3%, he will be charged 6.5%.) The participant invests his funds in one or more of a few diversified portfolios, with low administration costs.

The Commission estimates that workers at all income levels should experience higher benefits, with a "medium-earner" getting a benefit that's about 12% higher than he would without the PRA. National savings should increase as we set aside money to fund these PRAs. And, last but not least, workers might be motivated to work harder and longer (and to report those earnings), because they would be making meaningful investments that can be left to their loved ones when they die.

Would I support Proposal 1?

Definitely. As put forth by the Commission, it would be a commonsensical improvement for all concerned. As you can see from figures 21, 22 and 23 (for low, medium, and high earners), people of every wage bracket and of every age could expect to benefit from this proposal. (Note: all graphs show retirement at age 65.)

Figure 21: "Low earners" are helped.

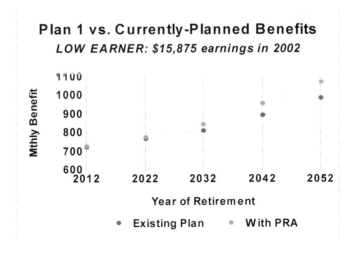

Figure 22: "Medium-earners" are helped.

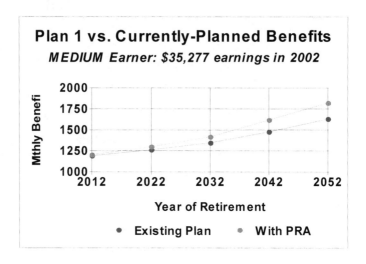

Figure 23: "High earners" are helped.

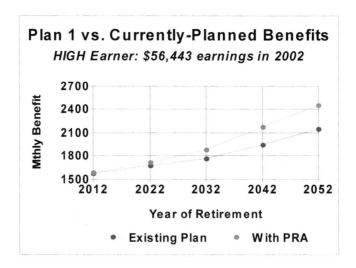

Commission Proposal 2

Graphs similar to the ones presented above can be found in the report issued by the Commission with respect to Proposal 1. Strangely, however, the Commission does not present comparable graphs with respect to Proposals 2 or 3.[262] The graphs presented below were constructed from information presented in tabular format in an attachment to the Commission's report.

Let's get right to the results. The first chart shows that a "low earner" would benefit significantly from Proposal 2. For example, a low earner retiring in 2022 would have a monthly benefit of $885, versus the currently-planned benefit of $767. That is an increase of more than 15%.

Figure 24: "Low earners" are helped.

The second chart (below) shows that medium-earners would not fare as well. Proposal 2 would significantly *decrease* the benefits of medium-earners retiring during the next 40 years. In other words, anyone presently age 25 or older would be seriously hurt by this proposal.

---

262. The graphs presented by the President's Commission for proposals 2 and 3 omit the "existing plan" line, which shows projected benefits as currently scheduled. Therefore, it is impossible for the user to see how badly he or she may be hurt by the proposed changes.

Figure 25: All "medium-earners" who retire in the next 40 years lose.

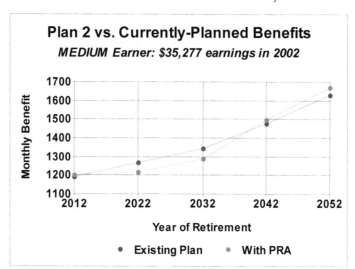

The last chart (for Proposal 2) shows that so-called high earners ($56,443 per year) lose big-time. Regardless of the year of retirement, their benefits under Proposal 2 would be substantially lower than their currently-planned benefits.

Figure 26: "High earners" lose — no matter when they retire.

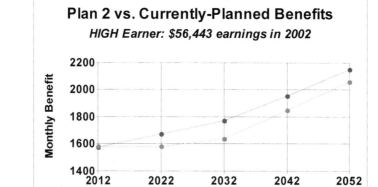

Commission Proposal 3

This proposal is almost as bad as the last one, as can be seen from the following.

Figure 27: It is good for "low earners"

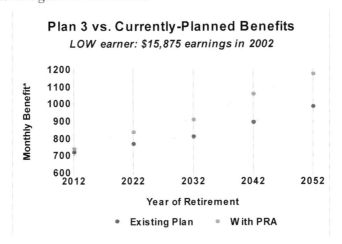

*Note: Benefits shown are those estimated to be attributable to a total of 12.4% payroll tax

Figure 28: But, it hurts all medium earners who retire in the next 30 years.

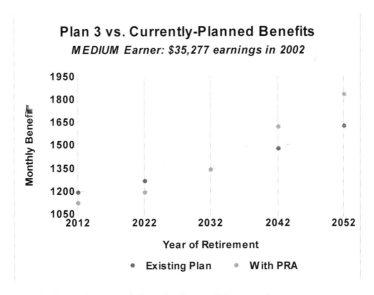

*Note: Benefits shown are those estimated to be attributable to a total of 12.4% payroll tax.

Figure 29: And it hurts all high earners who retire in the next 30 years.

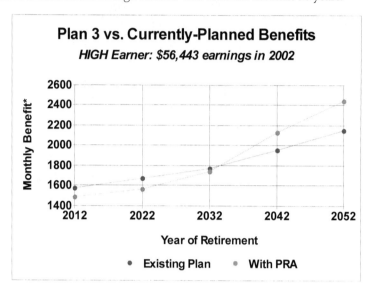

Note: Benefits shown are those estimated to be attributable to a total of 12.4% payroll tax

What's going on with regard to Proposals 2 and 3?

If PRAs are a good thing, why is it that medium-earners and high earners (who, together, are a majority of all workers) do poorly under Proposals 2 and 3? Are they hurt by Social Security privatization? No. It's the *political payola* we talked about earlier.

In Proposals 2 and 3, many workers are not eligible for the full PRA feature. For example, in Proposal 2, the PRA is available only with respect to the *first $25,000 of earnings*. Also, each of these proposals cuts the planned level of traditional benefits by changing the inflation index factor. And, in the case of Proposal 3, there is an *implicit payroll tax increase* of one percent (1%) for all but low earners.[263] Finally, Proposals 2 and 3 provide new benefits for certain married couples — financed by everyone else. These sneaky adjustments, slipped in the back door, more than offset the benefits of the PRAs.

They gave with one hand, and took back with the other

Do you see what's going on? Apparently, there's been some back-room wheeling and dealing, and you and I have been dealt out. What they propose to give us with their right hand, they plan to take back with their left hand. But, you can't say the President's Commission didn't warn us. It has the following citation at the beginning of its report:

> Like all federal entitlement programs, Congress can change the rules regarding eligibility — and it has done so many times over the years. The rules can be made more generous, or they can be made more restrictive. *Benefits which are granted at one time can be withdrawn ...* [emphasis added].[264]

The bottom line

PRAs can be of significant economic benefit to almost every worker, *but read the fine print!* They must be structured in a simple and straightforward manner.

If the average worker moved just 2% of his taxed wages from traditional Social Security to a simple PRA, such as that described as Proposal 1 in the Commission's Report, the system could gain the equivalent of more than $26 billion for each of the next 75 years due to the increased earnings on those PRA funds.[265] That would significantly enhance our retirement income.

But the most compelling argument for PRAs is reflected in the quotation about federal entitlement programs cited above. Presently, there is enormous political risk associated with Social Security. If properly structured, PRAs can reduce that risk by putting some of our money out of reach of the politicians.

---

263. To participate in proposal 3, the worker must contribute additional payroll taxes in the amount of 1% of earned wages. However, the President's Commission advocates that the additional payroll taxes (i.e., the 1%) be reimbursed in some unspecified manner targeting low earner workers (probably via a refundable tax credit that could offset payroll taxes as well as income taxes). Although it is possible that a fairly trivial rebate would also be directed towards medium and high—earner workers (up to $100 has been discussed), it seems unlikely that a significant portion of the 1% contribution, required under proposal 3, would be available to anyone except the low-earner workers. For this reason, the projected benefit values for medium and high earners have been reduced by applying the fraction 12.4/13.4 (to approximate the benefits which would be related to the normal 12.4% payroll taxes). In the case of low-earner workers, it is assumed that a full rebate of the 1% required contribution would be made. If not, the projected benefit values shown in Figure 27 are overstated.

264. "Strengthening Social Security and Creating Personal Wealth for All Americans, 30.

265. For an explanation of the related calculation, see Appendix A-14.

CHAPTER XIII: EAT YOUR HEART OUT

(A SAFE ALTERNATIVE PLAN THAT REALLY WORKS)

"A blessing from God"

That's what Burt Jamus calls the Galveston Plan, a Social Security alternative that is available to workers in three counties in south Texas. The funny thing is that he didn't like the plan very much when it was created, in 1981; he wanted to stay in Social Security, so he voted against the alternative plan.[266] Some of the luckiest people on earth are those who *don't* get what they wish for.

When the Galveston Plan was created, the usual groups were lining up to oppose it. According to Judge Holbrook, who set up the plan:

> There was considerable opposition from labor unions, minorities and other traditional supporters, including many elected officials.[267]
>
> The 22 percent who voted against it in 1980 are all supportive now and see the many benefits of having a retirement program other than Social Security....[268]

---

266. Rod D. Martin, "Social Security Excuses" [online] (Vanguard PAC, 15 December 1997 — [cited 22 August 2002]); available from *http://www.thevanguard.org/thevanguard/columns/971215.shtml.*

267. Ray Holbrook, "Privatize Social Security? Galveston County Did" [online] (San Antonio, Texas: Texas Public Policy Foundation, November 1998 — [cited 22 August 2002]); available from *http://www.tppf.org/government/perspect/holbrook.html.*

268. Ed Myers, "How Galveston Opted Out of Social Security," *The Freeman* [online] (Irvington-on-Hudson, New York: Foundation for Economic Education, Inc., May 1997 — [cited 25 August 2002]), vol. 47, no, 5; available from *http://www.libertyhaven.com/politic-sandcurrentevents/healthcarewelfareorsocialsecurity/galveston.shtml.*

The Galveston plan is a safe alternative to Social Security, with no risky stock investments — zero. All money is lent to top-rated financial institutions for *guaranteed* interest rates, which have averaged between 7.5 and 8% during these last 20 years. And, all of the money goes to the workers, in proportion to their contributions to the plan. The benefits are good — for most participants they are significantly higher than Social Security benefits. Yes, the Galveston Plan is a great alternative to Social Security, and that's why it has received a great deal of attention.

It's not the only alternative

Actually, there are lots of retirement alternatives used by the 5 million state and local workers who are exempt from Social Security. The Galveston Plan is not the only one, and it's not even the best of them. Ohio has its own alternative plan — older, bigger, with superior results. Not too many people know about it — outside of Ohio. They don't "toot their horn" as much as the Texans do.

THE OHIO PUBLIC EMPLOYEES RETIREMENT SYSTEM (OHIO PERS) VS. SOCIAL SECURITY

Ohio PERS was created in 1933, two years before Social Security, and 48 years before the Galveston Plan. This multi-employer system, with assets of over $50 billion, serves more than 500,000 members. It is not part of the State of Ohio; rather, it is administered by an *independent* Retirement Board, in accordance with sections of the Ohio Revised Code. Within Ohio PERS there are three distinct sub plans: for law enforcement workers, for state workers, and for local workers. For the sake of simplicity, this chapter will focus on the sub plan for state workers. But, before we talk about the details of Ohio PERS, let's get right to the bottom line. You may be shocked — and dismayed — to see just how pitiful Social Security benefits are in comparison to those of Ohio PERS.

In Chapter I, we compared the Social Security benefits received by hypothetical Mary and Jill. We tried to equalize the net amounts paid by each woman (after taxes) so that we could fully appreciate the disparity of their benefits. In the charts below, however, the emphasis is different. Here we are trying to eliminate the factors beyond the current control of either retirement system. For example, part of the Social Security payroll taxes collected are actually applied to implicit interest on the trillions of dollars owed in relation to earlier retirees who underpaid their share of benefits. Because this implicit interest is a drag on the Social Security system, an adjustment has been made to decrease Ohio PERS benefits by a proportional amount in the charts, below. For a detailed explanation of the methodology used, please refer to Appendix A. The bottom line is this: The charts in this chapter have been adjusted to make this a fair, system-to-system comparison. tell you this because the results are so one-sided, you may believe, *or may want to believe*, that smoke and mirrors are being used to skew the results. [269]

Figure 30

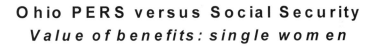

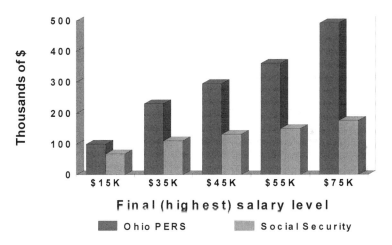

If it were a fight, they'd call it off

Figure 30 shows the total values (in 2002 dollars) of Ohio PERS retirement benefits vs. Social Security retirement benefits for women state workers at different levels of salary. (Similar disparities exist for men and married couples where both partners have significant earnings.) The differences are enormous.

---

269. For assumptions related to the calculation of Ohio PERS vs. Social Security benefits, see Appendix A-15.

The left side of the chart shows values for a woman who began her career at age 22, earning just $2800 per year (in 1973 dollars). In 2002, after 30 years of inflation and merit wage increases, this woman reached a peak salary of $15,000 per year, and retired. Under Ohio PERS, her benefits would be worth about $99,000; under Social Security they would be worth about $69,000. From there the differences get larger. The next column, second from the left, shows results for a 22 year-old woman who started with earnings of $6,500 in 1973, and who "maxed out" at $35,000, 30 years later. Her benefits would be worth $230,000 under Ohio PERS, but only $109,000 under Social Security. The losses further increase until we get to the extreme right, where we see results for a woman who ended her career with a salary of $75,000. Social Security steals $317,000 from this woman — the difference between benefits worth $493,000 under Ohio PERS and only $176,000 under Social Security. And remember, we're assuming that planned Social Security benefits are not cut due to insolvency problems.

They ought to require a disclosure by Social Security: *Warning. The Surgeon General has determined that this program could be hazardous to your financial health, your retirement plans, and your dreams.* A lot of people think Social Security is a marvelous example of efficiency in government, but it just makes me angry.

What about married people?

One would expect Social Security to do much better in an analysis involving married people, because it has lucrative spousal benefits that can increase the value of a worker's benefit by as much as 50%. However, it is important to remember that *most* married people don't qualify for *significant* spousal benefits and, therefore, get little more from Social Security than do single people. Why? Because the lucrative spousal benefits are only available where one spouse has minor earnings in comparison to those of the other spouse, and that is not typical for most couples today. Let's focus, however, on the relatively unusual situation where one partner earned all the income, and the other never worked outside of the home.

Figure 31 shows the same 5 women, only this time each is married to a man who never earned a nickel of wages in his life. (If the husbands earned any wages at all, we'd have to alter the chart by increasing the Ohio PERS column, proportionally. For instance, if a husband earned 10% as much as his wife, we would need to increase the Ohio PERS column by 10%.)

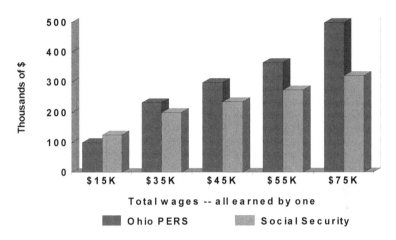

Ohio PERS versus Social Security
Value of benefits: 1-earner couples

Figure 31

As you can see, the couple whose total wage income peaked at $15,000 would get better benefits from Social Security (a $26,000 differential that would be wiped out if the husband earned just 26% of his wife's wages). In all other cases, benefits paid by Ohio PERS would be significantly better than those paid by Social Security, with the advantage ranging from $33,000 to $176,000[270].

What do we do about that "low-income" couple?

I'd like to briefly digress to discuss the one situation in the above chart, where Social Security outperforms Ohio PERS. It is the case of the married couple with a history of very low wages, and where one of the partners contributed little or nothing to those earnings. What do we do about this?

First, we need to be sure that, at the time of retirement, this truly is a low-income couple. To determine this, we can't simply look at the couple's taxable *wage* history. That couple could have had, and could presently have, all sorts of income from exempt wages (e.g., government salaries), pensions, rents,

---

270. For assumptions related to the calculation of Ohio PERS vs. Social Security benefits, see Appendix A-15.

dividends, interest, lottery, inheritance, etc. As pointed out in an earlier chapter, couples with a history of low wages are, statistically, the *wealthiest* couples upon retirement, when non-Social Security income is considered.

Let's assume, however, that this couple truly needs economic support (i.e., benefits beyond the normal amount that would be proportional to the payroll taxes they paid). What do we do? We give the needed support, but in a way that does not corrupt the basic benefit formula of the Social Security retirement program. The extra support must come from general income tax revenues (vs. payroll taxes), so that the integrity of the retirement program is maintained.

Disability and Survivor benefits

So far, we've seen that Ohio PERS has vastly superior *retirement* benefits in almost every case. What about disability and survivor benefits? Although these programs are difficult to directly compare (due to differing program features), the table below is an attempt to summarize key differences.

A few comments on Table 7:

Definition of disability: Table 7 shows that the definitions of disability are quite different. Whereas Social Security defines disability as an impairment that prevents any type of substantial employment that exists *anywhere* in the national economy, the Ohio PERS definition only specifies an impairment that prevents work in the *current occupation*, or a similar occupation. For example, if a teacher can no longer teach but can do telemarketing work, she would probably be disabled according to Ohio PERS, but not disabled according to Social Security. If you've ever priced disability insurance, you know that the Ohio PERS definition is associated with much more expensive policies.

Earnings limit: With the Ohio PERS plan your earnings from other (dissimilar) occupations are not limited. If that disabled teacher makes lots of money as a telemarketer, she still qualifies for benefits from Ohio PERS. With Social Security disability, on the other hand, any wages over the "SGA" limit (about $800 per month) would be a disqualifying event.

Table 7

Disability	**Ohio PERS***	**Social Security**
Definition of disability	Mental or physical incapacity for the performance of a member's present duty or similar service. Duration at least 12 months.	Inability to engage in any substantial gainful activity that exists anywhere in the national economy, due to "medically determinable physical or mental impairment." Duration at least 12 months.
Requirements	At least 5 years of covered service, and no greater than 2 years since the termination of that service.	At least 20 quarters of covered employment in the 10 years preceding the disability; however, special provisions allow younger workers to get benefits with as little as 6 quarters of covered employment in the 3 preceding years.
Basic benefit	A worker's "final average salary" (i.e., average of top three years of earnings) times number of years of service times 2.2%. However, minimum benefit is at least 45% of final average salary, and maximum is 60%.	Calculated in manner similar to retirement benefits. That is, there is a benefit formula that heavily favors workers with lower incomes, shorter work periods before disability, and dependents.
Earnings limit	No, however, the earnings must come from a different occupation.	Yes. Earnings from any occupation limited to about $800 per month.
Duration	Age 65, but workers who become disabled after age 60 can retain benefits to as long as age 70.	Until "retirement age," which will be as late as 67, eventually
Can nonsurgical treatment be required?	Yes	Yes, but only in limited circumstances

Survivors benefits	**Ohio PERS**	**Social Security**
General benefits	If a worker dies prior to reaching retirement age, or while on disability, his named beneficiaries are entitled, at the minimum, to a full refund of all contributions the worker made to the plan during his career. If the deceased worker had at least 10 years of service, qualified survivors are entitled to monthly benefits in lieu of the full refund. If the deceased worker had at least 5 years of service, an additional lump-sum death benefit of $500 to $2,500 is payable to beneficiaries.	Benefits are limited to family members - usually a spouse aged 60 or over, or a younger spouse and her minor children. Those benefits are paid monthly. In addition, there is a one-time monthly lump-sum payment of $255

All information in the table, above, is from the Ohio Revised Code, the Ohio Administrative Code, the Ohio PERS website, and the Ohio Retirement Study Council.

Required treatment: Ohio PERS requires nonsurgical treatment, where deemed appropriate by its medical examiners and consultants. Social Security requires nonsurgical treatment only where it has been prescribed by the disabled worker's own doctor.

Low earners: Ohio PERS pays disability benefits that are closely proportional to earnings, and range from 45 to 60% of those earnings. With Social Security disability, some people get very low benefits (relative to pre-disability earnings), while others — people who had low earnings and/or short work histories — get very high benefits: up to 90% of wages (tax free) — plus Medicare. This shifting of benefits takes place in both the Social Security disability and retirement programs, but it causes *a serious problem* with respect to the disability program. It reduces the incentive of the disabled beneficiary (with a low-wage history) to return to work. (See Chapter VIII for more discussion of this issue.)

Survivor benefits: If the deceased worker has at least 10 years of service credit, qualified beneficiaries are entitled to monthly Ohio PERS benefits in accordance with a sliding scale which is dependent on length of service. In addition, death benefits of $500 to $2,500 are payable if the worker has service credits of at least 5 years. In all cases, however, beneficiaries get a minimum payment equal to no less than the contributions made by the deceased worker.

With Social Security, a guaranteed return of worker payroll taxes is not made. There are, however, survivor benefits for a limited group of qualified beneficiaries. Most Social Security survivor benefits are paid to spouses, who have to be age 60 or older unless they are caring for a minor child. Other restrictions on Social Security survivor benefits are discussed in the previous chapter.

Other Ohio PERS plan design features

Type of plan: Like Social Security, Ohio PERS is a defined *benefit* plan, as opposed to a defined *contribution* plan. With a defined benefit plan, the worker generally knows how much the monthly retirement benefit will be (in relation to final salary and years worked), but he is not sure how much will be contributed to the plan while he is working. On the other hand, with a defined contribution plan, the worker doesn't know what his final monthly benefit will be, but he knows how much (in dollars or as a percentage of pay) he and his employer plan to contribute each month while he is working.

If properly managed, defined benefit plans can have less *investment* risk than defined contribution plans because downturns in the market can be spread across generations, as well as among current retirees. And, defined benefit plans are more appropriate for large populations that include relatively unsophisticated workers. This is because defined benefit plans give workers a better understanding of what their final benefits will be.

However, defined benefit plans can be susceptible to the risk of benefit shifting because they "make the connection between individual financing and individual benefits opaque."[271] Older workers may be promised unrealistically large benefits, and then "grandfathered" against reductions. To compensate, newer employees may be given lower benefits (or, in the case of Social Security, asked to pay higher payroll taxes). Eventually, there could be several "tiers" of workers getting more or less benefits, depending on when they were hired. And, if the younger workers don't stick around long enough, they really lose. They may forfeit everything, with the spoils going to the more senior employees. If you want a good example of a defined benefit plan gone rotten, think of Social Security. It is a defined benefit plan, and it is loaded with benefit shifting.

Pre-retirement cash out: The Ohio PERS defined benefit plan has a feature that is normally associated with defined contribution plans. That is, an employee's contributions to the plan are credited to a savings account on behalf of that individual employee, who can, at her option, withdraw the contribution balance if she leaves employment prior to retirement.

Optional savings plan: In addition to the core plan, Ohio PERS administers a state-sponsored optional savings plan, similar to a 401K plan. All contributions to this savings plan are made by the employee, who is given a choice of investment options. Social Security has no optional savings plan.

Prefunding and investments: Unlike Social Security, Ohio PERS is mostly prefunded, with assets invested in a variety of domestic stocks, bonds, real estate, and international stocks. During the 20 years ended in 2001, the annual nominal return averaged an impressive 10.74% (and, this included two loss years — 2000 and 2001.)[272] During the same time period, Social Security's nominal earnings rate was about 2 percentage points less.

Although Ohio PERS is not part of Ohio state government, Ohio state law directs the Retirement Board to "give consideration to investments that enhance

---

271. Peter A. Diamond, *Social Security Reform* (New York, NY: Oxford University Press, 2002), 11.

272. "Comprehensive Annual Financial Report 2001" (Ohio Public Employees Retirement System, 2002) 21.

the general welfare of the state." This sort of interference is common among public-sector plans, and can lead to waste and corruption. Carrie Lips, Analyst with the Cato Institute, notes:

> Approximately 42 percent of state, county, and municipal pension systems have restrictions targeting a portion of investment funds to projects designed to bolster the local economy. Twenty-three percent of pension systems prohibit investment in specific types of companies for "moral" reasons. The dangers of those types of investment practices are serious: they can expose the program participants to unnecessary risk and introduce the possibility of corruption and cronyism.[273]

Retirement ages and benefits: Participants in Ohio PERS (i.e., the subplan for state workers) can retire at age 60 if they have 5 years of service, at age 55 if they have 25 years of service, or *at any age* with 30 years or more of service. Imagine! A worker starting at age 18 can retire with full benefits at age 48. Full retirement age for Social Security is between 65 and 67, depending on year of birth. There is an option to retire at 62; however, if the election is made, benefits are reduced by about 20%.

For the first 30 years of service credit, Ohio PERS provides a benefit equal to the number of years worked times 2.2% times the average salary in the top three years of earnings. For years in excess of 30, the rate increases to 2.5% per year. Social Security benefits are based upon the average earnings over a 35 year period. A "progressive" formula is used, by which lower wages generate a benefit that is up to six times higher than the benefit generated on higher earnings.

Inflation adjustment: Just like Social Security, benefits are adjusted for inflation; however, the adjustment is limited to 3% per year.

Minimum benefit: Ohio PERS has a minimum benefit for the lowest earners. Those whose top earnings were just $4,095, and who worked less than 30 years, get a minimum benefit of $86 times the number of years worked. Aside from this, however, benefits are pretty much proportional to salary. Social Security has a similar minimum benefit for people who worked several years with very low

---

273. Carrie Lips, "State and Local Government Retirement Programs: Lessons in Alternative to Social Security," SSP no. 16 [online] (Washington, D.C.: Cato Institute, 17 March 1999 — [cited 2 February 2002]); available from *http://www.cato.org/pubs/ssps/ssp-16es.html.*

wage earnings. It involves multiplying the number of work years in excess of 10 times a specific dollar amount (according to a table).

The Ohio PERS success story

Ohio PERS is an example of a well-run defined benefit plan that has maximized investment returns while minimizing investment and political risk. The plan has avoided excessive benefit shifting and has an impressive record of investment earnings, despite the political pressures from the State of Ohio, previously noted. In short, it has kept its commitment to workers, the disabled, and retirees. How has it done it?

Since the participants of Ohio PERS are government workers, Ohio law sets the benefit rates. But, when it comes to investment decisions, Ohio PERS has significant independence. As noted, Ohio law requires that Ohio PERS "give consideration" to state investments; however, it also requires the system "to invest under an investment policy established by the Retirement Board under a prudent person standard." That standard requires the Board "to discharge their duties with respect to the funds solely in the interest of the participants and beneficiaries" (and not in the interest of politics or employers).

Ohio politicians have also avoided the micromanagement of contribution rates. There are contribution rate *caps* set by law, but, within those parameters, the independent Retirement Board has authority. Generally, the Retirement Board sets the contribution rates on the basis of recommendations made by professional actuaries.

What a shame!

Isn't it unfortunate that our federal leaders did not have the wisdom shown by Ohio legislators? What if Congress had, more than 65 years ago, vested authority in a truly autonomous Social Security Board — a Board that would set contribution rates in accordance with the recommendations of professional actuaries, make the tough decisions necessary to efficiently run the disability programs, and manage our money prudently (or, at least, allow us to manage our own money in PRAs)? In all likelihood, earnings would be up, and risk — investment and political — would be down.

Conclusion

No excuses from the Social Security apologists can explain why its benefits are so miserable in comparison to those of Ohio PERS. As we have shown, it is not simply due to different payroll tax rates. And, it is not because Social Security taxes go, in part, to pay for an older generation. Social Security has failed because it is loaded with waste, inequities, and poor investment earnings.

CHAPTER XIV: I HAVE A DREAM

(AMENDMENT XXVIII TO THE UNITED STATES CONSTITUTION)

Section 1. A well regulated and equitable retirement system being essential to the economic security and prosperity of the Nation, an independent retirement Trust, to regulate such a system, is hereby established.

Section 2. The Trust shall be administered by a Board of Trustees comprising seven individuals, each appointed for a six-year term. Three shall be appointed by the President, two by the House of Representatives, and two by the Senate. Except as specified in this Amendment, *neither Congress nor the President shall have authority with regard to any matters of the Trust.*

Section 3. The Trustees shall discharge their duties with respect to the Trust for the exclusive purpose of providing retirement and/or disability benefits to participants and their designated beneficiaries, and defraying reasonable expenses of administering the system with care, skill, and prudence.

Wake up! Wake up!

I'm sorry. I was in the middle of a recurring dream. It's about a *real* trust, constitutionally protected from the whims of Congress — a trust that handles our money *prudently*, to get the best possible benefits for us. Now, I am awake, and see that we have the same old Social Security system that wastefully redistributes our benefits, so politicians appear compassionate — and electable. I wish I could fall asleep again. But, let me tell you more of my dream.

Section 4. The Trust shall be funded by applying a uniform rate of tax to all covered employee wages (as defined by the Trustees), and the tax shall be applied to employee and employer in equal amounts. The rate of tax shall be established by the Trustees, but shall not exceed limits imposed by Congress. Administrative costs of the Trust shall be paid from this tax.

Section 5. To avoid undue influence in the private investment markets, the Trustees' role with regard to the investment of funds shall be limited. In general, Trust funds shall be invested solely in special bonds carrying market rates of interest, and issued by the Treasury's general fund. The preceding statement not withstanding, each participant shall be given the option of transferring part of his/her funds to a privately-owned Personal Retirement Account, to be used solely for retirement income purposes in accordance with guidelines to be established by the Trustees.

Section 6. The Trustees shall distribute benefits to each retired or disabled participant, *or his/her designated beneficiary*, in proportion to the total taxes collected from the participant, after reduction by the amount of his/her taxes (if any) transferred to a Personal Retirement Account. These benefits may be modified to appropriately reflect changes in actuary estimates of investment earnings and mortality rates during a rolling 75-year projection period. However, this system shall *not* be used as a vehicle for the distribution of general assistance, or for the promotion of social or political agendas.

That's my dream; here is how it would work

The core part of the Dream Trust (i.e., the part that is *not* in PRAs) would operate much like a cash balance plan, which is similar to a super-safe 401K plan. With a typical cash balance plan, virtually all of the risk is borne by the employer (or, in this case, by the Trust). The employee is promised benefits based upon the aggregate sum of his contributions to the plan (or, in this case, his payroll taxes), an estimated rate of earnings, and presumed longevity rates. If actual earnings are lower than the estimated earnings, he still gets the promised benefits. If people start living longer than estimated, he still gets the promised benefits. All or most risk is borne by the employer (or trust). In the case of the Dream Trust, actuaries would continually look 75 years into the future to ensure that estimated benefits were realistic, and to ensure that necessary adjustments to benefits or taxes were minor for any given generation of retirees. Unlike the current Social Security system, there would be no wholesale shuffling of benefits, or hiking of payroll taxes. Cash balance plans are for providing retirement benefits — not welfare.

To get higher benefits than available in the core program, many or most employees would probably elect the Dream Trust PRA option. These PRAs would be privately owned, but regulated by the trustees to ensure that investments were adequately diversified, and distributions were made for appropriate retirement or inheritance purposes.

The trustees — not politicians — would set policy for a wide range of matters including:
- tax rates (up to the cap set by Congress)
- the taxable wage base (the portion of your salary that is subject to tax)
- the minimum retirement age
- benefit payout options (e.g., joint lives, fixed period, lump-sum)
- PRA funding limits, diversification requirements, and distribution options
- disability definitions, treatment and vocational rehabilitation requirements, and income limits

The discretion of the trustees would be broad. For example, they might hire private insurance companies to administer the disability program, if convinced that it would lead to improved benefits or economy. Difficult decisions such as these would be made *sans* the politics that currently impedes the decision process.

Why would the Dream Trust be better than today's Social Security?

Investment earnings would be high. The trust would be entirely prefunded and, to the extent that Personal Retirement Accounts were elected, those funds would be invested in equities and bonds that would, over the long haul, yield higher earnings.

Investment risk would be low. As stated earlier, the core part of the Dream Trust would be a super safe cash balance plan, with investments limited to government bonds that would have virtually no risk. This part of the trust would be similar to the current Social Security program, but without the benefit shifting.

For those electing the Personal Retirement Account option there would be more risk, but within limits set by the trustees. It would be their fiduciary responsibility to set limits on the percentage of funds put into PRAs, and to advise participants to diversify their portfolios appropriately in light of their income levels, ages, retirement plans, and risk tolerance.

Political risk would be low. A constitutional amendment, coupled with a Personal Retirement Account option, is the best way to keep the hands of Congress off of our money. With constitutional protection your money, *whether or not placed into a Personal Retirement Account,* would have to be returned to you or to your heirs.[274] It couldn't be transferred to others, or used for some new fangled benefit dreamed up by politicians. The rules could not be changed (short of a repeal), and the principle of "individual equity" would become a reality for everyone.

It would be motivating. *Everything* an employee earned, from teen years right up to retirement age, would have a direct impact on his benefits. Today, we count 35 years and throw out the other 10 or 12 years. They mean nothing.

It would be good for the needy. Section 6 of the Amendment would take the welfare out of Social Security. We could then put it where it belongs — in a means-tested program, funded by income tax revenues. This would allow us to focus our assistance on those who really need it, and finance that assistance with the contributions of all taxpayers — not just wage earners. To avoid stigmatizing senior citizens, it might be possible to seamlessly add the extra assistance to normal Social Security benefits, as a "Part B" component.

It would be great for the economy. Comments of economist Martin Feldstein, cited earlier, are worth repeating:

> Although the transition to a funded system would involve economic as well as political costs, the net present value of the gain would be enormous — as much as $10-20 trillion.[275]

---

274. If you were to die prior to retirement, your heirs would get the value of your retirement account. If you were to die after retirement, the amount provided to heirs would depend on the benefit payout option selected.

It has been estimated that such a gain could result in a million new jobs and an increase of $5,000 per year in the annual income of a family of four.[276]

Could the Dream Trust become a reality?

Yes, but first we'd have to gain momentum for change. There are two ways to do this:

- Force all new state and local workers into Social Security. This is cruel, but very important. Most of these state and local workers lean toward the political party that is most resistant to changing Social Security. If these state and local workers are "invited" to join our wonderful Social Security system, their shrieking voices will be heard by the right people in the right places.
- Start disclosing, to each working American, how much of her benefits has been transferred away and wasted away by fraud, abuse, and error. When the average person realizes just how much of her money is lost, she will become motivated for change.

That's what we'd have to do to get the ball rolling. But, to make the plan politically feasible, we'd have to do more.

Offer a choice

We'd have to offer most workers an option, to ensure that everyone is happy. Depending on their ages, workers could stay in the old Social Security system or join the new Dream Trust. A possible plan for regulating admittance to the Dream Trust is suggested in the following table:

Table 8

Those electing or required to be in the new trust would have credits, equal to the present value of their accrued benefits, transferred from Social Security.

---

275. Martin Feldstein, "Privatizing Social Security: The $10 Trillion Opportunity." *SSP* no. 7 [online] (Washington, D.C.: Cato Institute, 31 January 1997 — [cited 21 May 2002]); available from *http://www.socialsecurity.org/pubs/ssps/ssp7es.html.*

276. Daniel Mitchell, "A Brief Guide to Social Security Reform," Heritage Foundation Talking Points no. 22, August 7, 1997, quoted in Peter J. Ferrara and Michael Tanner, *A New Deal For Social Security* (Washington, D.C.: Cato Institute, 1998), 207-8.

	Original Social Security	New(dream) Trust
Age 60 and older	mandatory	–
Age 32 to 60	optional	optional
Below age 32	–	mandatory

This would be accompanied by an actual transfer of funds from the old system to the new. Age 32 might be a good cutoff age since most of the payroll taxes paid by people before that age have little effect on their ultimate Social Security benefits.

Benefits under the original Social Security plan would be the same as those being projected today — guaranteed, and including the wage-indexed increases. People near retirement age would still have Social Security, and anyone age 32 or older could keep it if he wanted to. (Most probably would *not* want to.) For all others, the original Social Security plan would be closed and, eventually, phased out.

Why limit the trustees with regard to investment decisions?

As noted earlier, some of the retirement plans for public-sector workers, such as the Ohio PERS plan, have directly invested funds in the market with substantial success. So, initially, I was open to the idea of direct investment by the Social Security trust fund. In fact, I even tried to develop a plan — a scheme that would protect the markets from undo influence, promote competition, and prevent cronyism. But, it is not easy to develop such a plan for a program as large as the Social Security system and, as it evolved, it grew more and more complex until it became some sort of bureaucratic cobweb of checks and balances. I abandoned the effort when someone told me my scheme reminded her of the failed attempts to nationalize health care.

The problems of government investment are clearly outlined by Ferrara and Tanner in their book, *A New Deal for Social Security:*

> Allowing the government to own stock in corporate America is an open invitation for the government to interfere with the American economy. After all, what if a company whose stock is purchased by the Social Security trust funds decides to move its operations overseas? Should the administrators of the investments of the trust funds remain indifferent to the plight of the company's workers, who after all will be future beneficiaries of the system?

Ferrara and Tanner go on to note that the nature of the investment, in itself, could lead to conflicts:

> For example, cigarette smoking is a major health concern to many people and to the federal and state governments that spend public money to provide health care for those suffering from smoking-related diseases. Should Social Security be allowed to invest in cigarette companies? ...
>
> Other controversial issues are easy to imagine. Should Social Security invest in nonunion companies? Companies that make nuclear weapons? Companies that pay high executive salaries or do not offer health benefits? Companies that do business in Burma or Cuba? Companies with insufficient numbers of women and minorities in executive positions? ... The list is virtually endless.[277]

For these reasons, we must carefully limit the power of the trustees with regard to investment of funds.

But the trustees should have a role

The above arguments not withstanding, there is a role for the trustees to play in regard to the investment of PRA funds (as opposed to core trust funds). For participants concerned with keeping administration costs low, there should be the option of investing in a few broad index funds, organized by the trustees and directly managed by private companies hired via competitive contract. If patterned after the federal Thrift Savings Plan, we could expect such an arrangement to have very low administration costs — as low as one tenth of one percent (.001) of the value of assets managed. These trustee-organized funds should supplement, but not replace, private investment fund options.

What about the Insolvency problem?

The new Dream Trust would be self-sustaining; it wouldn't need financial help. But, the original Social Security system would, of course, still have its huge, unfunded liability — about $10.5 trillion. In addition, we would need to finance a means tested, low-income assistance program, to replace some of Social Security's wealth transfers (the ones that actually reach truly needy people). How would we pay for these expenses?[278] One way would be to use a "special assessment," comprising an across-the-board surtax on federal individual and

---

277. Peter J. Ferrara and Michael Tanner, *A New Deal For Social Security* (Washington, D.C.: Cato Institute, 1998), 207-8.

corporate *income* tax. This would have to be levied over a very long time — at least 75 years, but preferably 100 years. Interim cash flow problems could be handled via debt. If we did it over a 100-year period, and had modest cost savings in a couple of areas, the surtax might be in the area of 17% of current tax rates. In other words, a worker paying a 15% rate of tax would end up paying 17.6%, after the surtax (i.e., 15% times 117%). Someone who is now paying 25% would end up paying 29.2%. Part of this burden could be offset by a decrease in the payroll tax, because a prefunded system should yield significantly higher benefits, even if based on reduced payroll taxes. But the income tax burden on individuals and businesses would be significant — no doubt about it.[279]

Alternatives to a tax hike

Many economists feel that a hike in the income tax should be one of the last used options for financing. Ferrara and Tanner have proposed transitional financing that would not necessitate any increase in the federal income tax. Rather, their plan involves several sources of financing, including "revenue feedback" (tax on increased earnings from the private investments), forfeited retirement and disability benefits from those who opt to use personal retirement accounts, savings from delaying the retirement age, savings from using price indexing instead of wage indexing, a temporary (ten year) payroll tax on employees and their employers (to be imposed after the personal retirement account option is elected), and general cuts in other government spending.

---

278. If everyone currently age 15 or older opted to stay in Social Security, the system would be short $10.5 trillion, but there would be no need for additional (new) welfare funding; it is built (however inefficiently) into the present Social Security system. In reality, however, there probably would be a need to fund a separate welfare program because many workers would opt to get out of Social Security. The people most likely to switch to the Dream Trust would be the people who get the worst deal from Social Security (i.e., the people who presently fund Social Security's welfare transfers). For this reason, we must plan to fund the $10.5 trillion *plus* the amount needed to help low earners. There are, however, offsetting factors that should reduce the overall cost. As noted, there is much disability abuse and fraud in the current programs, and the cost of this waste is included in the $10.5 trillion projection. In addition, a more rationale and uniform manner of taxing benefits (as discussed in Chapter VI) would increase revenues to the Treasury's general fund. And, if we establish a senior citizen welfare assistance program that prudently employs means testing, the amount of required welfare should be diminish from present levels.

279. For an explanation of the required tax increase estimate, see Appendix A-16.

I suspect that there is no right or wrong solution when it comes to financing the transition, provided the burden does not fall exclusively on wage earners, and is not restricted to just one or two generations. We should all share in the cost. After all, most of this unfunded liability goes back decades. It is our collective, national obligation.

No matter what plan is used, there would be financial pain, but it would be greatly outweighed by the long-term benefits. The entire system would be prefunded, national savings and productivity would increase, and workers could look forward to substantial retirement benefits greatly in excess of current amounts. There would be "individual equity" instead of sneaky income-shifting games. And, the needy would get targeted, low-income assistance *and* a chance to accumulate benefits in a real retirement program. Best of all, there would *never* be a retirement crisis again. What a gift for our grandchildren!

There would be critics

I can hear it now. Social Security defenders would say, "This plan will end one of our most successful government programs and put millions of senior citizens on welfare." Wrong, because Social Security has not been successful; it has had the *illusion* of success, due to the Ponzi methodology used (as described in Chapter II). And wrong, because the plan would not put people on welfare — they are already on it. The difference is, we'd limit that welfare to people who really need it, and we'd fund it properly.

Plan B

While we're waiting for Congress to get started on the constitutional amendment, perhaps we should develop a "Plan B." Here are some specific ways to improve the system (a recap of the recommendations found at the end of the chapters):

- Allow workers to put part of their payroll taxes into a carve-out PRA option, similar to Proposal One, made by the President's Commission. In itself, this doesn't reform the core Social Security system, but it would give immediate relief to millions of workers who are presently getting little out of Social Security.
- Every American has a right to know how much of his retirement benefits have been shifted to or from others in the program. This information should be given annually, in unambiguous terms.

- Flatten out the benefit formula. Eliminate the 90%, 32%, and 15% rates and replace these with one flat rate or, at least, with rates less dissimilar. For those who are needy (as determined via intelligent means testing), let's replace any lost benefits with assistance financed from the Treasury's general fund. This could be seamlessly added to normal Social Security benefits (as a "Part B" component) so that retirees are not subjected to any stigma associated with the assistance.

- Count *all* payroll taxes paid — not just those related to 35 of the years worked. All other things being equal, a person who begins working at age 32 gets the same benefits under the current system as the person who begins working at age 18. Yet, one of them had his pay docked 12.4% for an extra 14 years for Social Security contributions. It isn't equitable.

- Eliminate spousal benefits. In most cases, they do not help the needy; rather, they help the affluent. Where a hardship is created, the benefit should be replaced by means-tested assistance (as described above). If we can't eliminate spousal benefits, let's at least reduce them. The American Academy of Actuaries estimates that a reduction of spousal benefits from 50% to 33% of the retired worker's benefit would eliminate about 10% of Social Security's long-term actuarial imbalance.[280]

- Give lower-age retirement options. If someone wants to retire at age 50, he or she should be allowed to, *provided* the benefit is appropriately reduced to compensate for the extra years of benefits, and the reduced benefit is sufficient to keep the individual well above the poverty line. Also, where a recipient dies prior to retirement, or early in the retirement period, the heirs should get a portion of the forgone benefits. These changes would be of tremendous help and comfort to people who do not have high longevity expectations.

- Eliminate the Government Pension Offset loophole. State and local workers should not be allowed to use sham employment schemes to rip off the Social Security program. If necessary, legal action should be taken against participants in these "shams in substance."

- All new state and local governmental workers should be brought into the system. You can't blame them for wanting to avoid Social Security, but we simply can't have retirement apartheid in America.

- Change the way we tax Social Security benefits. It is far too complex and confusing, and forces millions of seniors to use paid tax preparers. Everyone pays income tax on the payroll taxes withheld from his/her checks, but no one pays on the Social Security taxes paid by the employer. So, make one half of Social Security benefits taxable for everyone. (Those who have

---

280. "Social Security Benefits: Changes to the Benefit Formula and Taxation,'" [online] (American Academy of Actuaries, October 2002 — [cited 15 November 2002]), 5; available from *http://www.actuary.org/socsec/index.htm#2002.*

little income will not pay taxes anyway because of standard deductions and exemptions.) This is straightforward and fair. For new workers, on the other hand, let's start taxing benefits in the same manner we tax the benefits of other pension plans. That is, the worker would pay no income tax on the Social Security payroll taxes withheld from pay. However, benefits would be fully taxable, when received.

• Repeal the work penalty! Let's stop punishing people whose only crime is working.

By doing all of the above, we could almost make the current Social Security system decent. But, unfortunately, without the independent trust, the improvements could be quickly eroded by political currents.

Recommendations for the Disability Programs

It would be ideal to have the disability program under the auspices of a truly independent board of trustees (along with the retirement system). Then, perhaps, we could have an intelligent and nonpolitical evaluation of a plan of *optional privatization*. The arguments for using private insurance companies are well-stated by Christopher M. Wright, in a Cato Institute policy analysis entitled, "SSI: The Black Hole of the Welfare State:"

> The need for a government-administered disability insurance program has never been established and is particularly questionable given that a market for private disability insurance already exists. Under an opt-out approach to DI, many more Americans would be in the private market, which would summon forth an even greater variety of disability insurance options from private insurers.[281]

Mr. Wright notes that an advantage of privatizing disability would be the ability of workers to select insurance plans appropriate for their needs. For example, some workers might select high-cost plans that define disability in terms of a specific occupation, while others would seek low-cost plans that define disability as an inability to work in *any* occupation. There would also be

---

281. Christopher M. Wright, "SSI: The Black Hole of the Welfare State," Policy Analysis no. 224 [online] (Washington, D.C.: Cato Institute, 27 April 1995 — [cited 22 August 2002]), section entitled *Ultimately Privatize Disability Insurance*.; available from *http://www.cato.org/pubs/pas/pa-224.html*.

options regarding waiting periods, deductibles, types of impairments covered, and other matters. And, privatization would yield another benefit:

> Another virtue of private insurance is that, unlike DI, benefit costs are forced into line with policy premiums. Private insurers have a financial interest in controlling costs. A private insurance system, with strong cost-containment features, would save workers money through lower premiums than are now paid through the payroll tax.[282]

Plan B for disability

Once again, however, we'd better have a fall-back strategy. The following recommendations are less sweeping in scope, and involve modifications to the existing disability programs:

• Require the existence of a medically-verifiable impairment. To meet the "medically-verifiable" standard, there should be medical signs or symptoms that are *not* derived, directly or indirectly, from the claimant's own statements.

• For the no-brainer cases, have an expedited process so that obviously-impaired workers can quickly get relief.

• In judging a person's ability to perform in an occupation, we should assume the availability of a workplace that has the "reasonable accommodations" required by the ADA.

• Appeals should be submitted to independent panels comprising representatives of government, workers, employers, medical professionals, vocational experts, and insurance companies (not simply one lawyer with a week or two of medical training). These panels should be insulated from political influence, and their decisions should be a matter of public record, provided the identity of the claimants can be concealed. The public needs to know how well, or how poorly, the system works.

• Never give benefits that equal or exceed the claimant's pre-disability earnings. Disability income must not be as attractive as wages earned. The solution is to put a percentage cap on disability benefits, as related to past wages. The cap used by most private insurers is around 60%.

• The SGA earnings standard should not be used to judge whether a claimant can work. Instead, ability to work should be assessed on the basis of medical and vocational analysis, and on the basis of earnings in relation to pre-disability wage levels.

• Initially, disabled workers should be allowed to earn as much as possible, provided the combination of benefits and earnings is not in excess

---

282. *Ibid.*

of pre-disability earnings. After one or two years, however, benefits should be gradually reduced so that total income is less than pre-disability earnings. This would serve as an inducement for the disabled worker to return to work.

• Private insurers start with a liberal definition of disability, and gradually make the definition more restrictive over the two years following the onset of a claimant's disability. This gives the insurer leverage to induce the claimant to rehabilitate, and to return to work. In contrast, Social Security uses an "all-or-nothing" definition, which gives the applicant a strong incentive to emphasize his limitations, lest he lose everything. We need to adopt a flexible definition of disability that recognizes the potential of the disabled to gradually improve his skills, and adapt to the workplace.

• Currently, the SSI welfare program issues flat monthly checks to the parents of pre-work-age disabled children. Whether these funds are actually used for the children is unknown. (No one tracks expenditures.) This program should be replaced by an expense reimbursement program, in which families of disabled children receive reimbursement for disability-related expenses actually incurred, and documented.

• Give vocational rehabilitation guidance earlier, and require nonsurgical treatments and vocational training whenever they might be helpful. Any recipient of benefits who fails to comply with this requirement should be denied benefits.

• More qualified personnel should be hired by the SSA and state disability offices. College degrees should be required for disability examiners, and these people should be capable of assisting the disabled in returning to productive employment.

• Disability evaluation and review service contracts should be awarded to private companies as part of a pilot project. The results of the project should be studied to see where cost savings and improved services may be achieved.

• To monitor health trends — and abuse trends — track final awards by specific impairment. Deviations from the norm should be investigated.

Fraud

The following steps should be taken to control fraud and abuse.

• Start by developing meaningful estimates of fraud and abuse — program-wide and for each specific program. These estimates are essential to pin-point problem areas, to measure progress in fighting the problems, and to bring public attention to any problems.

• Expand the number of Continuing Disability Reviews and Cooperative Disability Investigations. These are very successful programs that save more money than they cost.

- The SSA should revise disability regulations that invite abuse and fraud due to the inclusion of conflicting, confusing and subjective standards. The burden of proof has to be shifted back to the claimant. That is, he must demonstrate via clear medical evidence that he has an impairment.
- The fraud "tip" line has been successful. Let's publicize it, and start paying *rewards* for tips that lead to convictions.
- Educate the public regarding the immorality of cheating, by using high-profile marketing campaigns with big-name stars, etc. Publicize the identities of flagrant cheats and law breakers.
- A national identity card, a topic of interest since 9/11, would greatly reduce identity theft. In addition, better data base sharing between the SSA and INS (Immigration) is needed.
- Utilize surreptitious testers to test the program for weaknesses. These testers should periodically evaluate different offices of Social Security, and different program areas.
- We need to clean up the Supplemental Security Income program (SSI) so it can play a more effective and efficient role in assisting the aged and disabled. The main problem here is the quality of SSA personnel. It appears that they are not qualified or, perhaps, not motivated to vigorously check applicant income and asset information, needed to determine eligibility for program benefits. Periodically, samples of the completed work of each SSA employee should be thoroughly reviewed by traveling teams of quality control experts. Advancement and promotions should be linked to the results.
- Recipients of public assistance, including SSI, have no right to misrepresent their finances by concealing beneficial relationships. At the very minimum, we need to get full and truthful disclosures from people seeking benefits, if we are to protect the public at large. Claimants should be asked pointed questions, and their answers should be verified whenever possible. Penalties and jail time should await those who provide blatantly false information.
- There are three ways to significantly reduce the size of the underground economy: lowering marginal tax rates, making Social Security more like a real investment (instead of a tax), and simplifying the reporting requirements of businesses, as related to employees. Decreasing the size of the underground economy would greatly strengthen Social Security, and decrease the strain on welfare programs.

Parting thoughts

Social Security is like an old house that hasn't been updated or repaired in nearly 70 years. The roof leaks, so we put a pot under the dripping water. Cold air comes through the broken windows, so we turn up the heat. We throw patches here and there, but never fix the core problem.

In the case of Social Security, the core problem is politics. *That* is what we have to fix. We must wring the politics out of this vital, essential program, and make it an efficient, effective, and equitable retirement system for all of us: A system that distributes to each retiree, his or her full share of benefits, and not one cent less. A system where investments are made with integrity and professionalism, to maximize the wealth of all participants. A system that has the flexible distribution options required to accommodate the needs and desires of each individual participant. And, finally, a system that has no tolerance for fraud or abuse, or anything else that wastes the hard-earned money of workers.

If that is the kind of Social Security system you'd like to see, I hope you will actively support efforts to discuss, analyze, and, eventually, reform the Social Security system. To this end, you will find, in Appendix B, a listing of government leaders, media sources, and other influential public figures. Tell them that we need to finally fix Social Security. The patient is sick, and time is not on our side.

A-1 Calculation of Jill's Ohio PERS benefits vs. Mary's Social Security benefits
(See page 4.)

For both Mary and Jill, it was assumed that career wage increases were 5.96% per year — a little over the annual increase in the average of total U.S. wages (5.26%) during that time period. The excess represents presumed merit increases (beyond inflation increases) that the women would have earned during their careers.[283] Jill's monthly retirement benefit was obtained by using the online benefit calculator at the Ohio Public Employees Retirement System website (*www.opers.org*), and by using her last three years of earnings (as prescribed). The payment option selected was C, which reduced her monthly benefit somewhat but allowed for a 50% benefit to her named beneficiary (Ted), in the event of Jill's death. Jill's benefit was then reduced by an assumed income tax rate of 20%.

Mary's monthly benefit was obtained by using the Social Security online benefit calculator (*www.ssa.org*), and was calculated on the basis of her adjusted indexed monthly earnings (AIME) through age 52. That result was increased by

---

283. Obviously, the average worker expects and gets wage increases related to improved skills, training, and experience. Therefore, the career wages of a given worker usually increases by an amount greater than wage inflation. Readers seeking a quantitative analysis of this phenomenon are referred to Barry Bosworth, Gary Burtless, and C. Eugene Steuerle, "Lifetime Earnings Patterns, the Distribution of Future Social Security Benefits, and the Impact of Pension Reform" (Chestnut Hill, MA: Center for Retirement Research at Boston College, December 1999).

an estimated real-wage differential of .75% per year, reflecting the excess of estimated wage inflation over general inflation for years between age 52 and her retirement at age 66. (This was done to simulate the effect of the wage indexing which is built into the Social Security benefit formula.) Mary's benefit was then reduced by income tax calculated by multiplying a 20% income tax rate times the taxable portion of the benefit — assumed to be 25%. (Depending on other income, the taxable portion of Social Security benefits can range from zero to 85%.)

In each case, longevity was estimated by use of Social Security period life tables. Since Ohio PERS and Social Security both adjust benefits for inflation, an after-inflation interest rate of 3% was used to obtain the present values of the monthly benefits. The present value of the Ohio PERS benefits was then reduced by multiplying it times 0an amount which was calculated as follows: Social Security payroll tax rates for years 1973 through 2002 were increased by the amount of income tax Mary would have paid on the portion (i.e., the half) withheld from her paychecks. (Remember, Social Security withholdings are not deductible for income tax purposes.) An assumed income tax rate of 20% was used. The adjusted Social Security payroll tax rates were then expressed in 2002 dollars, using an interest rate factor of 3%. Ohio PERS contribution rates for the same years (employer and employee) were also expressed in 2002 dollars, using the 3% interest factor. (The Ohio PERS contribution rates were not adjusted for worker income taxes, since they were fully tax deductible when withheld from Jill's paychecks.) The amount calculated for Social Security was divided by the amount calculated for Ohio PERS. That yielded the 0.6658 amount.

To estimate the value of Ted's benefits, it was assumed that he was the same age as Jill and had an expected lifespan of 15 years at age 66 (per Social Security Actuary period life tables). The value of his after-tax benefits was calculated as of age 66, using an after-inflation interest rate of 3%, and was then reduced by multiplying it times .6658. (See explanation in preceding paragraph.) Note that, if Ted were a female, the estimated value of his (her) benefits would increase significantly (from $85,000 to $99,000) due to the greater longevity of women in comparison to men.

It is important to understand the objective of this particular comparison between Mary and Jill. It is to illustrate that two individuals earning the same pay, and contributing the same amounts (after our adjustments), can have very different retirement fortunes even though each is in a government-sanctioned retirement system. Part of the difference in benefit values is directly related to the administrative performance of Social Security and Ohio PERS (e.g., controlling disability fraud, and investing prudently). But, some of the difference is due to factors beyond the purview of either retirement system (e.g., the income taxation of benefits). In Chapter XIII, you will again find comparisons between Social Security and Ohio PERS; however, those comparisons have been designed to eliminate, where possible, the factors that are presently beyond the control of either system. In that way we can better judge the performance of each system.

A-2 The Social Security shortfall: explanation
(See page 9.)

Generally speaking, there are three different estimates tossed around to describe the economic shortfall of Social Security: $3.5 trillion, $10.5 trillion, and about $24 trillion. Which is right? All three — sort of. The $3.5 trillion dollar estimate, known as the "open-group actuarial imbalance" (or "open-group unfunded obligation"), reflects the present value of future program costs, less future revenues for the next 75 years, less the present value of the Social Security trust fund.[284] This figure is misleading because it counts the payroll taxes collected from people for the next 75 years, but it *doesn't* count the amount that will be owed to those same people in years 76 through whenever they keel over (which, given health trends, will probably be an additional 200 years). And, it implies our right to commit future generations to the same, sick "pay-as-you-go" system. As the Concord Coalition states, "It suggests that government can exact enormous obligations from future generations without their consent — what Thomas Jefferson called 'binding the unborn.'"[285]

The "*closed*-group actuarial imbalance" (or "closed-group unfunded liability") is a better and truer measure of the status of the system. Essentially, that standard assumes that Social Security will be closed to new entrants. It reflects the cost, in current dollars, of paying all current retirees and future retirees who are age 15, or older, less the current value of payroll taxes that will

---

284. "2003 OASDI Trustees Report" (Social Security Administration, 2003), 61.

285. Neil Howe and Richard Jackson, "How to Measure Social Security's Financial Status," vol. IV, no. 6 of The Truth about Entitlements and the Budget [online] (The Concord Coalition, 15 June 1998 — [cited 24 August 2002]); available from *http://www.concordcoalition.org/facing_facts/alert_v4_n6.html*.

be collected from these same people, less miscellaneous revenues, less the value of the trust fund. When we use this method, we get an actuarial imbalance of about $10.5 trillion, as of January 1, 2003.[286] The closed-group method is, by the way, the method that private pension plans are *required* to use. But, when the Federal Accounting Standards Advisory Board (FASAB) proposed, in the late 1990s, to require the closed-group method for *governmental units*, such as Social Security, some of the Social Security defenders howled. They maintained that the Social Security commitment "is not a liability and should not be recognized as such." They noted the "political nature of the commitment," and noted that "terms can be and are changed by the Congress...."[287] (That's no lie!) Some of these closed-group opponents were even against having this dangerous information included as supplemental information in the footnotes to Social Security financial statements. Nevertheless, the FASAB issued a pronouncement that requires supplemental disclosure of information needed to calculate the closed-group method.[288] The 2003 Social Security Trustees Report includes (for the first time) disclosure of the closed-group actuarial imbalance. And, also, the information can be found in the very small print deep within the Social Security Administration's FY 2002 Performance and Accountability Report. (The SSA makes you supply the math, however.)[289]

Although the closed-group actuarial imbalance (the $10.5 trillion figure) is a reasonable estimate of the *program's* financial dilemma, it doesn't give us the full picture. This is best explained with an analogy. Let's say that a husband and wife each have a sole proprietorship business. The wife runs Pro Medical Clinic and the husband runs Acme Gas Station. Unfortunately, business has been bad for Acme Gas Station, so it borrows $50,000 from Pro Medical Clinic. Husband and wife now decide to take a world-wide vacation that will cost $50,000. Wife says, "The money will be no problem; my business will simply collect the loan it made to Acme Gas Station." Do you see the problem? Her cash will simultaneously go up and down because, by virtue of her marriage, her assets and debts are the

286. "2003 OASDI Trustees Report," 62.

287. "Statement of Federal Financial Standards No. 17: Accounting for Social Insurance," version 2.1 [online] (Federal Accounting Standards Advisory Board, October 2001 — [cited 24 November 2002]), 867; available from *http://www.fasab.gov/pdf/17_ss.pdf.*

288. "Statement of Federal Financial Standards No. 17: Accounting for Social Insurance," version 2.1, 872.

289. "FY 2002 Performance and Accountability Report" [online] (Social Security Administration, 2003— [cited March 2003]), 78; available from *http://www.ssa.gov/finance/.*

same as those of her husband. Likewise, the Social Security system is (unfortunately) part and parcel of the U.S. government. There is no separate legal entity, so we can't consider Social Security finances without considering the implications for the government as a whole. To estimate the entire amount owed by *both* Social Security and the U.S. Treasury's general fund, we need to compare the present value of all future Social Security inflows and outflows. If we do this for a 75-year period, we come up with a total obligation of over $24 trillion.[290] That is the total amount that will have to be paid via payroll taxes and general income taxes.

A-3 Calculating one universal replacement rate for all workers retiring at age 65 in 1999: explanation
(See page 20.)

Each year, the Social Security Administration (SSA) publishes the number and percentage of newly-retired workers, categorized by the value of their monthly benefits or, in other words, by their "Primary Insurance Amounts" (PIA). By using this information, which can be found in the Annual Statistical Supplements, and by using tables published by the Institute for Policy Innovation (IPI), it is possible to estimate the one universal benefit rate that would apply, were we to take the "bend points" out of the formula and eliminate non-worker benefits.[291,292] This was done in the following manner.

The mid-point of each 1999 PIA range was determined and then reduced to its 1996 value by dividing it by the CPI adjustment amounts for 1996, 1997, and 1998. This was necessary because PIA is computed at the eligibility date (generally age 62) and then increased by CPI up to retirement age. The Average Indexed Monthly Earnings (AIME) associated with each 1996 PIA value was deduced by applying the normal PIA calculation formula in reverse. The

---

290. David C. John, "A Guide to the New 2002 Social Security Trustees' Report," *WebMemo* no. 91 [online] (The Heritage Foundation, 29 March 2002 — [cited 20 October 2002]); available from *http://www.heritage.org/Research/SocialSecurity/WM91.cfm.*

291. "Annual Statistical Supplement, 2000" [online] (Social Security Administration, Office of Policy, 2001 — [cited 15 October 2002]), table 6.B4; available from *http:// www.ssa.gov/policy/docs/statcomps/supplement/2000/index.html.*

292. Aldona Robbins, "Social Security Reform and Tax Reform: Is One Possible Without the Other?," Policy Report no. 172 [online] (The Institute for Policy Innovation, 12 February 2002 — [cited 14 May 2002]), Table 5; available from *http://www.ipi.org/.*

calculated AIME amounts were then adjusted (increased) to reflect *wage* indexing (as opposed to CPI adjustments) up to the year of retirement (1999). This was necessary due to the fact that wages are indexed only through age 60 (in this case, 1994). Each 1999 PIA amount and each adjusted (1999) AIME amount was multiplied times the percentage of people awarded benefits (in 1999), related to those amounts. The weighted PIA amounts were totaled, and the weighted adjusted AIME amounts were totaled. The total of the PIA amounts was divided by the total of the AIME amounts to get an overall rate of about 35.6%.

Finally, the 35.6% amount was multiplied by a fraction, the numerator of which was total OASI benefit payments and the denominator of which was total OASI *worker* benefit payments. (This was done to eliminate the effect of dependency and survivor benefits.) This produced a total worker replacement rate of 45.5%.

Figure 5, on page 21, shows percentage increases that could be realized by people with differing amounts of earnings. In each case the percentage increase was calculated by subtracting the current replacement value for a given income level from the theoretical worker replacement rate of 45.5%.

A-4 Annual amount of savings needed to keep Social Security solvent for 75 years (See page 25.)

The Social Security trustees have estimated that the 75-year open-group actuarial imbalance is, in today's dollars, about $3.5 trillion.[293] Expressed as a fixed annuity for 75 years, using a 3% after-inflation interest rate, that amount is $117.8 billion per year.

---

293. "FY 2002 Performance and Accountability Report," 77-78.

A-5 Calculation of transferred spousal/survivor benefits
(See page 37.)

Gustman and Steinmeier studied more than 7,000 individuals who participated in a national, longitudinal study of older Americans, and who were born between 1931 and 1941.[294] To measure benefit redistribution, they started by arraying the individuals into ten groups (deciles) by the amount of their average indexed monthly earnings (AIME). They then compared each individual's actual benefits with those he or she would have received if benefits were distributed *pro rata* to payroll taxes paid. By doing this, they determined that a redistribution of about 10.6% of total benefits took place (from the upper 30% to the lower 70%). When spousal and survivor benefits were introduced, however, the percentage of total benefits redistributed dropped to only 6.8%.

By using these percentages and benefit payment amounts from the SSA's Annual Statistical Supplement for 2001, we can estimate that spousal and survivor benefits result in a net benefit transfer, from lower earners to high earners, equal in amount to 14% of the total cost of the spousal and survivor benefits. The 14% rate is calculated as follows.

If X = the amount of net transfers, in the form of spousal and survivor benefits, from higher to lower earners, then:

(10.6% x Worker Benefits) + X	=	6.8% x (Worker Benefits + Spousal Benefits)
(10.6% x $284 billion) + X	=	6.8% x ($284 billion + $52 billion)
$30.1 billion + X	=	$22.8 billion
X	=	negative $7.3 billion

There is a *negative* transfer of $7.3 billion to low earners or, in other words, there is a *positive* transfer of $7.3 billion to the upper 30% of earners. Expressed as a percentage of spousal and survivor benefits, this amount is 7.3/52 = 14%.

Now, we need to apply the 14% rate to an estimate of *future* spousal / survivor benefit amounts. know, from the 2003 Trustees Report, that the 75-year

---

294. Alan L. Gustman and Thomas L. Steinmeier, "How Effective is Redistribution Under the Social Security Benefit Formula?" *Journal of Public Economics* 82, no. 1 (Elsevier Science B.V., October 2001), table 5 and related explanations.

open-group actuarial imbalance is estimated to be $3.5 trillion. And, in the report the trustees state that a 13% reduction in all benefits payable during the next 75 years would eliminate that deficit.[295] That means that total projected benefits, expressed in a lump-sum (in today's dollars) must equal $3.5 trillion divided by 13%, which is about $26 trillion.[296] $26 trillion would be the equivalent of $875 billion per year, on average, for 75 years (using a 3% interest factor).

How much of the $875 billion in retirement benefits will be for worker retirement benefits, as opposed to spousal/survivor benefits and other dependency benefits? In 2001, 80.5% of retirement benefits went to retired workers, 14.9% went to spousal/survivor benefits, and 4.6% went to miscellaneous beneficiaries (children and parents).[297] But, it is expected that spousal/survivor benefits will decrease as more women expand their careers. To estimate the spousal/survivors benefit percentage of the future, I used a rough 50/50 average of two percentages. According to an estimate prepared by economist Yung-Ping Chen, by the year 2060, the percentage of workers getting part of their benefits from spousal/survival benefits will drop to 40%, from today's rate of 63%.[298] Therefore, I multiplied the current percentage of spousal benefits (14.9%) times 40/63 to get an adjusted (future) percentage of 9.5%. The 14.9 and 9.5 amounts were then averaged to get a (rough) estimate of 12.2%. Assuming that the miscellaneous benefits percentage stays the same, spousal/survivor benefits will be about $107 billion per year (12.2% times $875 billion); and worker retirement benefits will be $728 billion per year ((100%-12.2%-4.6%) times $875 billion). applying the 14% transfer rate, calculated above, to the projected spousal/survivor benefit level ($107 billion) we get an average net transfer amount of $15 billion.

---

295. "2003 OASDI Trustees Report," Highlights section, p. 3.

296. This amount reconciles closely to the "cost" amount shown in Table IV.B6 of the 2003 Trustees Report. That amount, $26.5 trillion, would be about $26 trillion after elimination of administration costs.

297. Based on amounts in Tables 4.A5 and 5.G4 of the 2001 Annual Statistical Supplement. Spousal/survivor benefits were decreased and worker benefits increased by the amount of benefits payable on both the basis of worker earnings and spousal/survivor status.

298. Yung-Ping Chen, "Changing Family Structure and Social Security Reform" [online] (Schaumburg, Illinois: Society of Actuaries, June 2002 — [cited 26 November 2002]), 9; available from *www.soa.org*.

Of course, if we only concentrate on *net* transfers, we don't get a complete picture of the amount of waste. We can determine the *gross* amount of transferred spousal and survivor benefits (to the lower and upper wage-earners) by adding a few more steps. The balance of the spousal and survivor benefits is $107 - $15 = $92 billion. That amount is allocated, *pro rata*, on the basis of payroll taxes paid. We can determine from Table 4 in the Gustman and Steinmeier study that 60.5% of the payroll taxes were paid by the top 3 deciles. Therefore, the total amount of spousal and survivor benefits distributed to the high earners (top 3 deciles) must be ... $15 + (60.5% x $92) = $70.7 billion.

That would leave the low earners with $107 - $70.7 = $36.3 billion.

A-6 The bottom line in the Gustman-Steinmeier study
(See page 37.)

As noted, the Gustman-Steinmeier study shows that much of the progressivity of Social Security is an illusion. Ostensibly, there is a transfer of 10.6% of benefits from upper wage earners to lower wage earners. But, when spousal benefits and earnings of family units are considered (rather than individuals) the transfer amount is about half that amount. It gets worse. The final step in the study is to classify families by earnings *capacity*. In the words of the researchers, "It is the average amount earned in years when the individual was seriously committed to work."[299] It excludes years with relatively insignificant earnings. An example of this might be a physician, attorney, or college professor who works 20 years and then chooses to live on investments or some other source of income. Although he has the capacity to earn high income, he has chosen not to.

Gustman and Steinmeier note that, when families are classified by earnings capacity, the amount of total benefits transferred to low wage earners drops to just 2.5%. Note, however, that the analysis of waste in this book does not include these extra benefits transferred to families with high earnings capacity, since we do not know whether the career interruptions were due to preference or necessity (and such factors are not readily subject to quantification).

---

299. Alan L. Gustman and Thomas L. Steinmeier, 21.

A-7 Calculation of extra benefits going to those with non-SS retirement incomes greater than 70% of retirees
(See page 40.)

This analysis was prepared in two different ways, each giving the same bottom-line results. The first approach is based on Tables 4.3 and 3.1 from "Income of the Population 55 or Older, 2000," a report based partly on Census data, and available on the Social Security website. Table 4.3 indicates the total money income of Social Security retirees age 65 and older, *excluding* Social Security benefits. Individuals and married couples are arrayed by Social Security benefit levels into quintiles. In other words, those with Social Security benefits below 80% of the population are in the first (lowest) quintile, and those with Social Security benefits above 80% of the population, are in the 5th (i.e., highest) quintile, etc. These Social Security benefit quintiles should *roughly* correlate to quintiles of historical wage levels.

The individuals or married couples *within* each quintile are also categorized, on a percentage basis, into various ranges of *non*-Social Security income. For example, the table indicates that, for married people in the lowest quintile of Social Security benefits, 3.1% have non-Social Security incomes (from wages, pensions, interest, rents, etc.) of $40,000 to $45,000 per year. Another 2.3% have non-Social Security incomes between $45,000 and $50,000 per year, and so forth.

Table 3.1 (from the "Income of the Population" report) lists the percentage of people aged 65 and older with *total* incomes (including Social Security) at various income levels. By studying this table, it can be determined that an individual aged 65 or older, with income from all sources of $20,000 or more (in 2000), was wealthier than 72% of other unmarried people of his age group. A married couple with total income of $45,000 or more (in 2000), was wealthier than 69% of other couples 65 years old or more. The $20,000 and $45,000 amounts were used as described below.

By using Table 4.3, it was possible to determine the percentage of individuals or couples in each of the quintiles with non-Social Security incomes in excess of the $20,000 and $45,000 levels for individuals and couples, respectively. These were the people or couples who had incomes, in 2000, in excess of about 70% of other retirees, even before they began collecting benefits. For each quintile, the appropriate percentage was multiplied times the dollar amount of extra benefits redistributed to that quintile. (The dollar amount of extra benefits redistributed was determined by using percentages per Table 5 in the Gustman and Steinmeier study, described in Appendix A-5 Calculation of transferred spousal/survivor benefits, multiplied times the total of worker retirement benefits and spousal and survivor benefits paid in 2001.) The results for each quintile were combined, and the aggregate amount was divided by total retirement benefits (worker and spousal/survivor) for 2001, to yield a "waste" factor of 14.3%. This percentage, multiplied times the $98 billion shown on line 5f of Table 2, on page 39, yields a dollar value of $14 billion. This is the amount of benefits shifted to those who appear to be poor, but are, in fact, wealthier than 70% their peers, even before collecting Social Security.

A second approach was used to confirm these results, due to concerns that the first method might be overstating the transfer amounts (to high earners) for a couple of reasons. First, the law concerning the work penalty was in transition in early 2000. Prior to that time, people ages 65 to 70 would have benefits reduced if their earned income exceeded certain levels. Although the work penalty was repealed in March, 2000, [300] and the repeal was made retroactive to January, 2000, there could have been delays in implementing the repeal. If this were the case, the lower Social Security quintiles might include people whose high Social Security benefits appeared to be small due to a work penalty reduction (and not because previous wage earnings were low). In addition, some beneficiaries are slow to claim benefits when they reach age 65 and, as a result, they don't get a full year of benefits (in that year). This might also cause benefits to appear lower than normal.

To remedy these two problems, and to recheck the SSA data generally, I obtained data directly from the Current Population Survey (March Supplement). All data selected were for year 2001 (to avoid problems associated with law changes in the year 2000). Also, retirees selected were limited to those aged 66 to 90 (to avoid problems associated with partial years of benefits for people aged 65).

For married people, I co-tabulated individual Social Security benefit amounts (within each of 5 quintiles) with total family income. Each individual Social Security benefit amount was then subtracted from the associated amount

---

300. The repeal was only for people who were at or above full retirement age.

of family income, and the percentage of benefits (within each quintile) going to people with high income (upper 30%) versus low income (lower 70%) was calculated.

The same procedure was used for non-married individuals; however, in this case individual Social Security benefit amounts were co-tabulated with individual *adjusted gross income* amounts. In the interest of being conservative, it was presumed that the full Social Security benefit was, in each case, included in adjusted gross income.[301] Therefore, Social Security benefits were subtracted from the associated adjusted gross income amounts. The percentage of benefits (within each quintile) going to people with high income versus low income was then determined.

The results of this method were virtually identical to the results of the first method. It was determined that just over 14% of extra benefits transferred, ostensibly to low-earners, go instead to people with high incomes in retirement. These people have more income *before* getting their benefits than 70 of the population has *after* getting Social Security benefits.

A-8 The Clinton double tax: explanation
(See page 77.)

The easiest way to explain this is with an illustration. Let's say that a man named Tim, born around 1950, earns wages of about $3,000 per month (expressed in today's dollars) for his entire 45-year career. Social Security tax of $186 (i.e., 6.2%) was and will be withheld from each of his monthly paychecks but, as is always the case with Social Security, this amount is *not* deductible from his wages for purposes of income tax. So, Tim has paid, and will continue to pay, income taxes on his full earnings of $3,000, even though he doesn't actually receive the $186 of Social Security taxes withheld. Tim's employer pays an additional $186 in Social Security tax, on which Tim does *not* pay income tax.

---

301. Direct correspondence with the CPS indicates that only the taxable portion of Social Security is included in its tabulation of adjusted gross income. By subtracting the full amount, I have slightly understated the transfer of benefits to those with income greater than 70% of the retired population. In other words, the actual waste may be slightly higher than estimated.

Assuming that the payroll taxes paid by Tim and his employer will grow within the Social Security system at the average rate of 1.5% (the average rate for people born around 1950), the value of Tim's Social Security benefits will be $286,650 after 45 years. Now, this is the important part. Anyone subject to the Clinton tax on 85% of benefits would, by definition, already be subject to the pre-Clinton tax on 50% of benefits. Let's assume that Tim pays an average income tax rate of 25%. (The rate doesn't affect the analysis.) His benefits, worth $286,650, will be reduced to $250,818 by the pre-Clinton benefits tax (i.e., $286,650 less (50% times $286,650 times 25%)). But, remember, Tim also paid income tax on the amounts withheld from his checks when he was a worker. Assuming that Tim could have invested those amounts (that he paid as income taxes) at a tax-free 1.5% rate (which he could have done, easily), those taxes cost Tim $35,830 by the time he retired. Subtracting that amount from the $250,818 net benefit amount reduces Tim's benefits to just $214,988. And, guess what? That is *exactly* the amount Tim would have had if he had simply paid tax on *all* of his benefits ($286,650 less 25% tax = $214,988). So, Tim paid his taxes — all of them, *before* Clinton came out with his new tax. Thus, the Clinton tax is a double tax.

Actually, I've put a rosy spin on this matter. Millions of Americans won't even earn 1.5% on their Social Security "investment," yet they could earn far more than 1.5% in a tax-free, safe investment. Those people will pay *more* than a double tax.

A-9 Age-adjusted disability rates: explanation of methods and sources (See page 116.)

Information regarding the number of worker disability awards, workers currently receiving awards, and insured workers by age bracket, was obtained from the Office of Actuary page on the Social Security website (www.ssa.gov). Age-specific rates were obtained from Actuarial Study 114, which is also available on the Office of Actuary page of the Social Security website. To age-adjust the rates, the age-specific disability rates for 1988 were multiplied times the percentages of insured workers in each age bracket for that year. Then, the same age-specific disability rates for 1988 were multiplied times the percentages of insured workers in each age bracket for 2001. The difference between the two calculations is the change between 1988 and 2001 that can be attributed to the aging of the population. A similar procedure was used to calculate the age adjustment between 1997 and 2001. Finally, the age-adjustment factors for 1988-2001 and 1997-2001 were subtracted from the gross rate increases for those time periods (per the Actuary page of www.ssa.gov), to obtain the net increase amounts.

It should be noted that the 2002 Trustees Report includes an apparently erroneous comment concerning the upward trend of worker disability awards. It states that there was:

> a special administrative activity undertaken by SSA beginning in 2001 that contributed to the upsurge in disabled worker awards. This special workload was the result of discovering roughly 200,000 recipients of Supplemental Security Income (SSI) benefits whose disability-insured status under the DI program [worker disability program] was not previously recognized.

According to the Trustees Report, processing this special workload resulted in several new awards starting in 2001. However, direct conversations with two Social Security analysts indicate that, in fact, none of these special cases was processed in time to affect the 2001 records. The first impact was noted in 2002. (And for this reason, trend statistics involving the year 2002 are not presented herein.)

A-10 SSI Age and population-adjusted disability rates: explanation of methods and sources (See page 119.)

The number of SSI awards by impairment category was obtained from the SSI Statistical Report 2001, tables 45 (children) and 46 (adults). The percentage increases in disability awards for adults and children were each reduced by the amount of increase attributable to population increases. In addition, an age adjustment (for the adults) was subtracted. Population information was obtained by dividing total disability numbers per Table IV B6 of the 2002 SSI Annual Report by the disability rates listed in Table IV B7 of that same report. The age-adjustment factor was made in a manner similar to that shown in Appendix A-9.

A-11 Estimation of potential disability savings: explanation
(See page 121.)

In their 2003 report, the Social Security trustees estimate that the ultimate long-term disability incidence rate will be 5.6%. That is, 5.6% of insured workers will be awarded disability benefits. To get that rate, they started with an assumed base rate of 5.2% (the rate that existed from 1994 through 1996), and they added 8% more (i.e., 8% of the 5.2%) to reflect the anticipated gender and age changes of the working population. We need to challenge the somewhat arbitrarily-selected base rate of 5.2%.

The disability incidence rate from 1985 through 1989, after being restated to reflect the age of the population at January 1, 1996, was just 4.0%.[302] If we could maintain a 4% age-adjusted average rate for five consecutive years in the 1980s, it seems reasonable to believe that we can achieve the same age-adjusted rate (4%) now. That would bring the ultimate rate down to 4.3% (i.e., 4% times 1.08), an amount which is slightly below the trustees' low-cost long-term rate (4.5%). The trustees tell us, in Table VI.D.7 of their report, that the low-cost rate would reduce the long-term actuarial imbalance from 1.92 to 1.68 (as a percentage of the taxable payroll). By extrapolation, we know that a rate of 4.3% would further reduce the actuarial imbalance to just 1.64% of taxable payroll. This would be a reduction in the actuarial imbalance of 14.6% (i.e., (1.92 — 1.64) divided by 1.92 = 14.6%). And, we know that the total estimated actuarial imbalance translates to about $117.8 billion per year, in constant dollars, for the next 75 years. (See Appendix A-4) A 14.6% reduction would save the worker disability program $17 billion per year (14.6% times $117.8 billion).

If we assume that the SSI welfare disability program will grow in proportion to the worker disability program, the annual SSI disability benefits will average $55 billion. That amount is $25 billion (the annual sum of SSI

302. To age-adjust the 1985-1989 rates, the gross incidence rate for each age category (in each of the 5 years), per Social Security Actuarial study 114, was multiplied by the percentage of workers insured in the same age group as of December 31, 1995, per Table 4c2DI on the Office of Actuary page of the Social Security Administration website (www.ssa.gov). The results for each of the 5 years were then combined and averaged. This resulted in a rate of 4.0.

disability benefits currently paid) times $145 billion (the long-term average of worker benefits that will be paid each year, as shown in Table 6 on page 143), divided by $66 billion (the 2002 sum of worker disability benefits paid). If the SSI welfare disability savings are proportional to the worker disability savings, an average of $6 billion (i.e., $55 billion times $17 billion, divided by $145 billion) will be saved in SSI disability funds.

A-12 Failure to report a change in earnings. Is it a crime?
(See page 127.)

In an article entitled "Prosecuting Social Security Fraud: Protecting the Trust Fund for Present and Future Generations," John K. Webb, Special Assistant U.S. Attorney, notes that criminal cases are not limited to the falsification of documents or direct misstatements. "Fraud can also be the result of an omission or when a beneficiary fails to report a change in circumstances." Mr. Webb cites the following case law:

> The Third Circuit, in upholding a conviction for Social Security fraud in a concealment case charged under 42 U.S.C. Section 408 (a)(4), identified the following elements:
>
> 1. The defendant had knowledge of an event affecting his or her right to receive or to continue to receive payments;
> 2. The defendant knowingly concealed or failed to disclose this event to the Social Security Administration;
> 3. The defendant concealed *or failed to disclose* this event to the Social Security Administration with the intent to fraudulently secure payment of disability benefits in an amount greater than was due him or her or when no payment was authorized (emphasis added).[303]

In addition to the specific Social Security fraud statutes, prosecution may be possible under the more general criminal statutes within Title 18. According to Mr. Webb, it is sometimes easier to prosecute under Title 18, because "[t]his statute does not require fraud as a necessary element." Title 18, Section 1001,

---

303. John K. Webb, "Prosecuting Social Security Fraud: Protecting the Trust Fund for Present and Future Generations," vol. 49, no. 6 of *United States Attorneys' Bulletin* (United States Department of Justice, Executive Office for United States Attorneys, November, 2001), 3.

makes "knowingly and willfully concealing a material fact...within the jurisdiction of a department or agency of the United States" a crime, punishable by five years or more in prison.[304]

With regard to civil monetary penalties (CMPs), there is pending legislation (H.R. 743), likely to become law in 2003, that would clarify that CMPs (up to $5,000) can be applied in cases where the beneficiary fails to notify SSA of changes in circumstances which affect his benefit amount.

A-13 Is Bush getting all of the facts?
(See page 127.)

In 2002, the Office of Management and Budget (OMB) asked each agency in the federal government, including the SSA, to provide "program-wide estimates of erroneous payments." It specifically noted that the term "erroneous payments" includes fraud. The request was made via OMB Circular No. A-11 (2002).

In its response (a copy of which was obtained via a Freedom of Information Request), the SSA completely ignores the issue of fraud. (Indeed, I don't think the word even appears, although there are redacted portions.) However, the report is worded in such an ambiguous way that this fact is not readily apparent. The SSA notes that it tests, on a monthly basis, statistical samples of its beneficiary records. Recipients are interviewed, and "collateral contacts are made, as needed, and all factors of eligibility are redeveloped." However, the SSA doesn't tell the OMB that these quality reviews are based primarily on beneficiary *self-reporting*, and are not designed to detect or measure fraud. The agency also fails to mention that its own Inspector General (IG) has repeatedly urged the SSA to make fraud estimates, and the SSA has repeatedly declined to do so. The IG has stated that, "[f]or SSA to fulfill its role as a steward of public dollars, it is imperative that the universe or magnitude of fraud be identified. For example, the insurance, retail, and banking industries have baselines to estimate potential dollars lost to fraud."[305] In response, the SSA has stated, on several

---

304. *Ibid.*

occasions, that "the universe of fraud cannot be known." Apparently so, given the recalcitrance of the SSA.

A-14 Estimation of system savings due to use of PRAs
(See page 179.)

To assist the President's Commission to Strengthen Social Security, SSA actuaries have prepared estimates of the impact of each Commission proposal on the system's actuarial imbalance, and on the value of personally-owned retirement assets, for each of the next 75 years.[306] If we were to implement the Commission's Proposal 1, the estimates show that, by 2076, total system assets would increase by about $725 billion in today's dollars (assuming that, on average, workers put 2% of wages into their PRAs). That would represent a reduction in the system's actuarial imbalance of about 22.5% (i.e., .725/3.230 trillion).[307] Since the current projected actuarial imbalance, based on the 2003 Trustees Report, is equivalent to about $117.8 billion per year for each of the next 75 years (See Appendix .), the annual savings to the system would be about $26.5 billion (i.e., 22.5% times $117.8 billion).

A-15 Estimation of Ohio PERS benefits versus Social Security benefits
(See page 185.)

The rationale behind the adjustments

Before getting into specifics concerning the methods used in the Chapter XIII comparison charts, a brief overview is in order. As noted in Chapter XIII, comparisons between Social Security and other systems can be made from different vantage points and for different objectives. In Chapter I, a comparison

---

305. "Inspector General Statement on the Social Security Administration's Major Management Challenges." [online] (Social Security Administration, December 2001- [cited 30 April 2003]); available from *http://www.ssa.gov/finance/2001/mgmtchallengez1.htm.* "

306. "Strengthening Social Security and Creating Personal Wealth for All Americans," Attached Memorandum dated January 31, 2002 from Stephen C. Goss, Chief Actuary to Daniel Patrick Moynihan and Richard D. Parsons, Co-Chairs, President's Commission to Strengthen Social Security, 44.

307. Using the Commission figures for total increase in assets and total actuarial imbalance as of 2076.

is made between the net, after-tax benefits of Mary and Jill, after equalizing (as much as possible) the amounts of their separate investments. The focus there is on the individual, and the rationale for that approach is revealed by a review of Column A in Table 9.

Table 9

Comparing Social Security and Ohio PERS — It depends on the point of view.

	A	B	C
Point of view:	Evaluation of net benefits — an individual SS retiree vs. an individual Ohio PERS retiree (rationale for Ch. I)	Evaluation of efficiency of current program management — SS vs. Ohio PERS (rationale for Ch. XIII)	Evaluation of public policy — Is SS system treated as fairly as a public employees retirement system?
Variable:			
1. About ¼ of SS tax goes to implicit interest on the unfunded liability, primarily for earlier generations who underpaid.	A given SS retiree is no more responsible for the unfunded liability than is any public employee. We should not expect him to get lower benefits because of this.	SS is saddled with this debt, and Ohio PERS is not. To evaluate efficiency of the current-day SS program, we have to make allowance for this unrecorded debt.	Were the retirees of the '40s and '50s all ancestors of current SS workers, or were they also ancestors of public employees? The debt belongs to everyone.
2. Income taxes are generally higher for Ohio PERS retirees, but many SS retirees pay the highest rates of all.	Even though income taxes are not a matter of retirement system policy, they can't be ignored in a comparison of net results between individuals.	Taxation of benefits is government policy, and not in the purview of either system. Performance must be evaluated on a pre-tax basis.	It's not fair that governmental retirees pay, in general, higher income taxes than SS retirees.
3. Ohio PERS rates have been fairly steady during the last 30 years (and have declined slightly); SS rates have climbed.	For anyone over age 30, this is a factor to consider when evaluating his/her rate of return on payroll taxes. (SS workers paid less prior to 1990s.)	Contribution rates must be considered when evaluating the performance of the retirement systems.	This is not a factor involving equity between the two systems; however, if SS workers pay lower payroll taxes, they must expect to get lower benefits.

| 4. Is current SS rate sufficient to prevent growth in unfunded liability; is current Ohio PERS rate sufficient to keep program prefunded? | This does not affect evaluation of individual results except to the extent that it affects the risk faced in regard to future benefit cuts or payroll tax increases. | Before we can compare the efficiency of the two programs, we have to determine the contribution rates that can hold each program in equilibrium (funding-wise). | This is not a factor involving fairness between the two systems. |

In Chapter XIII, on the other hand, an attempt is made to compare the current performance of the Social Security and Ohio PERS programs. The rationale used in making the Chapter XIII comparisons is manifest in Column B. Let's briefly review each column — row-by-row. Row 1 has to do with the implicit interest on the $10.5 trillion unfunded Social Security debt — a debt primarily attributable to generations of Americans who underpaid their share of Social Security tax (and attributable, to a lesser degree, to mismanagement in the disability program and elsewhere). There is an implicit expense (a de facto interest expense) on this debt, and it is shouldered by Social Security. To make our Chapter XIII comparisons fair, Ohio PERS benefit amounts were reduced to simulate the effect of implicit interest. On the other hand, no adjustment was made in the Chapter I comparison charts, since implicit interest is of no relevance in comparisons made from the perspective of individual participants.

Row 2 pertains to income taxes. Since taxation of benefits is government policy, beyond the control of either retirement system, all figures Chapter XIII were prepared on a pretax basis. On the other hand, individuals within each system have to consider taxes in order to meaningfully assess their benefits. For this reason, charts in Chapter I were prepared on an after-tax basis.

Rows 3 and 4 pertain to historical Social Security payroll tax rates, and the sufficiency of current rates to prevent the unfunded liability from growing. In Chapter I, the actual Social Security and Ohio PERS rates between 1973 and 2003 were used, since these were the rates relevant for the individuals working in that time period. In the Chapter XIII comparisons, the historical (lower) Social Security rates from the 1970s and 1980s were not used since it is clear that those low rates contributed to an increase in the unfunded liability. Instead, the current 12.4% rate was used, on the assumption (hope, really) that it is just sufficient to keep the unfunded liability from growing. (This is an optimistic assumption since the 2003 Trustees Report estimates a $10.5 trillion closed-group actuarial imbalance — the highest ever.) With regard to Ohio PERS, it seems reasonable to assume that current rates are sufficient to cover current costs, since the system's level of funding has increased significantly since the mid-1980s, when the ratio of actuarial assets to actuarial liabilities was less than 75%. Nevertheless, the 30-year average Ohio rate was used in the interest of conservatism. It is higher than the current rate and, thus, minimizes the apparent advantage of Ohio PERS over Social Security.[308]

Column C in the table is not reflected in any comparison chart. It simply addresses the fairness of our public policy as it pertains to workers in the Social Security system versus workers in the Ohio PERS system (or any governmental retirement system). For example, is the unfunded liability entirely the responsibility of the Social Security system? Or do governmental employees share this obligation (because their ancestors were just as likely to be beneficiaries of the Social Security system)? Is it fair that governmental employees pay, overall, a higher income tax rate on benefits than do Social Security workers (as a group)?

Details of the methods used

For the chart depicting *single* women, average wage levels during the 30 years from 1973 through 2002 were obtained by starting with the final (highest) salary levels, and projecting backward using an annual rate of 5.96%, which is a little higher than the actual average annual increase in total wages during that particular historical period (5.26%). As explained in Appendix A-1, the excess of the 5.96% rate used, over the increase in average wages (5.26%) reflects presumed merit increases, beyond inflation increases, during the 30 year period.

For Social Security, the entire 30-year average was incorporated into the calculation of benefits; for Ohio PERS, only the final three years were used (as

---

308. From 1986 through 2002, the combined (employer and employee) contribution rate for Ohio PERS averaged 17.59%, and this rate was sufficient to cover current costs and increase the funding level. However, the average Ohio PERS contribution rate for the 30 years from 1973 through 2002 was 18.29% (excluding the portion earmarked for health insurance). The comparison calculations in Chapter XIII use the higher (18.29%) figure in the interest of being conservative (i.e., to minimize the estimated advantage of Ohio PERS over Social Security).

dictated by the Ohio PERS plan). Monthly benefits were then obtained by using the benefit calculators at the Public Employees Retirement System of Ohio website (www.opers.org) and at the Social Security website (www.ssa.gov).

The present value of the Ohio PERS monthly benefits was obtained by assuming a 3% after-inflation interest rate and a 30-year payment stream (the estimated remaining lifespan of a female who is 52 years old). This amount was then reduced by the fraction 9.75/18.29, to compensate for the higher contributions paid by Ohio PERS workers, and to compensate for the fact that Social Security benefits are (effectively) reduced to cover the implicit interest on the long-term unfunded liability of Social Security. The numerator (9.75) is equal to the current combined employee and employer payroll tax rate of 12.4%, plus 0.35%, which reflects the approximate level of revenue from income taxes assessed on Social Security benefits, less 3.0%, which represents an estimate of the amount of Social Security which is, effectively, applied toward implicit interest on the long-term unfunded liability of Social Security. The 3% implicit interest factor is based on an analysis performed by economist Alicia H. Munnell.[309] The denominator (18.29) is equal to a simple average of the combined employee and employer contributions required by Ohio PERS (retirement and disability) since 1973.[310]

As stated previously, these estimates were prepared using current rates for Social Security, and average rates (over 30 years) for Ohio PERS. (See reasons given.) Also, no adjustment was made for income taxes on benefits since they are a product of government policy, and do not reflect on the efficiency or effectiveness of the retirement programs.

The present value of Social Security monthly benefits was calculated by increasing the monthly benefit obtained from the Social Security calculator by an estimated real-wage differential of .75%, to reflect the excess of estimated wage inflation over general inflation for the years between age 52 and age 66 (i.e., retirement age). The monthly benefits were then discounted by using a 3% after-inflation interest rate over a 16 year period (the estimated remaining lifespan).

---

309. Alicia H. Munnell, "Reform Social Security: The Case Against Individual Accounts," work paper no. 1999-04 [online] (December 1999 — [cited 24 November 2002]), 7; available from *http://www2.bc.edu/~munnell/wp_1999-04.shtml.*

310. Pre-1992 contribution rates to Ohio PERS provided by Glenn Kacic, the Ohio Retirement Study Commission, Columbus, Ohio, in telephone interview by with author.

That amount was further reduced to current (age 52) dollars by using a 3% annual interest factor.

The amounts in the chart for *married* females were obtained in a similar manner. However, it was assumed that the Ohio PERS retiree selected Option D, which specifies that payments will be constant in amount (except for inflation adjustments) over the joint lives of the spouses. In the case of Social Security, it was assumed that there would be a *full* spousal benefit. (Although the spousal benefit is normally reduced, if not eliminated, due to earnings of the spouse.) In both cases, it was assumed that the spouses were of equal age and, after age 52, at least one of the spouses would live another 38.5 years (the longevity of a joint life, per 4/17/02 IRS Regulation tables). For Social Security, it was assumed that the joint benefit rate (including the spousal benefit) would be in force for 14 years (i.e., until the death of the first spouse to die), and the single benefit rate would apply thereafter.

A-16 Estimation of required income tax increase, to eliminate long-term unfunded liability over a 100-year period
(See page 200.)

We can roughly estimate the required increase in individual and corporate income taxes in the following manner. Per the 2003 Trustees Report (Table VI.F.5), the 75-year open-group actuarial imbalance, as a percentage of Gross Domestic Product (GDP), is 0.73%. Since the open-group actuarial imbalance is estimated to be $3.5 trillion, and the closed-group actuarial imbalance is estimated to be $10.5 trillion (See Appendix A-2 The Social Security shortfall: explanation for explanation.), we can assume that, as a percentage of GDP, the closed-group actuarial imbalance is $10.5 trillion / $3.5 trillion times 0.73%, which is 2.2%. That is the average percentage of GDP that we will need in each of the next 75 years, if we are to pay benefits (or transfer account balances) to all current Social Security participants. You might say that it is the cost of transition to a new, completely-prefunded trust system.

Now, we will need to convert the percentage of GDP we just calculated (2.2%) into a percentage of individual and corporate income taxes, but first we need to make a few adjustments (These are savings and costs discussed elsewhere.).[311]

ADJUSTMENT	%
% GDP saved by reforming taxation of benefits ($28/117.8 billion X .73%GDP) (See Chapter VI.)	-0.17
% GDP saved by reducing disability abuse ($23/117.8 billion X .73%GDP)[a] (See Chapter IX.)	-0.14
% GDP needed for low-income assistance ($84/117.8 billion X .73%GDP)[b] (See Chapter III.)	+0.52
Net additional cost, as % of GDP	0.21

a. The $23 billion disability abuse savings comprises $17 billion in the worker disability program and $6 billion in the SSI welfare program.

b. In this book we use a very liberal definition of "low income," which includes anyone in the lower 70% of the population in terms of wage income or retirement wealth.

Therefore, the adjusted cost to pay all benefits associated with the existing plan, and to fund additional low-income assistance out of general revenues, is 2.2% plus 0.21%, which is 2.4% of GDP, for each of the next 75 years.

We also know, from the Congressional Budget Office website,[312] that individual and corporate income taxes, as a percentage of GDP, have averaged 8.7% and 1.9% of GDP, respectively (during the 12 years from 1990 through 2001). Therefore, the approximate increase in annual individual and corporate income tax rates required to eliminate the closed-group actuarial imbalance would be 2.4 divided by (8.7 + 1.9), which is 22.6%. That, however, is the increase needed over a 75 year period. For a 100-year period, the rate of increase would be closer to 17%. That increase is expressed as a percentage of tax — not of taxable income. In other words, someone currently paying 20% in taxes would end up paying 23.4% (20% times 117%).

---

311. In these calculations, it is assumed that all savings (except those related to disability reform and elimination of inconsistent taxation), are used to pay higher benefits to retirees (and are not used to lower income tax rates).

312. "Historical Budget Data," Table 4 (www.cbo.gov).

Admittedly, this is a rough estimate; however, I believe that it may be a conservative rough estimate. These calculations contemplate no savings whatsoever from a reduction in fraud in the retirement program and/or the SSI welfare program. The adjustment for revenues generated from a change in the method of taxing benefits is probably substantially understated, since taxable benefits from the new trust are likely to greatly exceed those from traditional Social Security. Disability savings may be understated because, once there is a decent pension plan in place, many people will be motivated to work and build up their pension plans; they will be less inclined to join the ranks of the disabled. And, the adjustment for the cost of funding welfare from general revenues is probably overstated, since many of these people (i.e., the lower 70% of earners) won't need help once they have a new pension, with good earnings. Finally, it has been assumed that all savings related to improved investment earnings, and from the curtailment of misguided welfare transfers, are used to provide increased benefits — not to reduce required income tax funding.

Get involved

If you have strong feelings regarding the Social Security program and want to express them, this appendix is for you. It makes it a snap to write pointed letters to the people who count — your political leaders and the media.

At the end of Chapter XIV, many recommendations are listed. You may wish to advocate some of those recommendations in letters to your elected representatives, and/or the media. In addition, you will find, below, twenty questions based on topics in this book. Please feel free to incorporate these questions into your own correspondence, if you wish.

Finally, you'll find a short list of websites that provide contact information to help you reach the President, Congressional leaders, newspapers, magazines, and TV and radio talk shows. These sites make it easy to deliver an e-mail, or print an addressed letter for mailing.

Whatever your point of view, Social Security is an important topic that warrants your active involvement.

Ask questions regarding the retirement program

1. Benefits are transferred from one retiree to another by means of spousal/survivor payments and the 3-rate benefit formula. This is done without notifying the affected parties, and without determining whether the extra benefits are going to people in financial need. Why?

2. Social Security often pays more benefits to a married couple with one wage earner than it pays to a married couple with two wage earners, even where total family wages are identical. Can you explain why this is good public policy?

3. People with low W-2 earnings are presumed to be poorer than those with high W-2 earnings, and are paid benefits at a higher rate. This is true even though many of these "low earners" receive large amounts of income in the form of interest, dividends, rents, capital gains, etc. Is this fair?

4. We're told that Personal Retirement Accounts would drain funds from Social Security. Yet, 5 million state and local government workers are completely exempt from Social Security and pay no payroll taxes at all. Should these public-sector workers be merged into Social Security to stop this draining of funds from the program?

5. The GAO estimates that $450 million will be paid to a few thousand teachers because they worked as janitors for a single day. It appears that these 8-hour career changes were "shams" because they were devoid of economic substance. What legal action will be taken to recover these funds?

6. Social Security retirees can lose their benefits — all of them — simply by supplementing those benefits with wages. Will you support a repeal of the work penalty?

7. Many people pay a double tax on their benefits. It is even possible for a retiree to pay an effective tax rate (counting the work penalty) of over 100% of earnings. Do you feel this is fair? If not, will you support income tax reform to reduce this tax?

8. The tax on Social Security benefits is so complex that millions of senior citizens are forced to use professional tax preparers. Are you in favor of tax simplification for senior citizens?

9. The SSA has refused to provide an estimate of the amount of fraud in its programs, despite the urgings of its own Inspector General. How can the SSA effectively manage the program without this information?

10. One of the stated goals of Social Security is to provide "Social Insurance" (extra benefits) to low-income retirees. However, Social Security is almost entirely funded by payroll taxes, and the burden for payroll taxes falls mainly on middle and lower class wage earners. If we took the "social insurance" out of Social Security, and put it in a program financed by revenues from general income taxes, our wealthiest taxpayers would start to share in this burden. Would you support such a change?

Ask questions regarding the disability programs

1. The percentage of workers receiving disability benefits increased by nearly 40% between 1988 and 2001, even after adjusting for population aging. Does this make sense in light of modern medical advances?

2. In the SSI welfare program, award rates for general mental impairments increased by 41% for adults and by 125% for children in just four years (1977-2001). What explains these huge increases? Is anyone investigating?

3. Since 1960, the average age of workers receiving disability benefits has declined by 6 years or more, despite enormous advances in healthcare, and despite ADA legislation. Why are people becoming disabled at younger ages?

4. In many cases, workers receiving disability benefits are not required to get medical treatment even though that treatment would eliminate the disability. Why?

5. Did you realize that disabled workers are not required to get vocational rehabilitation training that could help them get back into the work place? Should the law be changed to make vocational rehabilitation mandatory?

6. Only one disabled worker in every five hundred recovers and returns to work. Considering this statistic, do you believe that the SSA is doing a good job with regard to the rehabilitation of disabled workers?

7. One third of disabled workers claim to have mental impairments, and 60% of SSI disabled beneficiaries claim to have mental impairments. Do these high rates suggest the possibility of disability abuse? What steps are being taken to reduce these percentages?

8. Disability benefits are normally supposed to replace lost wages, yet we pay monthly disability benefits to children. The assumption is that the benefits will be used for disability related expenses; however, nobody actually checks to see how this money is spent. Should we replace these monthly benefits with a program of specific (and documented) expense reimbursements?

9. Employers are required, under ADA rules, to provide "reasonable accommodations" that make it easier for disabled people to work. Yet, in evaluating whether a disabled worker is, in fact, able to work, the SSA ignores the possibility of "reasonable accommodations." Why?

10. Social Security disability coverage is mandatory. The worker does not have the option to substitute a private disability insurance policy, tailored to his particular needs. Will you support the creation of a private disability insurance option?

Contact aids

Web sites that can help you contact media and government leaders:

E-mail Address	Name	Instructions
http://www.newspapersol.com/	Guide to Newspapers, Radio & TV	Click "USA Media" in upper left corner. Then, click one or more states. You will see a listing of newspapers, magazines, TV, and radio. You can e-mail or print a letter to one address or several addresses.
http://www.emailthecongress.com/	EmailThe-Congress.com	Click "Email Your Representative," and follow instructions.
http://www.emailyoursenator.com/	EmailY-ourSenator.com	Click "Who Are My Senators?" Names and contact information will appear.
http://www.emailthepresident.com/	EmailTheP-resident.com	Click "Send an Email to the President"
http://www.house.gov/	United States House of Representatives	Click "Write Your Representative" on the left panel.
http://www.senate.gov/	The United States Senate	Click your state, and a list of senators and contact information will appear.
http://www.visi.com/ juan/congress/	Contacting the Congress — Online Directory for the 108th Congress	Click your state, and a list of senators and congressmen and contact information will appear.

Web sites that list members of SS subcommittees:

E-mail address	Name
http:// waysandmeans.house.gov /members.asp?comm=4	Committee on Ways and Means: Subcommittee on Social Security
http://www.senate.gov/ ~finance/fin-sub.htm	Senate Finance Committee: Subcommittee on Social Security and Family Planning

INDEX